Beginning Rails

From Novice to Professional

Jeffrey Allan Hardy and Cloves Carneiro Jr.

with Hampton Catlin

Apress®

Beginning Rails: From Novice to Professional

Copyright © 2007 by Jeffrey Allan Hardy and Cloves Carneiro Jr.

ISBN-13 (pbk): 978-1-59059-686-9

ISBN-10 (pbk): 1-59059-686-2

Printed and bound in the United States of America 9 8 7 6 5 4 3 2 1

Trademarked names may appear in this book. Rather than use a trademark symbol with every occurrence of a trademarked name, we use the names only in an editorial fashion and to the benefit of the trademark owner, with no intention of infringement of the trademark.

Lead Editor: Chris Mills
Technical Reviewer: Hampton Catlin
Editorial Board: Steve Anglin, Ewan Buckingham, Gary Cornell, Jonathan Gennick, Jason Gilmore, Jonathan Hassell, Chris Mills, Matthew Moodie, Jeffrey Pepper, Ben Renow-Clarke, Dominic Shakeshaft, Matt Wade, Tom Welsh
Project Manager: Sofia Marchant
Copy Edit Manager: Nicole Flores
Copy Editor: Marilyn Smith
Assistant Production Director: Kari Brooks-Copony
Production Editor: Ellie Fountain
Compositor: Gina Rexrode
Proofreader: Lori Bring
Indexer: Broccoli Information Management
Artist: Kinetic Publishing Services, LLC
Cover Designer: Kurt Krames
Manufacturing Director: Tom Debolski

Distributed to the book trade worldwide by Springer-Verlag New York, Inc., 233 Spring Street, 6th Floor, New York, NY 10013. Phone 1-800-SPRINGER, fax 201-348-4505, e-mail orders-ny@springer-sbm.com, or visit http://www.springeronline.com.

For information on translations, please contact Apress directly at 2855 Telegraph Avenue, Suite 600, Berkeley, CA 94705. Phone 510-549-5930, fax 510-549-5939, e-mail info@apress.com, or visit http://www.apress.com.

The information in this book is distributed on an "as is" basis, without warranty. Although every precaution has been taken in the preparation of this work, neither the author(s) nor Apress shall have any liability to any person or entity with respect to any loss or damage caused or alleged to be caused directly or indirectly by the information contained in this work.

The source code for this book is available to readers at http://www.apress.com in the Source Code/ Download section. You will need to answer questions pertaining to this book in order to successfully download the code.

For my best friend, Amy.
—Jeff

For Jane; you inspire me every morning.
—Cloves

Contents at a Glance

Contents

About the Authors

 **JEFFREY ALLAN HARDY** is a web developer, programmer, and occasional speaker with more than seven years of experience building large-scale web applications. He began working with Rails shortly after its first public release in 2004 and hasn't looked back. He is a partner at Unspace Interactive in Toronto, blogs at `http://quotedprintable.com`, and lives somewhere in the deep Canadian wilderness with his wife, his dog, and a cat.

 **CLOVES CARNEIRO JR.** is a software engineer and web application developer with ten years of experience creating enterprise-level web applications for companies in the telecommunication and financial industries, including Cablevision, MTS, and Bell Canada. Born in Brazil and then living for some years in Canada, he now lives in Dubai, United Arab Emirates, with his wife Jane. He owns and runs SpinBits, a Rails consulting and training company, and blogs at `http://ccjr.name`.

About the Technical Reviewer

HAMPTON CATLIN was born in Jacksonville, Florida, in 1982, on a sunny day with highs in the mid-80s and only a 20% chance of precipitation. He has been developing web applications since high school and fell in love with the web all over again when he found the Rails framework. The creator of the Haml markup language and Sass (Haml for CSS), Hampton blogs at http://hamptoncatlin.com and is currently a partner at Unspace Interactive in Toronto.

Acknowledgments

You read this at the beginning of every book, and now we're painfully aware of how true it is: writing a book is an enormous amount of work. Although their names don't appear on the cover, without the help, support, and encouragement of several people, this book would never have been completed.

We would like to thank all the folks at Apress who made this book a reality. Thanks to Elizabeth Seymour and Sofia Marchant, who worked tirelessly to keep us on schedule despite our best efforts to keep writing forever; our editor, Chris Mills, for supporting and encouraging us; our copy editor, Marilyn Smith, for her countless suggestions and valuable advice; and our production editor, Ellie Fountain, for patiently dealing with our last-minute modifications.

Any book on an open source project owes a debt of gratitude to the community that produced it. Thanks to David Heinemeier Hansson, the Rails core team, and the hundreds of contributors worldwide, for developing, supporting, and continually improving upon such a beautiful framework.

We would like to thank our families and friends for their patience in tolerating our long nights and mysterious absences while writing this book. We're sincerely looking forward to being able to spend more time with you again.

Jeff would like to thank Unspace, for allowing him the time to work on this project. Without your support and encouragement, this book would never have been possible. Also, thanks to Hampton Catlin for sanity-checking the code, text, and, occasionally, me. I would especially like to thank my wife, Amy, for putting up with me while writing this book consumed my life. Your love and support are nothing short of inspirational, and I count myself lucky to have met you.

Cloves would like to thank two great software developers, mentors, and friends who have taught him a lot about being a great programmer: Mircea Oancea and Alex Katsnelson. I would like to thank Rida Al Barazi for keeping up with deadlines when I had to spend time working on the book, instead of hacking on SpinBits' projects. I would like to thank my friend and coauthor Jeffrey Hardy for the quality work and all the uncountable nights dedicated to this book. I would like to thank Hampton Catlin for making sure the quality of this work was up to high standards. Above all, I would like to thank my wife Jane, for the encouragement and support provided during the long route that we literally traveled together; all your love and friendship made finishing this book possible.

Preface

Thinking back, it's hard to remember what web development was like before Rails came on the scene. I still remember using Basecamp for the first time (the application by 37signals from which Rails was extracted) and wondering what it was created with. It obviously wasn't PHP, and until then, PHP was my tool of choice for web applications. At the time that the rumors about Rails began to circulate on the Web, PHP had reached a significant level of maturity, having gained stronger object-oriented abilities. While Rails was being born in Basecamp, similar frameworks for PHP were beginning to crop up as well. Still, when I heard about how quickly Basecamp was constructed, I couldn't help but be intrigued by the technology that powered it.

When I first installed Rails, I eagerly followed a long-since perished tutorial on the wiki and gave the framework a spin. I was, to say the least, impressed. After having used similar frameworks in PHP, I was amazed at the level of abstraction and intuition displayed in the Rails code. I had never seen Ruby before, and immediately thought to myself that this is the language I've been seeking. When I learned that 37signals was offering a workshop titled "The Building of Basecamp," I promptly registered. I wrote my first Rails application on the plane ride home from Chicago, and I never looked back.

Typical of disruptive technologies, when Rails first hit the scene, it accumulated its fair share of detractors. A former PHP and Java developer, David Heinemeier Hansson had formed a clear opinion on the problems that plagued his trade, and with Rails, he set out to change things. It turns out that his way of thinking really shook up the industry. Never before had one technology so arrogantly asserted its position, and near holy wars erupted between proponents of more mature frameworks over this new kid on the block. It seemed that every day, Rails gained supporters, eventually achieving the perfect pro-portion of thought leaders to trigger a tip in the scale. Even the detractors were eventually conceding defeat, having been won over by Ruby, or the community, or the enthusiasm, or the forgotten pleasure of writing beautiful code.

At this late stage, unless you've been living under a rock, you've heard about the Rails framework. In the neighborhood of web development, it's a household name. At the time of this writing, Rails has displaced, or at least had influence on, every major web application construction framework in use today. Nearly every language—from Java and .NET to PHP and Python—has a framework similar in philosophy to Rails. Rails has completely changed the landscape of web development.

I'm proud of Rails. Having seen it grow from its earliest incarnations through to its current position as a modern, mature framework, I think the story of the little engine that could is an apt metaphor. In a lot of ways, Rails is the little framework that could. It pulled through and prevailed in face of disbelief. And I feel somewhat vindicated that the early adopters were right about what we were saying so long ago: Rails would revolutionize web development.

Jeffrey Allan Hardy

Introduction

By now, there are a number of books about getting started with Rails. We've read a lot of them, and found a few to be quite helpful. But what we've found to be lacking is a resource that, while tailored to the complete beginner, still imparts enough of the Rails culture and philosophy to be a useful building block. Rails is a large topic, and too many books spread themselves sufficiently thin so as to render themselves ineffective at conveying the core functionality of Rails. This book is different.

This book is particularly well suited to those with little or no experience with web application development, or who have some experience but are new to Rails. We assume that you're familiar with the technologies that make up the web, including HTML, and that you're comfortable installing software. But you don't need to know how to program, how to use web servers, how state is maintained on the web, or how to create and connect to a database. This book will teach you the basics of how web applications work and how Rails makes their construction easier.

Everyone starts out as a beginner. We certainly did. And when we began writing this book, we thought about the information we would have found most useful when we were first starting out with Rails. What do we wish we would have known? What would have made things easier? And we set out to write a book that would make sense of the complexities of web development and get beginners started on the right foot.

If you're seeking a book full of advanced techniques for experienced Rails programmers, you're going to be disappointed. This book does not delve into every arcane detail of Ruby or Rails. You will not find a discussion of Rails' support for self-referential polymorphic joins or advanced caching techniques. Instead, we focused on the pieces of the framework that will get you the most mileage. Rather than bury you with a lot of details, we want you to be comfortable in the Rails environment as soon as possible. That's why we've designed each chapter in this book around a specific component of the framework and focused on the most useful features of each piece.

If you've never programmed before, you should start by reading the introduction to Ruby in Appendix A. If you're new to data-driven applications, you should read the introduction to relational databases in Appendix B. When you're ready, Chapter 1 will introduce you to "the Rails way," and Chapter 2 will walk you through installing Ruby and Rails on your machine. The rest of the book will take you on a tour through the components of the Rails framework as we incrementally build a working application.

This book spends more time on the features you'll use the most, and less time on those that you'll use less often. Most everything you do in Rails is related to your models, so you'll need to understand Active Record, the library that Rails uses to communicate with your database. Active Record is easily the largest component of the Rails framework, so it makes sense that you'll spend a lot of your time working with it and that we spent a lot of time writing about it (Chapters 4 and 5). If you know how to model your domain and how to effectively work with database objects, you'll be in good shape when it comes to building the rest of your application. By the time we delve into Action Pack (Chapter 6), the web component of Rails, we'll have built our entire model and taken it for a test run. In Chapter 6, you'll learn how to build controllers and views that will expose your model objects via the web. Chapter 7 will explain how to use Ajax and other techniques to improve the user interface. Chapter 8 will show you how your applications can send and receive mail using Action Mailer. The remaining chapters will teach you the most important things you need to know about testing your application; installing, using, and creating plugins; and finally, deploying your application and making it available to the world.

Rails is a fast-moving target. During the creation of this book, several features have been added, refined, deprecated, and removed, and we've struggled to keep the text up-to-date and relevant. This book covers Rails 1.2.3 (the current stable version at the time of this writing), and we've included notes and tips on what to expect in future versions where applicable. If you're using a newer version of Rails, you might notice that a few things have changed, but for the most part, you shouldn't have any trouble.

To be sure, Rails is a big framework, and it's capable of much more than any one book can cover. However, despite its size and capabilities, Rails is conceptually easy to grasp. And therein lies its strength. With this book, you'll learn everything you need to know to get started building web applications with Rails.

The Beginning Rails Website

Be sure to check out this book's website at `http://beginningrails.com`. In addition to the most up-to-date version of the source code used in the book, you'll find errata, notes, tips, and other important updates. You'll be able to connect with the authors, ask technical questions, and receive help when you need it.

CHAPTER 1

■ ■ ■

Introducing the Rails Framework

Rails is a web application framework for the Ruby programming language. Rails is well thought out and practical. It will help you build powerful web sites quickly, with code that's clean and easy to maintain.

The goal of this book is to give you a thorough and complete understanding of how to build dynamic web applications with Rails. This means more than just showing you how to use the specific features and facilities of the framework, and more than just a working knowledge of the Ruby language. Rails is quite a bit more than just another tool. It represents a way of thinking. To completely understand Rails, it's essential that you know about its underpinnings, its culture and aesthetics, and its philosophy on web development.

If you haven't heard it already, you're sure to notice the phrase "the Rails way" cropping up every now and again. It echoes a familiar phrase that has been floating around the Ruby community for a number of years: "the Ruby way." The Rails way is usually the easiest way—the path of least resistance, if you will. This isn't to say that you can't do things your way, nor is it meant to suggest that the framework is constraining. It simply means that if you choose to go off the beaten path, don't expect Rails to make it easy for you. If you've been around the UNIX circle for any length of time, you might think that this idea bears resemblance to the UNIX mantra: "Do the simplest thing that could possibly work." You would be right. This chapter's aim is to introduce to you the Rails way.

The Rise and Rise of the Web Application

Web applications are increasingly gaining in importance. As our world becomes more and more connected, more and more of what we do is on the web. We check our email on the web, and we do our banking on the web. We take courses, share photos, upload videos, manage projects, and connect with people all over the world from the comfort of our browsers. As our connections get faster, and as broadband adoption grows, web-based software, and similarly networked client/server applications, are poised to displace software distributed by more traditional (read, outdated) means.

1

As consumers, web-based software affords us greater convenience, allowing us to do more from more places. Web-based software works on every platform that supports a web browser (which is to say, all of them), and there's nothing to install or download. And if Google's stock value is any indication, web applications are really taking off. In fact, the change in the web has been so dramatic in recent years that its current incarnation has been dubbed Web 2.0. All over the world, people are waking up to the new web and the beauty of being web-based. From email and calendars, photos and videos, to bookmarking, banking, and bidding, we are living increasingly inside the browser.

Due to the ease of distribution, the pace of change in the web-based software market is fast. Unlike traditional software, which must be installed on each individual computer, changes in web applications can be delivered quickly and features can be added incrementally. There's no need to spend months or years perfecting the final version or getting in all the features before the launch date. Instead of spending months on research and development, you can go into production early and refine in the wild, even without all the features in place.

Can you imagine having a million CDs pressed and shipped, only to find a bug in your software as the FedEx truck is disappearing into the sunset? That would be an expensive mistake! Software distributed this way takes notoriously long to get out the door because before a company ships a product, it needs to be sure the software is bug-free. Of course, we all know there's no such thing as bug-free software. And web applications are themselves not immune to these unintended features. But with a web application, bug fixes are easy to deploy.

When a fix is pushed to the server hosting the web application, all users get the benefit from the update at the same time, usually without any interruption in service. That's a level of quality assurance you just can't offer with store-bought software. There are no service packs to tirelessly distribute and no critical updates to install. A fix is often only a browser refresh away. And as a side benefit, instead of spending large amounts of money and resources on packaging and distribution, software developers are free to spend more time on quality and innovation.

Web-based software has the following advantages:

- Easier to distribute

- Easier to deploy

- Easier to maintain

- Platform-independent

- Accessible from anywhere

The Web Is Not Perfect

As great a platform as the web is, it's also fraught with constraints. One of the biggest problems is the browser itself. When it comes to browsers, there are several contenders, all of which have a slightly different take on how to display the contents of a web page. While there is a movement toward unification, and the state of standards-compliance among browsers is steadily improving, there is still a lot left to be desired. Even today, it's nearly impossible to achieve 100% cross-browser compatibility. Something that works in Internet Explorer won't necessarily work in Firefox, and vice versa. This lack of uniformity makes it difficult for developers to create truly cross-platform applications, as well as harder for users to work in their browser of choice.

Browser issues aside, perhaps the biggest constraint facing web development is its inherent complexity. A typical web application has dozens of moving parts: protocols and ports, the HTML and CSS, the database and the server, the designer and the developer, and a multitude of other players, all conspiring toward complexity.

But despite these problems, the new focus on the web as a platform has meant that the field of web development is evolving rapidly and quickly overcoming obstacles. As it continues to mature, the tools and processes that have long been commonplace in traditional, client-side software development are beginning to make their way into the world of web development.

The Good Web Framework

Among the tools making their way into the world of web development is the framework. A *framework* is a collection of libraries and tools intended to facilitate development. Designed with productivity in mind, a good framework will provide you with a basic but complete infrastructure on top of which to build an application.

Having a good framework is a lot like having a chunk of your application already written for you. Instead of having to start from scratch, you start with the foundation already in place. If there is a community of developers using the same framework, you have a community of support when you need it. You also have greater assurance that the foundation you're building upon is less prone to pesky bugs and vulnerabilities, which can slow down the development process.

A good web framework can be described as follows:

- **Full stack:** Everything you need for building complete applications should be included in the box. Having to install various libraries or configure multiple components is a drag. The different layers should fit together seamlessly.

- **Open source:** A framework should be open source, preferably licensed under a liberal, free-as-in-free license, like BSD or MIT.

- **Cross-platform:** A good framework will be platform-independent. The platform on which you decide to work is one of personal choice. Your framework should remain as neutral as possible.

A good web framework will provide you with the following:

- **A place for everything:** Structure and convention drive a good framework. In other words, unless a framework offers a good structure and a practical set of conventions, it's not a very good framework. The idea is that everything should have a proper place within the system. This eliminates the guesswork and increases productivity.

- **A database abstraction layer:** You shouldn't have to deal with the low-level details of database access, nor should you be constrained to a particular database application. A good framework will take care of most of the database grunt work for you, and it will work with almost any database out there.

- **A culture and aesthetic to help inform programming decisions:** Rather than seeing the structure imposed by a framework as constraining, see it as liberating. A good framework encodes its opinions, gently guiding the developer. Often, a difficult decision has been made for you by virtue of convention. The culture of the framework helps you make fewer menial decisions and helps you to focus on what matters most.

Enter Rails

Rails is a best-of-breed framework for building web applications. It's complete, open source, and cross-platform. It provides a powerful database abstraction layer called Active Record, which works with all popular database systems. It ships with a sensible set of defaults and provides a well-proven, multilayer system for organizing program files and concerns.

Above all, Rails is opinionated software. It has a philosophy on the art of web development that it takes very seriously. Fortunately, this philosophy is centered around beauty and productivity. You'll find that as you learn Rails, it actually makes writing web applications pleasurable.

Originally created by David Heinemeier Hansson, Rails first took shape in the form of a wiki-wiki application called Instiki. The first version of what is now the Rails framework was actually extracted from a real-world, working application: Basecamp, by 37signals. The Rails creators took away all the Basecamp-specific parts, and what remained was Rails.

Because it was extracted from a real application and not built as an ivory tower exercise, Rails is practical and free of needless features. Its goal as a framework is to solve 80% of the problems that occur in web development, assuming that the remaining 20% are the problems that are truly unique to the application's domain. It might be surprising that as much as 80% of the code in an application is infrastructure, but it's not as far-fetched as it sounds. Consider all the work that's involved in application construction, from directory structure and naming conventions, to the database abstraction layer and the maintenance of state.

You'll see that Rails has specific ideas about directory structure, file naming, data structures, method arguments, and, well, nearly everything. When you write a Rails application, you're expected to follow the conventions that have been laid out for you. Instead of focusing on the details of knitting the application together, you get to focus on the 20% that really matters.

Rails Is Ruby

There are a lot of programming languages out there. You've probably heard of many of them. C, C#, Lisp, Java, Smalltalk, PHP, and Python are popular choices. And then there are others you've probably never heard of: Haskel, IO, and maybe even Ruby. Like the others, Ruby is a programming language. You use it to write computer programs, including, but certainly not limited to, web applications.

Before Rails came along, not many people were writing web applications with Ruby. Other languages like PHP and ASP were the dominant players in the field, and a large part of the web is powered by them. The fact that Rails uses Ruby is significant because Ruby is considerably more powerful that either PHP or ASP in terms of its abilities as a programming language. This is largely another symptom of the web's maturity. Now that it's attracting a larger audience, more powerful languages and tools are falling into the fold.

Ruby is a key part of the success of Rails. Rails actually uses Ruby to create what's called a *domain-specific language*, or a DSL. Here, the domain is that of web development, and when you're working in Rails, it's almost as though you're writing in a language that was specifically designed to construct web applications—a language with its own set of rules and grammar. Rails does this so well that it's sometimes easy to forget that you're actually writing Ruby code. This is a testimony to Ruby's power, and Rails takes full advantage of Ruby's expressiveness to create a truly beautiful environment.

For many developers, Rails is their introduction to Ruby, a language whose following before Rails was admittedly small at best, at least in the west. While Ruby had been steadily coming to the attention of programmers outside Japan, the Rails framework is what brought Ruby to the mainstream.

Invented by Yukihiro Matsumoto in 1994, it's a wonder Ruby remained shrouded in obscurity for as long as it did. As far as programming languages go, Ruby is among the most beautiful. Interpreted and object-oriented, elegant and expressive, Ruby is truly a joy to work with. A large part of Rails's grace owes to Ruby and to the culture and aesthetics that permeate the Ruby community. As you begin to work with the framework, you'll quickly learn that Ruby, like Rails, is rich with idioms and conventions, all of which make for an enjoyable, productive programming environment.

In summary, Ruby can be described as follows:

- An interpreted, object-oriented scripting language

- Elegant, concise syntax

- Powerful metaprogramming features

- Well suited as a host language for creating DSLs

Appendix A of this book includes a complete Ruby primer. If you want to get a feel for what Ruby looks like now, go ahead and skip to that appendix and take a look. Don't worry if Ruby seems a little unconventional at first. You'll find it quite readable, even if you're not a programmer. It's safe to follow along in this book learning it as you go, referencing the appendix when you need clarification. If you're looking for a more in-depth guide, Peter Cooper has written a fabulous book titled *Beginning Ruby: From Novice to Professional* (Apress, 2007). You'll also find the Ruby community more than helpful in your pursuit of the language. Be sure to visit `http://ruby-lang.org` for a wealth of Ruby-related resources.

Rails Encourages Agility

Web applications are not traditionally known for agility. They have a reputation of being difficult to work with and a nightmare to maintain. It is perhaps in response to this diagnosis that Rails came on to the scene, helping to usher in a movement toward agile programming methodologies in web development. Rails advocates and assists in the achievement of the following basic principles when developing software:

- Individuals and interactions over processes and tools

- Working software over comprehensive documentation

- Customer collaboration over contract negotiation

- Responding to change over following a plan

So reads the Agile Manifesto[1], the result of a discussion between 17 prominent figures (including Dave Thomas, Andy Hunt, and Martin Fowler) in the field of what was then called "lightweight methodologies" for software development. Today, the Agile Manifesto[1] is widely regarded as the canonical definition of agile development.

---

1. `http://agilemanifesto.org`

Rails was designed with agility in mind, and it takes each of the agile principles to heart, almost obsessively. With Rails, you can respond to the needs of customers quickly and easily, and Rails works well during collaborative development. Rails accomplishes this by adhering to its own set of principles, all of which help make agile development possible.

Dave Thomas and Andy Hunt's seminal work on the craft of programming, *The Pragmatic Programmer* (Addison-Wesley, 1999) reads almost like a roadmap for Rails. Rails follows the *don't repeat yourself* (DRY) principle, the concepts of rapid prototyping, and the *you ain't gonna need it* (YAGNI) philosophy. Keeping important data in plain text, using convention over configuration, bridging the gap between customer and programmer, and above all, postponing decisions in anticipation of change are institutionalized in Rails. These are some of the reasons that Rails is such an apt tool for agile development, and it's no wonder that one of the earliest supporters of Rails was Dave Thomas himself.

In the sections that follow, we're going to take a tour through some of Rails mantras, and in doing so, demonstrate just how well suited Rails is for agile development. While we want to avoid getting too philosophical, some of these points are essential to grasping what makes Rails so important.

Less Software

One of the central tenets of Rails philosophy is the notion of *less software*. What does less software mean? It means using convention over configuration, writing less code, and doing away with things that needlessly add to the complexity of a system. In short, less software means less code, less complexity, and fewer bugs.

Convention Over Configuration

Convention over configuration means that the programmer needs to define only configuration that is unconventional.

Programming is all about making decisions. If you were to write a system from scratch, without the aid of Rails, you would have a lot of decisions to make: how to organize your files, what naming conventions to adopt, and how to handle database access are only a few. If you decided to use a database abstraction layer, you would need to sit down and write it, or at least find an open source implementation that suits your needs. You would need to do all this before you even got down to the business of modeling your domain.

Rails lets you get started right away, by encompassing a set of intelligent decisions about how your program should work, alleviating the amount of low-level decision-making you need to do up front. As a result, you can focus on the problems you're trying to solve and get the job done quicker.

Rails ships with almost no configuration files. If you're used to other frameworks, this fact might surprise you. If you've never used a framework before, you should be surprised. In some cases, configuring a framework is nearly half the work.

Instead of configuration, Rails relies on common structures and naming conventions, all of which employ the often-cited *principle of least surprise* (POLS). Things behave in a predictable, easy-to-decipher way. There are intelligent defaults for nearly every aspect of the framework, relieving you, the developer, from having to explicitly tell the framework how to behave. This isn't to say that you can't tell Rails how to behave. In fact, most behaviors can be customized to your liking and to suit your particular needs. But you'll get the most mileage and productivity out of the defaults, and Rails is all too willing to encourage you to accept the defaults and move on to solving more interesting problems.

While you can manipulate most things in the Rails setup and environment, the more you accept the defaults, the faster you can develop applications and predict how they will work. The speed with which you can develop without having to do any explicit configuration is one of the key reasons why Rails works so well. If you put your files in the right place and name them according to the right conventions, things will *just work*. If you're willing to agree to the defaults, you generally have less code to write.

The reason Rails does this comes back to the idea of less software. Less software means making fewer low-level decisions, which will make your life as a web developer a whole lot easier. And easier is a good thing.

Don't Repeat Yourself

Rails is big on the DRY principle. DRY stands for *don't repeat yourself*, a principle that states information in a system should be expressed in only one place.

For example, consider database configuration parameters. When you connect to a database, you generally need credentials, such as a username, password, and the name of the database you want to work with. It might seem acceptable to include this connection information with each database query, and would surely hold up fine if you were making only one or two connections. But as soon as you need to make more than a few connections, you would end up with a lot of instances of that username and password littered throughout your code. Then if your username and password for the database changed, you would have a lot of finding and replacing to do. It would be a much better idea to keep the connection information in a single file, referencing it as necessary. That way, if the credentials should change, you need to modify only a single file. That's what the DRY principle is all about.

The more duplication there is in a system, the more room there is for bugs to hide. The more places that the same information resides, the more that has to be modified when a change is required, and the harder it becomes to track these changes.

Rails is organized in such a way as to remain as DRY as possible. You generally specify information in a single place, and move on to better things.

Rails Is Opinionated Software

Frameworks encode opinions. It should come as no surprise then that Rails has strong opinions about how your application should be constructed. When you're working on a Rails application, those opinions are imposed on you, whether you're aware of it or not. One of the ways that Rails makes its voice heard is by gently (sometimes, forcefully) nudging you in the right direction. We've already mentioned this form of encouragement when we talked about convention over configuration. You're invited to do the right thing by virtue of the fact that doing the wrong thing is often more difficult.

Ruby is known for making certain programmatic constructs look more natural by way of what's called *syntactic sugar*. Syntactic sugar means that the syntax for something is altered in such a way as to make it appear more natural, even though it behaves the same way. Things that are syntactically correct but otherwise look awkward when typed are often treated to syntactic sugar.

Rails has popularized the term *syntactic vinegar*. Syntactic vinegar is the exact opposite of syntactic sugar: awkward programmatic constructs are discouraged by making their syntax look sour. When you write a snippet of code that looks bad, chances are it is bad. Rails is good at making the right thing obvious by virtue of its beauty, and the wrong thing equally obvious by virtue of ugliness.

You can see Rails's opinion in the things it does automatically, the ways it encourages you to do the right thing, and the conventions it asks you to accept. You'll find that Rails has an opinion on nearly everything about web application construction: how you should name your database tables, how you should name your fields, which database and server software to use, how to scale your application, what you're going to need, and what is a vestige of web development's past. If you subscribe to its world view, you'll probably get along with Rails quite well.

Like a programming language, a framework needs to be something you're comfortable with—something that reflects your personal style and mode of working. It's often said in the Rails community that if you're getting pushback from Rails, it's probably because you haven't experienced enough pain from doing web development the old-school way. This isn't meant to deter developers, rather it's meant to say that in order to truly appreciate Rails, you might need a history lesson in the technologies from whose ashes Rails has risen; sometimes until you've experienced the hurt, you can't appreciate the cure.

Rails Is Open Source

The Rails culture is steeped in open source tradition. The Rails source code is, of course, open. And it's significant that Rails is licensed under the MIT license, arguably one of the most "free" software licenses in existence.

Rails also advocates the use of open source tools, and encourages the collaborative spirit of open source. The code that makes up Rails is 100% free and can be downloaded, modified, and redistributed by anyone at anytime. Moreover, anyone is free to submit patches for bugs or features, and hundreds of people from all over the world have contributed to the project over the past two years.

You'll probably notice that a lot of Rails developers use Macs. The Mac is clearly the preferred platform of the core Rails team, and you'll find in general that most Rails developers are using UNIX variants (of which Mac OS X is one). The UNIX operating system is hailed by hackers and used almost exclusively among the hacker elite. There are several reasons for this, not least of which is the fact that UNIX is a well-tested and proven operating system, forged in an open source ecosystem, with contributions from some of the smartest programmers on the planet. Having been born in the 1970s, at this late stage, the UNIX operating system has evolved into lean and powerful example of open source craftsmanship. The beauty, simplicity, and singularity of purpose of UNIX is not lost on the creators of Rails.

Although there is perhaps a marked bias towards UNIX variants when it comes to Rails developers, make no mistake, Rails is truly cross-platform. It doesn't matter which operating system you choose, you'll be able to use Rails on it. Rails doesn't require any special editor or IDE to write code. Any text editor will do just fine, as long as it can save files in plain text. The Rails package even includes a built-in, stand-alone web server called WEBrick, so you don't need to worry about installing and configuring a web server for your platform. When you want to run your Rails application in development mode, simply start up the built-in server and open your web browser. Why should it be any more difficult than that?

The next chapter will take you step by step through the relatively painless procedure of installing Rails and getting it running on your system. But before we go there, and before you start writing your first application, we would like to talk a bit about how the Rails framework is architected. This is important because, as you'll see in a minute, it has a lot to do with how you organize your files and where you put them. Rails is actually a subset of a category of frameworks that are named for the way in which they divide the concerns of program design: the Model-View-Controller (MVC) pattern. Not surprisingly, the MVC pattern is the topic of our next section.

The MVC Pattern

Rails employs a time-honored and well-established architectural pattern that advocates a division of application logic and labor into three distinct categories: the model, view, and controller. In the MVC pattern, the model represents the data, the view represents the user interface, and the controller directs all the action. The real power lies in the combination of the MVC layers, which is something that Rails handles for you. Place your code in the right place and follow the naming conventions, and everything should fall into place.

Each part of the MVC—the model, view, and controller—is a separate entity, capable of being engineered and tested in isolation. A change to a model need not affect the views; likewise, a change to a view should have no effect on the model. This means that changes in an MVC application tend to be localized and low impact, easing the pain of maintenance considerably, while increasing the level of reusability among components.

Contrast this to the situation that occurs in a highly coupled application that mixes data access, business logic, and presentation code (PHP, we're looking at you). Some folks call this spaghetti code because of its striking resemblance to a tangled mess. In such systems, duplication is common, and even small changes can produce large ripple effects. MVC was designed to help solve this problem.

MVC isn't the only design pattern for web applications, but it does happen to be the one that Rails has chosen to implement. And it turns out that it works great for web development. By separating concerns into different layers, changes to one of them don't have an impact on the others, resulting in faster development cycles and easier maintenance.

The MVC Cycle

Although MVC comes in different flavors, control flow generally works as follows (see Figure 1-1):

1. The user interacts with the interface and triggers an event (for example, submits a registration form).

2. The controller receives the input from the interface (for example, the submitted form data).

3. The controller accesses the model, often updating it in some way (for example, by creating a new user with the form data).

4. The controller invokes a view that renders an updated interface (for example, a "welcome" screen).

5. The interface waits for further interaction from the user, and the cycle repeats.

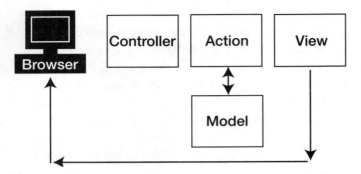

Figure 1-1. *The MVC cycle*

If the whole MVC concept sounds a little involved at first, don't worry. While entire books could be written on this pattern, and people will argue over its purest implementation for all time, you'll find that it's really quite easy to grasp, especially the way Rails does MVC.

Next, we'll take a quick tour through each letter in the MVC, and then describe how Rails handles it.

The Layers of MVC

The three layers of the MVC pattern work together as follows:

- **Model:** The information the application works with.

- **View:** The visual representation of the user interface.

- **Controller:** The director of interaction between the model and the view.

Models

In Rails, the model layer represents the database. While we call the entire layer the model, Rails applications are usually made up of several individual models, each of which (usually) maps to a database table. For example, a model called User would map to a table called users. The User model assumes responsibility for all access to the users table in the database, including creating, reading, updating, and deleting rows. So, if you wanted to work with the table and, say, search for someone by name, you would do so through the model, like this:

```
User.find_by_name('Linus')
```

This snippet, while very basic, would search the users table for the first row with the value Linus in the name column and return the results. To achieve this, Rails uses its built-in database abstraction layer, Active Record. Active Record is a powerful library, so needless to say, this is only a small portion of what you can do with it.

Chapters 4 and 5 will give you an in-depth understanding of Active Record and what you can expect from it. For the time being, the important thing to remember is that models represent data. All rules for data access, associations, validations, calculations, and routines that should be executed before and after save, update, or destroy operations are neatly encapsulated in the model. Your application's "world" is populated with Active Record objects: single ones, lists of them, new ones, and old ones. And Active Record lets you use Ruby language constructs to manipulate all of them, meaning you get to stick to one language for your entire application.

Controllers

We're going to rearrange the MVC acronym a bit here and put the *C* before the *V*. As you'll see in a minute, in Rails, controllers are responsible for rendering views, so it makes sense that we should introduce them first.

Controllers are the conductors of an MVC application. In Rails, controllers accept requests from the outside world, perform the necessary processing, and then pass control to the view layer to display the results. It's the controller's job to do the fielding of web requests, like processing server variables and form data, asking the model for information, and sending information back to the model to be saved in the database. While it may be a gross oversimplification, controllers generally perform a request from the user to create, read, update, or delete a model object. You'll see these words a lot in the context of Rails, most often abbreviated as CRUD. In response to a request, the controller typically performs a CRUD operation on the model, sets up variables to be used in the view, and then proceeds to render or redirect to another action once processing is complete.

Controllers typically manage a single area of an application. For example, in a recipe application, you would probably have a controller just for managing recipes. Inside the recipes controller, you would define what are called *actions*. Actions describe what a controller can do. If you wanted to be able to create, read, update, and delete recipes, you would create appropriately named actions in the recipes controller. A simple recipes controller might look something like this:

```
class RecipesController < ApplicationController
  def index
    # logic to list all recipes
  end
```

```ruby
  def show
    # logic to show a particular recipe
  end

  def create
    # logic to create a new recipe
  end

  def update
    # logic to update a particular recipe
  end

  def destroy
    # logic to delete a particular recipe
  end
end
```

Of course, if you wanted this controller to do anything, you would need to put some instructions inside each action. When a request comes into your controller, it uses a URL parameter to identify the action to execute, and when it's done, it sends a response to the browser. The response is what we'll look at next.

Views

The view layer in the MVC is the one that makes up the visible part of the application. In Rails, views are the templates that (most of the time) contain HTML markup to be rendered in a browser. It's important to note that views are meant to be free of all but the simplest programming logic. The idea is that any direct interaction with the model layer should be delegated to the controller layer so as to keep the view clean and decoupled from the application's business logic.

Generally, views have the responsibility of formatting and presenting model objects for output on the screen, as well as providing the forms and input boxes that accept model data, such as a login box with a username and password, or a registration form. Rails also provides the convenience of a comprehensive set of helpers that make connecting models and views easier, such as being able to prepopulate a form with information from the database, or the ability to display error messages if a record fails any validation rules, such as required fields.

You're sure to hear it eventually if you hang out in Rails circles, but a lot of folks consider the interface to *be* the software. We agree with them. The idea is that since the interface is all the user sees, it's the most important part. Whatever the software might be doing behind the scenes, the only parts that an end user can relate to are the parts they see and interact with. The MVC pattern helps by keeping programming logic out of the view. With this strategy in place, programmers get to deal with code, and designers get to deal with HTML. Having a clean environment in which to design the HTML means better interfaces and better software.

The Libraries That Make Up Rails

Rails is a collection of libraries, each with a specialized task. Assembled together, these individual libraries make up the Rails framework. Of the several libraries that compose Rails, three map directly to the MVC pattern:

- **ActiveRecord:** A library that handles database abstraction and interaction.

- **ActionView:** A templating system that generates the HTML documents that the visitor gets back as the result of a request to a Rails application.

- **ActionController:** A library for manipulating both application flow and the data coming from the database on its way to being displayed in a view.

These libraries can be used independently of Rails and of each other. Together, they make up the Rails Model-View-Controller development stack. Since Rails is a "full-stack" framework, all the components are integrated, so you do not need to set up bridges between them manually.

Rails Is No Silver Bullet

There is no question that Rails offers web developers a lot of benefits. In fact, after having used Rails, it's hard to imagine going back to web development without it. Fortunately, it looks like Rails will be around for a long time, so there's no need to worry. But it brings us to an important point.

As much as we've touted the benefits of Rails, it's important that you realize that there are no silver bullets in software design. No matter how good Rails gets, it will never be all things to all people, and it will never solve all problems. Most important, Rails will never replace the role of the developer. Its purpose is merely to assist developers in getting their job done. Impressive as it is, Rails is merely a tool, which when used well can yield amazing results. It is our hope that as you continue to read this book and learn how to use Rails, you'll be able to leverage its strength to deliver creative and high-quality web-based software.

Summary

This chapter provided an introductory overview of the Rails landscape, from the growing importance of web applications to the history, philosophy, evolution, and architecture of the framework. You learned about the features of Rails that make it ideally suited for agile development, including the concepts of less software, convention over configuration, and DRY. Finally, you learned the basics of the MVC pattern, and received a primer on how Rails does MVC.

With all this information under your belt, it's safe to say you're ready to get up and running with Rails. The next chapter will walk you through Rails installation, so you can try it for yourself and see what all the fuss is about. You'll be up and running with Rails in no time.

CHAPTER 2

■ ■ ■

Getting Started

For various reasons, Rails has gained an undeserved reputation of being difficult to install. We want to dispel this myth. The truth is that installing Rails is relatively easy and straightforward, provided you have all the right ingredients. Here, we'll begin with an overview of what you'll need to get Rails up and running, and then provide step-by-step instructions for actual installation. Finally, we'll get you started with your first Rails application.

An Overview of Rails Installation

The main ingredient you need for Rails is, of course, Ruby. If you're lucky, Ruby might already be installed on your system, in which case, you're halfway there. Most likely, however, it's not. You'll therefore need to install it. Once you have Ruby installed, you'll be able to install a package manager (a program designed to help you install and maintain software on your system) called RubyGems. You'll use that to install Rails.

Note If you're using a version of OS X prior to 10.4.7, the Apple-provided version of Ruby on your computer might be ill-configured. You should follow the instructions for compiling your own version of Ruby to bypass the built-in one, as outlined in this chapter. Building your own Ruby installation is probably a good idea in any case, as it will keep you from being bitten by any changes to the built-in version of Ruby by future system updates from Apple.

If you're a Ruby hacker and already have Ruby and RubyGems installed on your computer, Rails is ridiculously easy to get up and running. Since it's packaged as a gem, you can install it with a single command:

```
$ gem install rails --include-dependencies
```

That's all it really comes down to—installing Rails is a mere one-liner. The key is in having a working installation of Ruby and RubyGems. Before we get there, though, there's one other ingredient you'll need to use Rails, and that's a database server.

As you're well aware by now, Rails is specifically for building web applications. Well, it's a rare web application that isn't backed by a database. In fact, Rails is so sure you'll be using a database for your application that it's downright stubborn about working very nicely without one. While Rails works with nearly every database out there, we'll be using one called MySQL. MySQL is open source, easy to install, and incredibly well supported for web development. Perhaps that's why it's the most popular database among Rails developers.

You'll start by installing MySQL and making sure it's working properly. Then you'll install Ruby and RubyGems, and finally you'll get to use the magical one-liner and install Rails. Here are the steps in order:

- Install MySQL

- Install Ruby

- Install RubyGems

- Install Rails

Before we begin, we should point out that the "many ways to skin a cat" adage applies to Rails installation. For as many platforms as the Rails stack runs on, there are as many ways to install it. Here, we describe what we feel is the easiest and most reliable way to install Rails for your platform. While we'll go about the process differently for OS X, Linux, and Windows, you'll find they all amount to the same thing.

No matter which platform you're using, you'll need to get familiar with the command line. This likely won't be a problem for the Linux crowd, but it's possible that some OS X users and certainly many Windows users won't have much experience with it. If you're using OS X, you can find a terminal emulator in /Applications/Utilities/Terminal.app. If you're on Windows, you can open a command prompt by clicking Start ➤ Run, typing cmd, and clicking OK. Note that we'll be using the command line extensively in our travels with Rails.

Also, a quick note for OS X/Linux/UNIX users: your instructions are nearly inter-changeable. If you're using a Mac and would prefer to use a package manager such as Fink or MacPorts (see the sidebar on the next page), the Linux instructions will prove useful. The same is true for Linux/UNIX users who wish to compile everything them-selves: the OS X instructions should prove a drop-in replacement.

Go ahead and flip to the section that describes your platform (OS X, Linux, or Windows), and we'll begin!

Installing on Mac OS X 10.4 Tiger

You would think that given the prevalence of OS X among Rails developers (the entire core team uses OS X) that installing it would be easy. Alas, it's not. Due to the existence of a slightly crippled instance of Ruby preinstalled on most OS X 10.4 systems, we'll go through the steps for building almost everything from scratch. The exception is MySQL, which has a good installer.

■**Note** According to Apple, OS X 10.5 Leopard will ship with Rails preinstalled. If you're lucky enough to be reading this book in the future and have Leopard installed on your system, you can skip the steps outlined here. For more information, see `http://blog.rubyonrails.org/2006/8/7/` `ruby-on-rails-will-ship-with-os-x-10-5-leopard`.

Don't let the word *compile* scare you. While it's slightly more involved than a one-click install, it's a relatively painless experience.

To make things easier, we've even provided a script that you can run that will take care of most of the work for you. It's at the end of this section. Be aware, though, that the script won't install MySQL for you—you have to do that yourself—and you'll still need the Apple Developer Tools installed for the script to work, so be sure you don't skip the first few steps. (Can you see now why we put the script at the tail end of the section?)

■**Note** For an in-depth description of building Ruby, Rails, Subversion, Mongrel, and MySQL on Mac OS X, see Dan Benjamin's popular how-to article: `http://hivelogic.com/narrative/articles/` `ruby-rails-mongrel-mysql-osx`.

WHY NOT USE A PACKAGE MANAGER ON OS X?

In the installation instructions for Linux, we describe using a package manager to install the Rails stack. So why not for OS X? The short answer is that there are too many inconsistencies among various tools and versions to make a worthwhile guide. While this is slowly beginning to change, as of the time of this writing we feel that the only way to easily overcome the various subtleties of installing Rails on OS X is to go straight to the metal. That said, if you're on a Mac and want to use a package manager to install Rails, you wouldn't be alone.

On OS X, you have two choices for a package manager: Fink (`http://finkproject.org`) or MacPorts (`http://macports.org`) (formerly DarwinPorts). James Duncan Davidson has written the definitive guide on using the latter to set up a complete Rails environment, which you might want to read: `http://blog.duncandavidson.com/2006/04/sandboxing_rail.html`.

Installing the Apple Developer Tools (Xcode)

Before you can compile source code on your Mac, you need to install a compiler. Apple's Developer Tools package, Xcode Tools, includes a compiler and provides the easiest way to set up a development environment on your Mac. Xcode comes on your OS X 10.4 installation DVD, but if you can't find your installation media, you can always download it from Apple at `http://developer.apple.com/tools/xcode/`.

■**Note** Before proceeding, be aware that Xcode is a large download. Weighing in at a hefty 800MB, it's not the sort of thing you want to be downloading over a dial-up connection. Before you start downloading, you might want to try to find it on your installation DVD.

Xcode is packaged as a regular Apple installer (look for it on the 10.4 installation DVD as a package called Xcode 2.4 or Xcode Tools), so all you need to do is double-click its icon, answer a few basic questions, and you should be on your way. If you run into trouble and are looking for an in-depth guide to the whole process, try this article on the Macworld site, which has a good write-up:

`www.macworld.com/weblogs/macosxhints/2005/08/installxcode/index.php`

Installing MySQL

Thanks to a decent installer for OS X, MySQL is a breeze to set up. You can download the latest installer package from MySQL's web site:

`http://dev.mysql.com/downloads/mysql/5.0.html`

Scroll all the way down the page until you reach the section titled Mac OS X downloads. There, you'll see downloads for the latest version (5.0.27 at the time of this writing) in Standard, Max, and Debug variants. You'll want to download the Standard package, and depending on the processor in your Mac, you'll need either the PowerPC distribution (if you have a PowerPC processor) or the x86 distribution (if you have an Intel processor). If you don't know which processor is in your Mac, you can click the Apple icon in the top-left corner of your screen and choose About This Mac from the menu. This will open a window that will show you the type of processor onboard, as shown in Figure 2-1.

Figure 2-1. *About This Mac window showing an Intel processor*

The file you download will be a compressed disk image with the extension .dmg. Double-click its icon to extract and mount the image, and the Finder should open a window with icons for three files:

- mysql-standard-5.x.x.pkg: This is the main installer.

- MySQLStartupItem.pkg: This makes sure MySQL starts up when your computer does.

- MySQL.prefPane: This installs a preference pane in the Apple System Preferences, where you can start and stop the MySQL server.

You need to install all three of these. Kick off the process by double-clicking the main installation package, mysql-standard-5.x.x.pkg. After you move through the initial introductory and license screens, you'll start the simple installation steps, as shown in Figure 2-2.

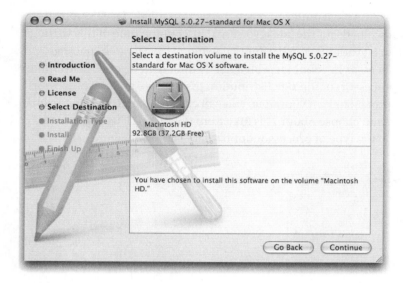

Figure 2-2. *MySQL Installer for OS X*

When MySQL is finished installing, double-click MySQLStartupItem.pkg to install the necessary startup scripts. Finally, double-click the MySQL.prefPane icon to install the preference pane. This last step should open the preference pane (if it doesn't open it from Apple ➤ System Preferences ➤ MySQL), which you can use to start and stop the server, as shown in Figure 2-3.

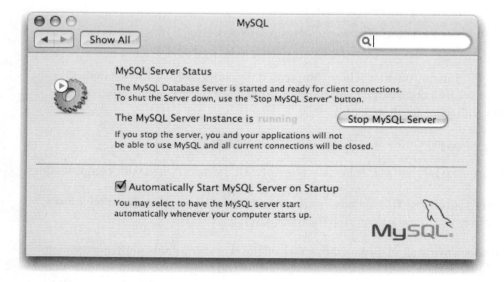

Figure 2-3. *MySQL preference pane*

Make sure the server is running and close the preference pane. You can eject the MySQL disk image and delete the .dmg file you downloaded. Now you're ready for the next step: adding MySQL to your PATH.

Adding MySQL to Your PATH

After MySQL is installed, you'll want to add the MySQL install directory (/usr/local/mysql) to your PATH. The PATH is a special variable that contains all the locations your shell should search for programs when you type them on the command line. If you add MySQL's directory to your PATH, you'll be able to issue commands right from the Terminal, which as you'll see later, is quite convenient.

To figure out your PATH, the shell looks in a special file residing in the root of your home directory that provides startup instructions. Assuming you're using the stock bash shell in OS X, this file should be called .bash_profile (but it might be called .bash_login, .profile, or something entirely different if you're not using bash). Because it begins with a dot (.), it's hidden from the Finder, so you'll need to use the Terminal in /Applications/Utilities/Terminal.app if you want to see it. You can use the ls program with -a (which means *all*) to show all files in a directory, including hidden ones. This file may or may not exist. If it doesn't, and you don't have a similar file (like .bash_login, or .profile), you'll need to create it. Even if you do have a .bash_login or .profile, .bash_profile has precedence and will override the others, so if you're not sure, choose .bash_profile.

You can edit .bash_profile using any text editor. Entering the following command should open the file if it exists, or create a new one if it doesn't. You can replace the word pico with your favorite command to launch your editor of choice (such as mate, vim, or emacs):

```
$ pico ~/.bash_profile
```

Look for a line with the word PATH in it and replace it with the following line. If you don't already have a .bash_profile file and are creating a new one, this is the only line you need to add. In either case, when you're all finished, it should look like this:

```
export PATH="/usr/local/bin:/usr/local/sbin:/usr/local/mysql/bin:$PATH"
```

The PATH variable tells your shell where to look for programs by taking a list of directories to be searched, separated by the colon character (:). The directories are searched by the shell in order, from left to right. As you can see, it will look first in /usr/local/bin. If it doesn't find a match, it will try /usr/local/sbin. Finally, it will try /usr/local/mysql/bin. If it still can't find the program you're looking for, it will tell you the command couldn't be found. By adding MySQL's binary directory (/usr/local/mysql/bin) to the path, you ensure that when you type things like mysql at the prompt, the shell will find the mysql program.

Note The PATH is searched in order from left to right. That means if you have a program with the same name in both /usr/local/bin and /usr/local/sbin, the one in /usr/local/sbin will never be run with the order shown. When you type the name of the program, you'll always get the one the shell finds first.

Make sure you save the changes to .bash_profile and exit your text editor. Remember that .bash_profile is a startup script and, as such, is run only when you start a new Terminal session. This means the shell doesn't know about the changes you've made yet. To cause the startup script to be read again, just close the Terminal window and open up a new one.

If you created a new shell and your PATH was read correctly, you should be able to run the mysql program and request its version number:

```
$ mysql --version
```

```
mysql  Ver 14.12 Distrib 5.0.27, for apple-darwin8.5.1 (i686) using readline 5.0
```

If this fails with an error like -bash: mysql: command not found, then your PATH might be set up incorrectly. Read over the previous paragraphs one more time and make sure you've followed the instructions.

Tip To find out where a program is being run from, use the which command: which mysql.

Installing Ruby

The first thing we like to do when compiling software is to make a place to work. In UNIX tradition, the place to compile and build sources is in the directory /usr/local/src. From the Terminal, enter the following command to create and change into /usr/local/src.

```
$ sudo mkdir -p /usr/local/src
$ cd /usr/local/src
```

You'll stay inside this directory for the next few steps. You can check which directory you're currently in at any time by typing pwd and pressing Enter.

```
$ pwd
```

```
/usr/local/src
```

The steps for compiling and installing packages are pretty standard:

1. Download the source package (`curl`).

2. Unarchive the source package (`tar`).

3. Configure compilation parameters (`configure`).

4. Compile the source files (`make`).

5. Install the software (`install`).

Start by installing Readline, a prerequisite for Ruby on OS X systems. Make sure you're in the `/usr/local/src` directory, and type each of the following commands on its own line, pressing Enter after each one. The Terminal will respond to each command by spitting out a bunch of text on the screen, but when it's all over, you'll be back at the prompt and ready to enter the next command. Ready? Let's go!

```
$ curl -O ftp://ftp.gnu.org/gnu/readline/readline-5.2.tar.gz
$ tar xzvf readline-5.2.tar.gz
$ pushd readline-5.2
$ ./configure --prefix=/usr/local
$ make
$ sudo make install
$ popd
```

The `popd` on the last line takes you back up a directory, so that you're in `/usr/local/src` again, ready to tackle the next package.

Note If you get an error like `configure: error: no acceptable C compiler found in $PATH`, it means that your system wasn't able to find a compiler and therefore can't compile the source files. If you see this, you likely don't have the Xcode Tools installed correctly. Take a quick look back at the "Installing the Apple Developer Tools" section and make sure you've followed all the directions.

With Readline successfully installed, you'll perform a similar procedure for installing Ruby. Again, make sure you're in the directory `/usr/local/src`, then issue the following commands at the prompt.

```
$ curl -O ftp://ftp.ruby-lang.org/pub/ruby/1.8/ruby-1.8.5-p12.tar.gz
$ tar xzvf ruby-1.8.5-p12.tar.gz
$ pushd ruby-1.8.5-p12
$ ./configure --prefix=/usr/local --enable-pthread --with-readline-dir=/usr/local
```

```
$ make
$ sudo make install
$ popd
```

You can test to see if Ruby is installed correctly (and that your PATH is set up correctly) by asking Ruby for its version number:

```
$ ruby --version
```

```
ruby 1.8.5 (2006-08-25) [i686-darwin8.8.2]
```

Next, make sure that the instance of Ruby the shell is finding is the one you expect, which should be in /usr/local/bin/ruby.

```
$ which ruby
```

```
/usr/local/bin/ruby
```

Great! Ruby is installed and working correctly. You can now move on to the next step: installing RubyGems.

Installing RubyGems

Ruby uses a package management system called RubyGems (http://rubyforge.org/ project/rubygems) to manage the installation and maintenance of Ruby programs and libraries. As you'll see, RubyGems makes the installation of the various Rails libraries a piece of cake, but first, you need to get RubyGems running. The current stable version at the time of this writing is 0.9.1. Depending on when you're reading this book, there may be a newer version available, which you should use.

Make sure you're in /usr/local/src and issue the following commands at the prompt.

```
$ curl -OL http://rubyforge.org/frs/download.php/16452/rubygems-0.9.1.tgz
$ tar xzvf rubygems-0.9.1.tgz
$ pushd rubygems-0.9.1
$ sudo ruby setup.rb
$ popd
```

Installing Rails

With RubyGems in place, Rails is a cinch to install. Simply use the gem command, and RubyGems will take care of the rest.

```
$ sudo gem install rails --include-dependencies
```

The include-dependencies argument tells RubyGems to automatically download and install all the libraries and programs that Rails depends on. If you don't include dependencies in the command, it will still work, but you'll need to answer Yes to install each additional dependency as it comes up.

When RubyGems is finished installing Rails, you can check to see if everything went smoothly by testing the rails command, just as you did with MySQL.

```
$ rails --version
```

```
Rails 1.2.3
```

```
$ which rails
```

```
/usr/local/bin/rails
```

Now that Rails is installed, it's time to take it for a spin! Unless you feel like reading the installation instructions for Windows and Linux, you're free to skip ahead to the "Creating Your First Rails Application" section.

Automating Installation

Here's a script you can use to automate all the steps we just covered for installing on Mac OS X. To use it, save it with an extension of .sh (we recommend install_rails.sh), and make sure you run it as a superuser using sudo. Remember that you need Apple's Developer Tools package, Xcode Tools, to run this script.

```
#!/bin/sh

PREFIX="/usr/local"
READLINE_VERSION="5.2"
RUBY_VERSION="1.8.5-p12"
GEM_VERSION="0.9.1"
```

```
curl -O ftp://ftp.gnu.org/gnu/readline/readline-${READLINE_VERSION}.tar.gz
tar xzvf readline-${READLINE_VERSION}.tar.gz
pushd readline-${READLINE_VERSION}
./configure --prefix=${PREFIX}
make
make install
popd

curl -O ftp://ftp.ruby-lang.org/pub/ruby/1.8/ruby-${RUBY_VERSION}.tar.gz
tar xzvf ruby-${RUBY_VERSION}.tar.gz
pushd ruby-${RUBY_VERSION}
./configure --prefix=${PREFIX} --enable-pthread --with-readline-dir=${PREFIX}
make
make install
popd

curl -OL http://rubyforge.org/frs/download.php/16452/rubygems-${GEM_VERSION}.tgz
tar xzvf rubygems-${RUBYGEMS_VERSION}.tgz
pushd rubygems-${RUBYGEMS_VERSION}
ruby setup.rb
popd

gem install rails –include-dependencies
```

Assuming you named this script `install_rails.sh`, you would run it using the following command.

```
$ sudo install_rails.sh
```

Installing on Windows XP

Installation on Windows is easy thanks to installer packages. While this is the norm for Windows, few installation procedures are without their "gotchas," so be sure to check out the latest information on the Rails wiki (http://wiki.rubyonrails.org/) for help with specific problems. We'll start by installing MySQL.

Installing MySQL

MySQL is easy to install on Windows thanks to a one-click installer provided by MySQL AB. You can find a link to download the latest package here:

`http://dev.mysql.com/downloads/mysql/5.0.html`

Make sure you download the latest stable Standard release. When it's finished downloading, double-click the installer to start the installation. You'll be presented with a list of options to fill in. The defaults will suffice, so click Next to proceed through the install wizard until you reach the option to configure your server. Make sure the option to Configure Your Server Now is checked, and then click Next.

The configuration step of the wizard is important. As shown in Figure 2-4, here you set up MySQL as a Windows service, which lets you use the Microsoft Management Console (MMC) to configure startup options and other useful commands. Make sure the "Launch the MySQL Server Automatically" check box is selected. Also make sure the Include BIN Directory in Windows PATH check box is selected, so the installer will add the MySQL utilities directory to the command-line PATH variable. This allows you to call the MySQL utilities from the command line.

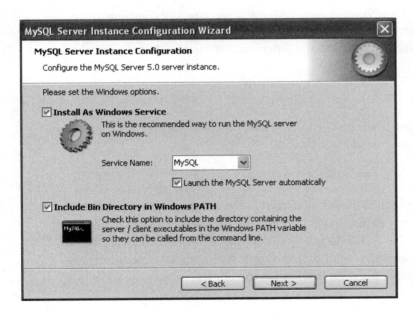

Figure 2-4. *MySQL Server Instance Configuration*

You can set a root password for your installation if you wish, but since you'll likely only be using this database for development, it's not really necessary. You might even find it's easier just to leave it at the default (blank) when working with Rails, since you'll have even less configuration to do when creating a new application. (Rails assumes you'll be accessing your database in development with the username root and a blank password.)

If all has gone according to plan, you'll be able to test your MySQL installation and the configuration of your Windows environment by opening the command prompt (click Start ➤ Run, type cmd, and click OK) and typing the following command.

```
> mysql --version
```

```
> mysql Ver 14.12 Distrib 5.0.27
```

With MySQL installed, it's time to tackle the next step: installing Ruby. Fortunately, it's even easier than installing MySQL.

Installing Ruby

Installing Ruby on Windows is marvelously easy thanks largely to Curt Hibb's one-click installer for Ruby. You can read more and download the installer from its RubyForge project page:

```
http://rubyforge.org/projects/rubyinstaller/
```

The current version of the installer at the time of this writing is 1.8.5-21, for Ruby 1.8.5, which you can download using this URL:

```
http://rubyforge.org/frs/download.php/12751/ruby185-21.exe
```

After you've downloaded the installer, start the installation by double-clicking its icon. What follows is standard installer fare, and the defaults are all sufficient for our purposes. All you need to do is select the location where you would like to put Ruby (usually c:\ruby), as shown in Figure 2-5, and the installer will take care of the rest. You'll have a fully functioning Ruby installation in minutes.

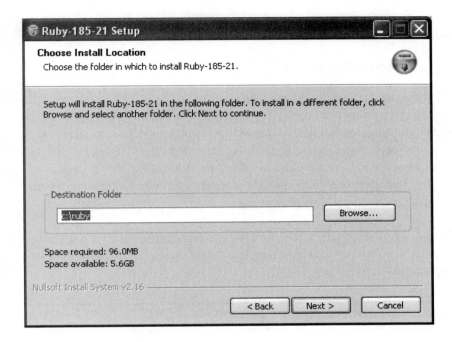

Figure 2-5. *Ruby installer*

When the installer is finished, you can test to see if Ruby is working and that your environment is correctly configured by opening your command prompt and asking Ruby its version number.

```
> ruby --version
```

```
ruby 1.8.5 (2006-08-25) [i386-mswin32]
```

Installing Rails

You'll be pleased to know that the one-click installer also installed RubyGems, a package management system for Ruby (http://rubyforge.org/project/rubygems), which makes installing Ruby libraries, utilities, and programs a breeze. This includes Rails installation.

To install Rails using RubyGems, open your command prompt and issue the gem command, as follows.

```
> gem install rails --include-dependencies
```

Be forewarned that the gem command can take some time, so don't be discouraged if it seems to be sitting there doing nothing for a few minutes; it's probably just updating its index file. It's worth pointing out that RubyGems searches for gems in its remote repository (http://gems.rubyforge.org), so you need to be connected to the Internet for this command to work. Also, if you have a firewall or other network settings that restrict communication with the Internet, you might have problems. For more information and troubleshooting tips, see the RubyGems project page at http://rubyforge.org/project/rubygems.

After spitting out some text to the screen and generally chugging away for a few minutes, the gem program should exit with something like the following before dumping you back at the command prompt.

```
Successfully installed rails-1.2.3
```

That's all there is to it! The one-click installer took care of most of the work by installing and configuring Ruby, and since Rails is distributed as a RubyGem, installing it was a simple one-liner!

You can double-check that Rails was installed successfully by issuing the rails --version command at the command prompt.

```
> rails --version
```

```
> Rails 1.2.3
```

With Ruby and Rails happily installed, it's time to take it for a test drive. Unless you feel like reading the installation instructions for Linux, you're free to skip ahead to the "Creating Your First Rails Application" section.

Installing on Linux

Linux, and UNIX-based systems in general, come in a variety of different flavors, but all share a lot in common. For these instructions, we're using a Debian-based variant called Ubuntu Linux (specifically, Dapper Drake), but they should apply to most UNIX systems with varying mileage. Check out the latest information on the Rails wiki (http://wiki.rubyonrails.org/) for help with specific problems.

■Note Ubuntu Linux is a top-notch distribution that's rapidly gaining mindshare in the Linux community. At the time of this writing, it is poised to become the most popular Linux distribution for general use and is largely responsible for the increased viability of Linux as a desktop platform. It's freely available from http://unbuntu.org and highly recommended. Keir Thomas has written an excellent book titled *Beginning Ubuntu Linux* (Apress, 2007). If you're new to Ubuntu (or to Linux in general), you might want to check it out.

Just about all Linux distributions (including Ubuntu) ship with a package manager. Whether you are installing programs or code libraries, they usually have dependencies, and a single program could depend on dozens of other programs in order to run properly, which can be a struggle to deal with yourself. A package manager takes care of these tasks for you, so you can focus on better things.

Ubuntu Linux includes the Debian package manager apt, which is what we'll be using in our examples. If you're using a different distribution, you'll likely have a different package manager, but the steps should be reasonably similar. If you're looking for a more do-it-yourself method, you can refer to the OS X installation instructions earlier in this chapter, which describe the process of building and installing the necessary packages yourself.

Before you begin installing MySQL, Ruby, RubyGems, and Rails, update the package library using apt-get update.

```
$ sudo apt-get update
```

The apt-get program keeps a cached index of all the programs and their versions in the repository for faster searching. Running the update command ensures that this list is up-to-date, so you'll be getting the most recent versions of the software you need.

Installing MySQL

To install MySQL with apt-get, issue the following command.

```
$ sudo apt-get install libmysql-ruby1.8 mysql-server-5.0
```

If all has gone according to plan, you'll be able to test your MySQL installation by invoking the mysql program and asking for its version number:

```
$ mysql --version
```

```
mysql Ver 14.12 Distrib 5.0.27
```

To stop and start MySQL, you can run the /etc/init.d/mysql program with an argument of start, stop, or restart. To start the server if it isn't already running, use this command:

```
$ /etc/init.d/mysql start
```

MySQL should now be running, and you're ready to move on to the next step: installing Ruby and its friends.

Tip You can set a root password for your installation using the mysql_secure_installation program if you wish, but since you'll likely be using this database only for development, it's not really necessary. You might even find it's easier just to leave it at the default (blank) when working with Rails, since you'll have even less configuration to do when creating a new application. (Rails assumes you'll be accessing your database in development with the username root and a blank password.)

Installing Ruby

Enter the following command to install Ruby and its friends.

```
$ sudo apt-get install ruby irb rdoc libruby1.8 ruby1.8-dev
```

This instructs apt to get the latest list of files that the online repository holds, and then requests Ruby, Ruby header files, rdoc, and the Ruby library files.

All you need to do now is link the filename that Ubuntu has used with the typical ruby command, so you don't have to type ruby1.8 every time you want to use it.

```
$ sudo ln -s /usr/bin/ruby1.8 /usr/bin/ruby
```

You can test that this is working by asking Ruby for its version number.

```
$ ruby --version
```

```
ruby 1.8.5 (2006-08-25) [i486-linux]
```

Next, make sure that the instance of Ruby the shell is finding is the one you expect, which should be in `/usr/bin/ruby`.

```
$ which ruby
```

```
/usr/bin/ruby
```

Installing RubyGems

Ruby uses a package management system called RubyGems (`http://rubyforge.org/ project/rubygems`) to manage the installation and maintenance of Ruby programs and libraries.

As you'll see, RubyGems makes the installation of the various Rails libraries a piece of cake, but first, you need to get RubyGems running. The current stable version at the time of this writing is 0.9.1. Depending on when you're reading this book, there may be a newer version available, which you should use.

To begin installing RubyGems, change to `/usr/local/src` and issue the following commands.

```
$ curl -O http://rubyforge.org/frs/download.php/11289/rubygems-0.9.1.tgz
$ tar xzvf rubygems-0.9.1.tgz
$ cd rubygems-0.9.1
$ sudo ruby setup.rb
```

Installing Rails

Now that RubyGems is installed, you can use it to install the Rails framework. Enter this command:

```
$ sudo gem install rails --include-dependencies
```

The `include-dependencies` argument tells RubyGems to automatically download and install all the libraries and programs that Rails depends on. If for some reason you forget to use the `--include-dependencies` argument, the command will still work, but RubyGems will prompt you to approve each additional library.

After spitting out some text to the screen and generally chugging away for a little while, the gem program should exit with a message like the following:

```
Successfully installed rails-1.2.3
```

You can verify this claim by asking Rails for its version number:

```
$ rails --version
```

```
Rails 1.2.3
```

```
$ which rails
```

```
/usr/local/bin/rails
```

With Ruby and Rails happily installed, it's time to take it for a test drive.

Creating Your First Rails Application

We'll start off by using the rails command to create a new Rails project. The rails command takes the name of the project you want to create as an argument and creates a Rails skeleton in a new directory by the same name. We'll demonstrate by creating a new project called (what else?) hello.

```
$ rails hello
```

```
create
create    app/controllers
create    app/helpers
create    app/models
create    app/views
create    config/database.yml
create    config/routes.rb
create    script/server
create    public/images
create    public/javascripts
```

```
create  log/production.log
create  log/development.log
create  log/test.log
```

We've trimmed the output here to point out a few items that were generated, namely the app/ directory and its subdirectories. If you look closely, you'll see the subdirectories of app/ are named after the MVC pattern we introduced in Chapter 1: models, views, and controllers. You'll also see a name we also mentioned briefly in Chapter 1: helpers. Helpers help bridge the gap between controllers and views, and we'll talk about them in Chapter 5.

Rails generated a new directory called hello, so let's change into it and have a quick look around. If you look at the folder structure, you'll see the following.

```
$ cd hello
hello$ ls
```

README	app	config	doc	log	script	tmp
Rakefile	components	db	lib	public	test	vendor

Starting the Built-In Web Server

Next, let's start up a local web server so we can test our new project in the browser. True, we haven't written any code yet, but Rails has a nice welcome screen that we can use to test whether our new project is set up correctly. It will even give you some information about your Ruby environment.

Rails ships with a built-in, zero-configuration, pure Ruby web server that makes running your application in development mode incredibly easy. You start up the built-in web server using the server command in the script directory. To start the server now, enter the following command.

```
$ ruby script/server
```

```
=> Booting WEBrick...
=> Rails application started on http://0.0.0.0:3000
=> Ctrl-C to shutdown server; call with --help for options
[2006-11-27 17:24:26] INFO  WEBrick 1.3.1
[2006-11-27 17:24:26] INFO  ruby 1.8.5 (2006-08-25) [i686-darwin8.6.1]
[2006-11-27 17:24:26] INFO  WEBrick::HTTPServer#start: pid=5181 port=3000
```

The message from the `server` script tells us that a web server is running at the IP address 0.0.0.0 on port 3000. Don't be alarmed by this all-zeros address. It simply means that the server is running locally on your machine. The hostname `localhost` also resolves to your local machine, and is thus interchangeable with the IP address. We prefer to use the hostname variant.

■Note The specific server Rails uses will depend on what you have installed. If you have Mongrel installed, it will use that; if not, it will look for LightTPD. If you don't have either Mongrel or LightTPD, Rails will use WEBrick, which is built right in. In the preceding sample output, you can see we're using WEBrick. WEBrick is great for development, and since it's bundled with Rails, you always have a web server around to fire up your application.

With the server now running, if you open `http://localhost:3000/` in your browser, you'll see the Rails welcome page, as shown in Figure 2-6. Congratulations! You've put Rails.

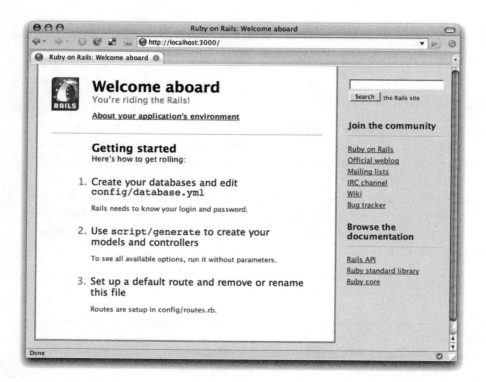

Figure 2-6. *Rails welcome page*

The welcome page is nice, but it doesn't really teach you much. In fact, it's really just a static HTML page sitting in the `public/` directory. The first step in learning how Rails works is to generate something dynamic. You're about to learn why we called this project "hello"!

We're sure it would be in violation of the law of programming books if we didn't start off with the ubiquitous "Hello World" example. And who are we to disobey? In the next few steps, we'll make our Rails application say hello, and in doing so, introduce a few new concepts. What's our goal? To have a request with the URL `http://localhost:3000/salutation/hello` respond with a friendly "Hello World!" message.

First things first: stop the web server by pressing Ctrl+C. That should bring you back to your prompt.

Note Notice how easy it is to start and stop a local server? That's the whole point of the built-in server in a nutshell. The idea is that you shouldn't need to be a sysadmin in order to develop your Rails application.

Generating a Controller

We're going to use another command in the `script/` directory now: the `generate` command. You use the `generate` command to create certain files within your project. Since we're dealing with the request and response cycle (you request a URL, and the browser receives a response), you'll generate a controller that will be responsible for handling salutations.

```
hello$ ./script/generate controller salutation
```

```
exists  app/controllers/
exists  app/helpers/
create  app/views/salutation
exists  test/functional/
create  app/controllers/salutation_controller.rb
create  test/functional/salutation_controller_test.rb
create  app/helpers/salutation_helper.rb
```

Not unlike the `rails` command, the `generate controller` command creates a bunch of new files. These are mostly empty, containing only skeletal code (*stubs*, as we often call them). You could easily have created all these files on your own. The generator merely saves you time and the effort of needing to remember which files to create and where to put them.

Our salutation controller was created in the `app/controllers` directory and is quite sensibly named `salutation_controller.rb`. If you open it with a text editor, you'll see there's not much to it, as shown in Listing 2-1.

Listing 2-1. *The app/controllers/salutation_controller.rb File*

```
class SalutationController < ApplicationController
end
```

Creating an Action

Controllers respond to actions. If we want our `SalutationController` to respond to a request for `hello`, we'll need to make an action for it. Open `salutation_controller.rb` in your text editor and add the `hello` action, as shown in Listing 2-2.

Listing 2-2. *The app/controllers/salutation_controller.rb File*

```
class SalutationController < ApplicationController
  def hello
    @message = 'Hello World!'
  end
end
```

Actions are implemented as Ruby methods. You can always tell a method definition because of the `def` keyword. Inside the action, we're setting a Ruby instance variable called `@message`, the value of which we'll output to the browser.

Creating a Template

With our action successfully defined, our next move is to add some HTML into the mix. Rails makes it easy by separating the files that contain HTML into their own directory as per the MVC pattern. In case you haven't guessed, HTML is the responsibility of the view.

If you look in the `app/views` directory, you'll see another product of the controller generator: a directory called `salutation`. It's linked to the `salutation` controller, and it's where you put template files that correspond to your `salutation` actions.

■**Note** Because Rails allows you to embed Ruby code in your HTML, you use the `.rhtml` (Ruby + HTML) extension for your templates.

The default way to render a template in response to a request for an action is remarkably simple: just name it the same as the action. Since we want to show a response to the `hello` action, we'll name our file `hello.rhtml`, and Rails will render it automatically. This is quite easy to grasp in practice. Take a look at Figure 2-7 for a visual cue as to how controllers and templates correspond.

Figure 2-7. *Controllers correspond to a directory in app/views*

Start by creating a new, blank file in `app/views/salutation/`. Name it `hello.rhtml` and add the code shown in Listing 2-3. Notice the `<%= %>` syntax that surrounds the `@message` variable. These are known as ERb (Embedded Ruby) output tags. We'll talk more about ERb in Chapter 6. For now, it's only important that you know that whenever you see `<%= %>` in a template, whatever is between the tags will be evaluated as Ruby and the result will be printed out.

Listing 2-3. *The app/views/salutation/hello.rhtml File*

```
<html>
  <body>
    <h1><%= @message %></h1>
  </body>
</html>
```

It looks like we're all set. The salutation controller will field the request for hello and automatically render the hello.rhtml template. Start up the web server again using the script/server command and request the URL http://localhost:3000/salutation/hello in your browser. You should see the result shown in Figure 2-8.

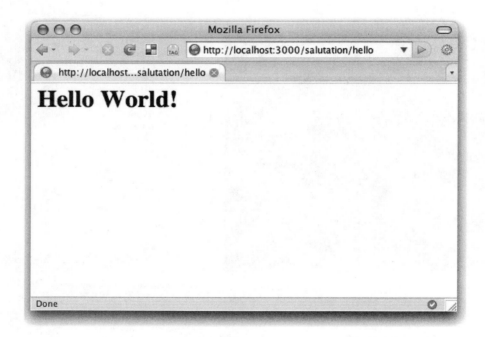

Figure 2-8. *The "Hello World" application*

Sure enough, there's our greeting! The hello template read the @message variable that we set in the controller, and with a little help from ERb, printed it out to the screen.

Now, we should mention something here in case you didn't notice. The URL `http://localhost:3000/salutation/hello` maps directly to the controller and action we created. This is no mere coincidence. It's just another example of convention over configuration, most succinctly expressed by the default URL pattern:

```
:controller/:action/:id
```

We're not sending anything along in the `:id` placeholder, but if we were, it would be available to us as a parameter by the same name (`params[:id]`). We'll talk about parameters more in Chapter 6, but for now, it's enough that you understand the default URL format so you can make the mental connection between URL segments and the code in your application. When you read the URL `http://localhost:3000/salutation/hello`, you can translate it into a request for the `hello` action on the `salutation` controller.

Summary

We covered a lot in this chapter, so you should be proud of yourself. We went from not having Rails installed to getting a basic Rails application up and running. You learned how to install Ruby and how to manage packages with RubyGems (which we used to install Rails). You also learned how to create a new Rails project using the `rails` command, and how to use the generator to create a new controller. And you learned how controller actions correspond to templates. The stage is now set for the next chapter, where we'll begin building a more full-featured project.

CHAPTER 3

■ ■ ■

Getting Something Running

The best way to learn a programming language or a web framework is to dig in and write some code. After reading the first two chapters, you should have a good understanding of the Rails landscape. This chapter builds on that foundation by walking you through the construction of a basic application. You'll learn how to create a database and how to connect it to Rails, as well as how to use a web interface to get data in and out of the application.

You'll receive a lot of information in this chapter, though not more than you can absorb, we hope. Our goal here is demonstrate, not to overwhelm. As you'll see, Rails makes it incredibly easy to get started, and that's a feature we want to highlight. There are a few places where Rails really shines, and getting something running is one of them. By the end of this chapter, you'll have a working web application to play with, explore, and learn from. We'll build on this application throughout the rest of the book, adding features and refining functionality.

An Overview of the Project

We're going to build a simple event-management system that will let us create and manage upcoming events, not unlike Upcoming.org or Evite. Our first iteration will focus on the basics: creating and editing events.

Before we start coding though, let's sketch out a brief summary of the goals and flow of the application. We're going to stay at a very high level. The idea is not to focus on the nitty-gritty, but instead to concentrate on the general case.

Our application will have two kinds of users: those who create events and those who wish to attend events. In some cases, people will play both roles. All users will need to create an account by registering on the site. It would also be nice if people could notify their friends of interesting events with a "send to friend" feature that sends out a friendly email notification to interested parties.

These are some of the features we will add in later chapters. Other application requirements will likely come up as we continue, but these will be enough to get started. In the real world, specifications are seldom correct the first time around, so it's best not to dwell on them. You'll see right away that Rails doesn't penalize you for making changes to an application that's already under construction, so we can engage in an iterative style of development, adding and incrementing functionality as we go.

We'll start with what matters most: events. You might be wondering why we don't start with users. After all, without users, who will create the events? We could begin with users, but if you think about it, without events, what could users do? Events are clearly the epicenter of the application, so it makes the most sense to start there and work out the details as we go. Ready? Let's get started!

Creating the Events Application

As you saw in the previous chapter, the first step is to create a new Rails application. We could try to come up with a fancy Web 2.0 name, but instead we'll keep it simple and just call the application events. It's not going to win any awards for creativity, but it works.

To get started, issue the rails command to generate the application skeleton and base files.

```
$rails events
```

```
create
create    app/controllers
create    app/helpers
create    app/models
create    app/views/layouts
...
```

As you'll recall from our little example in Chapter 2, the rails command takes the name of the project you want to create as an argument and generates a directory of the same name that contains all the support files. In this case, it will create a subdirectory in dev called events. Change into the events directory and get oriented. Figure 3-1 shows the directory structure.

Figure 3-1. *The Rails directory structure*

Our first stop is the config directory. Of the little configuration there is to do in a Rails application, most of it takes place in this aptly named location. To get an idea about what Rails is expecting as far as databases go, open the database.yml file in your editor and take a peek. You should see something like the file shown in Listing 3-1 (we're omitting the comments here).

Listing 3-1. *The config/database.yml File*

```
development:
  adapter: mysql
  database: events_development
  username: root
  password:
  host: localhost

test:
  adapter: mysql
  database: events_test
  username: root
  password:
  host: localhost

production:
  adapter: mysql
  database: events_production
  username: root
  password:
  host: localhost
```

The first thing you should notice is the different sections: development, test, and production. Rails understands the concept of *environments* and assumes you'll be using a different database for each environment. Therefore, each has its own database connection settings, and different connection parameters will be used automatically. Rails applications run in *development* mode by default, so we really only need to worry about the development section here. Still, other than the database names (events_*), there should be little difference between the connection parameters for each environment.

The rails command has prefilled the database parameter based on the project name: events. If you gave your application a different name (say, a snazzy Web 2.0 name, like, event.ilicio.us *beta), you would see something different here. In reality, it doesn't matter what you name your databases, as long as database.yml references the correct one for each environment. We'll stick with the convention and create the databases using the default names.

WHAT IS YAML?

The .yml extension refers to a YAML file. YAML is a special language for expressing objects in plain text. Rails can work with YAML natively and is able to turn what looks like plain text into Ruby objects that it can understand. It's a recursive acronym that stands for YAML Ain't Markup Language.

YAML is whitespace-active. It uses spaces (not tabs) to convey structure and meaning. Make sure your editor knows the difference between tabs and spaces, and make sure that when editing YAML files, you're using only spaces. If you find yourself getting an error like /usr/lib/ruby/1.8/yaml.rb:119:in `load': parse error, you're probably using tabs.

Creating the Project Databases

To create a new database, you can use your favorite database administration tool, or you can use the mysqladmin program from the command line. Since we're command-line junkies, we'll do the latter.

```
$ mysqladmin -uroot create events_development
```

We give the mysqladmin program two arguments: an action (create) and the name of the database we want to create. That should be sufficient to create a new database called events_development.

Note Depending on how your environment is set up, you might not need to specify the username under You might also need to supply a password, which you can do using the -p option. Here, we're using MySQL's default `root` user (with no password), which should work on most installations.

While we're only concerned with the development environment at this time, it won't hurt to create the other databases while we're at it. Go ahead and create two more databases, one each for the test and production environments.

```
$ mysqladmin -uroot create events_test
$ mysqladmin -uroot create events_production
```

You can confirm the creation of the database using the `mysqlshow` program to take a look at all the MySQL databases currently on your system.

```
$ mysqlshow
```

```
+--------------------------+
|        Databases         |
+--------------------------+
| information_schema       |
| events_development       |
| events_test              |
| events_production        |
| mysql                    |
| test                     |
+--------------------------+
```

For most MySQL installations, the default connection parameters in `database.yml` (a username of `root` and no password) will work out of the box. If you've set up a password for the root account, or if you prefer not to use the root account at all and instead use a different username, you'll need to fill in that information if you want your connection to work.

You can test to see if your connection is working by running the following command.

```
$ rake db:migrate
```

If you see nothing exceptional returned, congratulations! Rails can connect to your database. However, if you see something like this:

```
rake aborted!
Access denied for user 'root'@'localhost' (using password: NO)
```

then you need to adjust your connection settings. If you're having problems, make sure that the database exists and that you've entered the correct username and password.

Creating the Event Model

Now that we can connect to the database, we're going to create a model. Remember that models in Rails correspond to database table names. Since we want to model events, we're going to create a model named Event. By convention, model names are singular and correspond to plural table names. So, an Event model will expect a table named events; a Person model will expect a table named people.

Like most things in Rails, models have their own generator script that makes it easier to get started. The generator will automatically create a new model file in the app/models directory, and will create a bunch of other files to boot. Among these are a unit test (for testing your model's functionality, as we'll discuss in Chapter 9) and a database migration. A *database migration* contains instructions for building the database table and the fields to create. Whenever you generate a new model, a migration will be created along with it.

■Note If you want to skip generation of the migration when generating a new model, you can pass the --skip-migration argument to the generator.

To see the generator's usage information, run it without arguments.

```
$ ./script/generate model
```

```
Usage: ./script/generate model ModelName [options]
```

As you can see from the usage banner, the generator takes a model name as its argument. The model name may be given in *CamelCase* or *under_score* format, and options can be provided if you want to automatically populate the resulting migration with column information.

Let's run the generator now to create our first model: Event.

```
$ ./script/generate model Event
```

```
exists   app/models/
exists   test/unit/
exists   test/fixtures/
create   app/models/event.rb
create   test/unit/event_test.rb
create   test/fixtures/events.yml
create   db/migrate
create   db/migrate/001_create_events.rb
```

If you look at the lines that start with create, you'll see that the generator created an event model, an event test, an events fixture (which is a textual representation of table data that you can use for testing), and a migration named 001_create_events.rb. With that, our model is generated.

Creating a Database Table

We need to create a table in the database. We could do this with a database administration tool, or even manually using SQL, but Rails provides a much more efficient facility for table creation and maintenance called migrations. It's called a migration because it allows you to evolve, or migrate, your schema over time. (If you're not familiar with databases, tables, and SQL, consult Appendix B for the basics.)

Schema is the term given to the properties that make up a table: the table's name, its columns, and column types, as well as any default values a column is to have. And what's the best part about migrations? You get to define your schema in pure Ruby. This is all part of the Rails philosophy that you should stick to one language when developing. It helps eliminate context switching and results in higher productivity.

As you can see from the output of the model generator, it created a new file in db/migrate called 001_create_events.rb. Notice that migrations are named with a numeric prefix, starting at 001. Since migrations are run sequentially, this number represents their position in the queue.

Let's open this file and take a peek. It's shown in Listing 3-2.

Listing 3-2. *The db/migrate/001_create_events.rb File*

```
class CreateEvents < ActiveRecord::Migration
  def self.up
    create_table :events do |t|
    end
  end

  def self.down
    drop_table :events
  end
end
```

In its initial, generated form, the migration is a blank canvas. But before we go any further, let's note a few important items. First, notice the class methods: up and down. For each migration, you define instructions for updating in the up method, and use the down method to roll back any changes. So, if you were to, say, create a new table in the up method, you would drop the table in the down method, thereby reversing your changes. In fact, that's exactly what the generator did for us already: The events table gets created on up and dropped on down. Pretty slick, isn't it?

■**Note** You can easily spot the difference between class and instance method definitions in a Ruby class by looking for the self prefix. For more about Ruby classes, see Appendix A.

We've gone ahead and filled out the details for you. Without having seen a migration before, you should be able to tell exactly what's going on by looking at Listing 3-3.

Listing 3-3. *Completed db/migrate/001_create_events File*

```
class CreateEvents < ActiveRecord::Migration
  def self.up
    create_table :events do |t|
      t.column :title,     :string
      t.column :location,  :string
      t.column :occurs_on, :date
    end
  end
```

```
  def self.down
    drop_table :events
  end
end
```

Let's step through the code. First, we use the `create_table` method, giving it the name of the table we want to create. Inside the code block, we use the `column` method to create columns in the table. The `column` method takes the name of the column and its type. (For a full description of the available field types you can create in your migrations, see `http://api.rubyonrails.org/classes/ActiveRecord/Migration.html`.)

On its own, this migration does nothing. Really, it's just a plain-old Ruby class. If we want it to do some work and create a table in the database for us, we need to run it. To run a migration, you use the built-in Rake task that Rails provides called `db:migrate`.

■**Note** Rake is a build language for Ruby. Rails uses Rake to automate several tasks, such as running database migrations, running tests, and updating Rails support files. You can think of Rake tasks as little utility programs. For a list of all available Rake tasks, run `rake -T` from your Rails project directory. For more information about Rake, including complete documentation, see `http://rake.rubyforge.org/`.

From the command line, type the following to run the migration and create the `events` table. You'll recognize this command as the same one we used to test the database connection. We sort of hijacked it for our test, knowing that it will attempt to connect to the database and thus prove whether the connection works. Since there were no existing migrations when we first ran it, it didn't do anything. Now that we have our first migration, running, it will result in a table being created.

```
$ rake db:migrate
```

```
== CreateEvents: migrating ===================================================
-- create_table(:events)
   -> 0.0314s
== CreateEvents: migrated (0.0316s) ==========================================
```

Just as the output says, the migration created a new table. If you were to try to run the migration again (go ahead, try it!), you would see that nothing happens. That's because Rails keeps track of the current migration version and it knows that you're at version 1, so there's nothing left to do.

Generating a Controller

We've created a model and its supporting database table, so our next step is to work on the controller and view side of the application. We'll create a controller named (wait for it) events to control the operation of the events functionality of the application. Just as with models, Rails provides a generator that we can use to create controllers. Let's start using it.

```
$ ./script/generate controller events
```

```
exists   app/controllers/
exists   app/helpers/
create   app/views/events
create   test/functional/
create   app/controllers/events_controller.rb
create   test/functional/events_controller_test.rb
create   app/helpers/events_helper.rb
```

The controller generator created three files:

- app/controllers/events_controller.rb: The controller that will be responsible for handling requests and responses for anything to do with events.

- test/functional/events_controller_test.rb: The class that will contain all functional tests for the events controller (we'll cover testing applications in Chapter 8).

- app/helpers/events_helper.rb: The helper class in which you can add utility methods that can be used in your views.

The controller generator also created an empty directory in app/views called events. This is where we'll place the templates for the events controller.

Up and Running with Scaffolding

One of the killer features that gave a lot of exposure to Rails is its scaffolding capabilities. Scaffolding allows you to create a boilerplate-style set of actions and templates that make it easy to manipulate data for a specific model. The scaffold provides methods and pages that allow you to insert, update, and delete records in your database.

To scaffold the Event model, open the file app/controllers/events_controller.rb in your editor and add scaffold :event inside the class body. When you're finished, the file should look like Listing 3-4.

Listing 3-4. *The app/controllers/events_controller.rb File*

```
class EventsController < ApplicationController
  scaffold :event
end
```

That's all you need to generate a working scaffold of the Event model. Let's fire up the web server and test it. Start your local web server from the command line (./script/server) and browse to the events controller in your browser.

```
http://localhost:3000/events
```

You should see the results displayed in your browser, as shown in Figure 3-2.

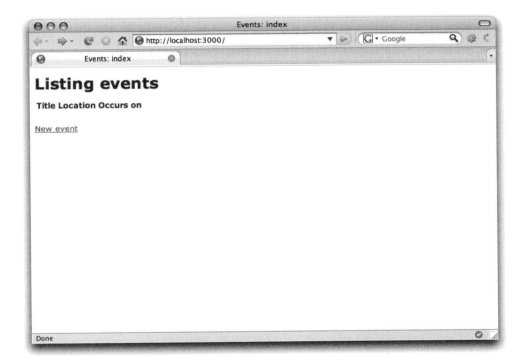

Figure 3-2. *Events scaffolding*

Click the New event link, and you'll be taken to a screen where you can enter events. Notice that the URL is http://localhost:3000/events/new, which means you're invoking the new action on the events controller. Go ahead and add a few events and generally play with it. Figure 3-3 shows an example of an event entered on this screen.

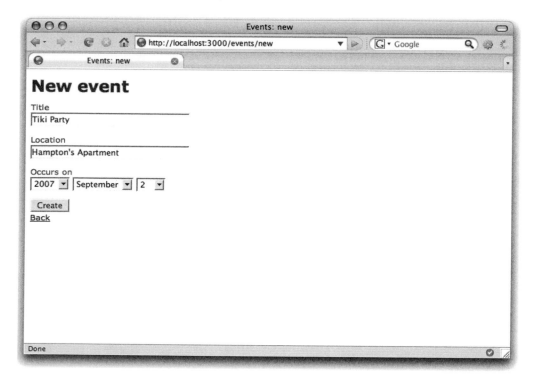

Figure 3-3. *Adding an event*

You'll notice that every time you add an event, you're redirected back to the index action, where you can see all your events listed. You can edit them, delete them, or create new ones. If you click the show link, you'll be taken to the detail page for that event. You've got to admit, that's a lot of functionality for only a single line of code!

Speed is the key benefit here. The scaffold declaration allows you to quickly get something running, which is a great way to test your assumptions.

■**Caution** Scaffolding comes with an important disclaimer. You shouldn't be using it in production. It exists to help you do exactly what we just did: get something running.

Adding More Fields

Now that you can see the model represented in the browser, we think it would be a good idea to add some more fields to make it a little more interesting. Whenever you need to add or modify database fields, you should do so using a migration. In this case, we'll add the url and description fields to the events table.

We didn't need to generate the last migration (the one that we used to create the events table), because the model generator took care of that for us. This time around, we'll use the migration generator. It works just like the model and controller generators, which you've already seen in action. All you need to do is give the migration generator a descriptive name for the transformation.

```
$ ./script/generate migration add_url_and_description_to_events
```

As you've already seen, the generator creates a migration class in db/migrate prefixed by its number in the queue. In this case, since this is our second migration, the prefix is 002. If you open the migration file, you'll see that it's just an empty stub. Unlike with the model generator, which prefilled the migration to some extent, we'll need to add the information manually here. To do this, use the add_column method with arguments.

```
class AddUrlAndDescriptionToEvents < ActiveRecord::Migration
  def self.up
    add_column :events, :url, :string
    add_column :events, :description, :text
  end

  def self.down
    remove_column :events, :url
    remove_column :events, :description
  end
end
```

The first argument is the table name (events), the second is the field name, and the third is the field type. You'll also want to fill in the self.down method to reverse the changes that this migration will make. While it's unlikely at this point that you'll want to remove these fields, it's a good idea to maintain reversibility. The remove_column method is the opposite of add_column. The only difference in its arguments is that you don't need to specify the field type.

With this new migration in place, use the Rake task to apply it and make the changes to the database.

```
$ rake db:migrate
```

```
== AddUrlAndDescriptionToEvents: migrating ======================================
-- add_column(:events, :url, :string)
   -> 0.0083s
-- add_column(:events, :description, :text)
   -> 0.0079s
== AddUrlAndDescriptionToEvents: migrated (0.0164s) ===========================
```

If all went according to plan, your events table will have two new fields. Now, here comes the fun part. Make sure your web server is still running and try adding a new event. Presto! Rails knows about the new fields, as you can see in Figure 3-4.

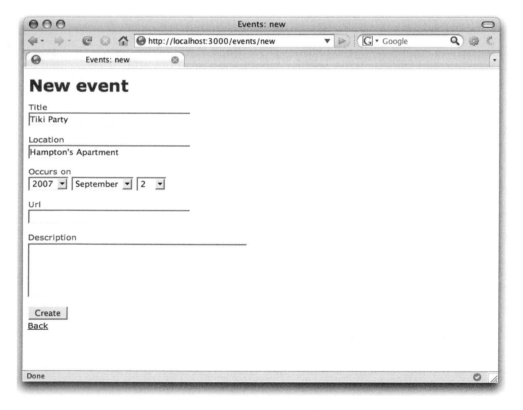

Figure 3-4. *Additional fields added to the new event form*

This exposes the central advantage of this type of scaffolding: you don't need to generate new versions of the scaffold files as your domain model evolves. Because the scaffold is generated dynamically at runtime, it's always a fresh representation of the fields in your table.

Adding Validations

You might be wondering what would happen if you tried to save a new event without giving it any information. Go ahead and try doing that. You'll see that Rails doesn't care. In fact, it's the Event model that doesn't care. This is because in Rails, the rules for data integrity (such as required fields) are the responsibility of the model.

To add basic validation for required fields, open the Event model in app/models/event.rb and add the validator methods shown in Listing 3-5 inside the class body.

Listing 3-5. *Validation Added to the app/models/event.rb File*

```
class Event < ActiveRecord::Base
  validates_presence_of :title, :location
end
```

Save the file and try creating an empty event again. Instead of saving the record, Rails will display a formatted error message, as shown in Figure 3-5.

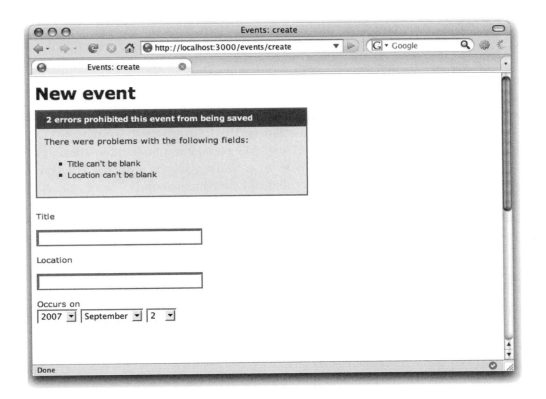

Figure 3-5. *Error messages for an event*

If you've done any web development before, you know that validating fields is a major nuisance. Thankfully, Rails makes it easy.

■**Note** Notice that you don't need to restart the web server when you make changes to your project files. This is a convenience provided by Rails when running in development mode.

We'll go through all the specifics of model validations in Chapter 5. For now, we're using only the most primitive methods of protecting our data. It shouldn't surprise you that Active Record is capable of much more involved validations, such as making sure that a numeric value was entered, validating that data is in the correct format using regular expressions, and ensuring unique values, among other checks.

■**Note** Regular expressions (*regex* for short) are expressions that describe patterns in strings. They are usually used to give a concise description of a set, without having to list all elements. Like most programming languages, Ruby has built-in support for regular expressions.

At this stage, you might be wondering how all this works. We added a single line to the events controller, and as if by magic, Rails took care of the rest. When you made your first controller in the previous chapter, you created actions and templates. Where are the actions and templates here? The answer is that they're all generated dynamically, at runtime. It's as if you created each individual action and template manually. We already talked about the advantages of this type of scaffolding (that it responds automatically to changes to the underlying model), but this won't do you much good if you need to modify the actions and templates to customize them for your application.

Now that we have pinned down our model and are confident that it's reasonably complete, we can pull back the curtain and have Rails *generate* the scaffolding, creating physical actions and templates that we can explore and tweak to our heart's content.

Generating a Scaffold

You generate scaffolding using the scaffold generator. You're probably getting pretty used to generators by now. Rails makes heavy use of them because they help automate repetitive tasks and generally remove the chances for errors when creating new files. Unlike us, the generator won't ever forget exactly how to name a file, nor will it make a typo when creating a class. Let's use the scaffold generator now and solve the mystery of how all this works.

```
$ ./script/generate scaffold Event
```

Since you've already generated a few of these files, Rails will prompt you before it tries to overwrite any that already exist. Specifically, it will warn about the events controller and the events functional test. Since all we added to the events controller was the scaffold declaration, it's safe to overwrite it. The same goes for the test, so go ahead and answer Y when you're asked.

With that out of the way, let's take a look at the events controller again. As you can see in Listing 3-6, our controller is now chock-full of actions. There's one for each of index, list, show, new, create, edit, update, and destroy—the basic CRUD actions.

Listing 3-6. *The app/controllers/events_controller.rb File*

```ruby
class EventsController < ApplicationController
  def index
    list
    render :action => 'list'
  end

  # GETs should be safe (see http://www.w3.org/2001/tag/doc/whenToUseGet.html)
  verify :method => :post, :only => [ :destroy, :create, :update ],
         :redirect_to => { :action => :list }

  def list
    @event_pages, @events = paginate :events, :per_page => 10
  end

  def show
    @event = Event.find(params[:id])
  end

  def new
    @event = Event.new
  end

  def create
    @event = Event.new(params[:event])
    if @event.save
      flash[:notice] = 'Event was successfully created.'
      redirect_to :action => 'list'
    else
      render :action => 'new'
    end
  end
```

```
  def edit
    @event = Event.find(params[:id])
  end

  def update
    @event = Event.find(params[:id])
    if @event.update_attributes(params[:event])
      flash[:notice] = 'Event was successfully updated.'
      redirect_to :action => 'show', :id => @event
    else
      render :action => 'edit'
    end
  end

  def destroy
    Event.find(params[:id]).destroy
    redirect_to :action => 'list'
  end
end
```

If you refresh the application in your browser, you'll notice that nothing has changed. The generated scaffold is identical in every way to the dynamic type. The big difference, though, is that once you've generated scaffolding, if you change your model, you'll have to regenerate it if you want your application to follow suit. Most of the time, however, you'll make the changes by hand.

It's important that you realize why scaffolding exists and that you're aware of its limitations. As we've just demonstrated, scaffolding helps when you need to get something running quickly to test your assumptions. It won't take you very far in the real world, and eventually you'll end up replacing most (if not all) of it.

Explore the generated code and see if you can figure out how it hangs together. Don't worry if you can't understand all of it. We'll discuss it in depth in the chapters that follow. With everything you know about Rails already, you should be able to piece together most of it.

Try changing a few things to see what happens. If you inadvertently break something, you can always run the scaffolding generator again to revert to the original. Can you see how the views in app/views/events are related to the actions? What about the response messages, like Event was successfully created? What happens when you change them? See if you can find where the error messages for failed validations are rendered. If you remove the message, does the record still get saved? You'll learn a lot by exploring, so take as much time as you need.

Summary

We started this chapter by outlining the basics of our sample application. Then we rolled up our sleeves and created our database and configuration files. Based on the goals of our application, we began by creating the tables necessary to run the core of our Event model and got a first look at the simplicity and flexibility that migrations give our development processes. Then the scaffolding allowed us to test our assumptions about the model and table we created by getting a firsthand look at it in action. Also, we took a first crack at adding in validations that ensure that we maintain the integrity of our data. In the chapters that follow, we will investigate each of these concepts in depth.

CHAPTER 4

■■■

Working with a Database: Active Record

In the previous chapter, we took a whirlwind tour through creating a basic Rails application using the built-in scaffolding feature. We sketched out a basic model for our sample application, an event manager, and created the project databases. We used the built-in web server to deploy the application locally, and practiced adding and managing events from the web browser. In this chapter, we're going to take a more in-depth look at how things work, starting with what is arguably the most important part of Rails: Active Record.

You might recall from Chapter 1 that Active Record is the Ruby library that handles database abstraction and interaction for Rails. In fact, whether you realized it or not, in the previous chapter, all the access to the database—adding, editing, and deleting events—happened through the magic of Active Record.

Active Record is the name given to the object-relational mapping library that ships with Rails. If you're not sure what exactly object-relational mapping is, don't worry. By the end of this chapter, you will know. For now, it's best if you think of Active Record as being an intermediary that sits between your code and your database, allowing you to work with data effectively and naturally. When you use Active Record, you communicate with your database using pure Ruby code. Active Record translates the Ruby you write into a language that databases can understand.

The purpose of this chapter is to teach you how to use Active Record to talk to your database and perform basic operations. We'll introduce you to the concepts you need to know about communicating with databases and object-relational mapping. Then we'll take a look at Active Record and walk you through the techniques you need to know to effectively work with a database from Rails. If you don't have a lot of database experience under your belt, you needn't worry. You'll find that working with databases through Active Record is a painless and even enjoyable experience. If you're an experienced database guru, you'll find that Active Record is an intelligent and efficient way to perform database operations without the need for low-level database-specific commands.

Introducing Active Record: Object-Relational Mapping on Rails

The key feature of Active Record is that it maps tables to classes, table rows to objects, and table columns to object attributes. This practice is commonly known as object-relational mapping, or ORM for short. To be sure, Active Record isn't the only ORM in existence, but it may well be the easiest to use of the bunch.

One of the reasons that Active Record is so easy to use is that there is almost no configuration required to have it map a table to a class. You just need to create a Ruby class that's named after the table you want to map and extend the Active Record Base class.

```
class Event < ActiveRecord::Base
end
```

Notice the part that reads < ActiveRecord::Base. That less-than sign indicates that the class on the left is a subclass of the one on the right. In Ruby, when you extend a class like this, you automatically gain access to all the functionality in the parent class. There's a lot of code in the ActiveRecord::Base class, but we don't need to look at it. Our class merely extends it, and our work is finished.

Assuming Active Record knows how to find our database and that we have a table called events (note that the table name is plural while the class name is singular), the table is automatically mapped. If our events table contained the fields title, location, and occurs_on, we could do this:

```
event = Event.new

event.title = "BBQ at Hampton's House"
event.location = "471 230 King Street"
event.occurs_on = "2006-10-13"

event.save
```

Those five lines would write a new record to the events table. That's a lot of ability we gained just by the simple act of subclassing! And that's what we mean when we say that Active Record is easy to use. Notice how the table's fields (title, location, and occurs_on) can be read and written to using methods on the object we created (event). And we didn't need to tell Active Record what our fields were named, or even that we had any fields. It figured that out all on its own. Of course, Active Record doesn't just let you create new records. It can also read, update, and delete records, plus a lot more.

Active Record is database-agnostic, so it doesn't care which database software you use, and it supports nearly every database out there. Since it's a high-level abstraction, the code you write remains the same no matter which database you're using. For the record (no pun intended), we'll be using MySQL. As explained in Chapter 2, MySQL is open source, easy to use, fast, and arguably the most popular database used for Rails development. (Along with the MySQL site, `http://mysql.com`, the Wikipedia entry on MySQL is an excellent resource: `http://en.wikipedia.org/wiki/Mysql`.)

What About SQL?

To be sure, you don't need Active Record (or any ORM) to talk to and manipulate your database. In fact, databases have their own language called Structured Query Language, popularly referred to as SQL, which is supported by nearly every database in existence. Using SQL, you can view column information, fetch a particular row or a set of rows, and search for rows containing certain criteria. You also use SQL to create, drop, and modify tables and insert, update, and destroy the information stored in those tables. The problem with SQL is that it's not object-oriented.

Object-oriented programming and relational databases are fundamentally different paradigms. The relational paradigm deals with relations and is mathematical by nature. The object-oriented paradigm, however, deals with objects, their attributes, and their associations to each other. As soon as you want to make objects persistent using a relational database, you will notice something: there is a rift between these two paradigms—the so-called object-relational gap. An ORM library like Active Record helps you bridge that gap.

■**Note** Active Record is based on a design pattern. Design patterns are standard solutions to common problems in software design. Well, it turns out that when working in an object-oriented environment, the problem of how to effectively communicate with a database (which is not object-oriented) is quite common. Therefore, many smart people have wrapped their heads around the problem of how best to bring the object-oriented paradigm together with the relational database. One of those smart people is Martin Fowler, who in his book, *Patterns of Enterprise Application Architecture* (Addison-Wesley, 2002), first described a pattern that he called an *Active Record*. In the pattern Fowler described, there is a one-to-one mapping between a database record and the object that represents it. When Rails creator David Heinemeier Hansson sought to implement an ORM for his framework, he based it on Fowler's pattern.

Active Record lets you model real-world things in your code. Rails calls these real-world things *models*—the *M* in MVC. A model might be named `Person`, `Product`, or `Event`, and would have a corresponding table in the database: `people`, `products`, or `events`. Each model is implemented as a Ruby class and is stored in the `app/models` directory. Active Record provides the link between these classes and your tables, allowing you to work with what look like regular objects, which, in turn, can be persisted to the database. This frees you from having to write low-level SQL to talk to the database. Instead, you work with your data as if it were an object, and Active Record does all the translation into SQL behind the scenes. This means that in Rails, you get to stick with one language: Ruby.

■**Note** Just because we're using Active Record to abstract our SQL generation doesn't mean that SQL is evil. In fact, Active Record makes it possible to execute SQL directly whenever that's necessary. The truth is that raw SQL is the native language of databases and there are some (albeit rare) cases when an ORM simply won't cut it.

Active Record Conventions

Active Record achieves its zero-configuration reputation by way of convention. Most of the conventions it uses are easy to grasp. After all, they're conventions, so they're already in wide use. While you can override most of the conventions to suit the particular design of your database, you'll save a lot of time and energy if you stick to them.

Let's take a quick look at the two main conventions you need to know:

- Class names are singular; table names are plural.

- Tables contain an identity column named id.

Active Record assumes that the name of your table is the plural form of the class name. If your table name contains underscores, then your class name is assumed to be in *CamelCase*. Table 4-1 shows some examples.

Table 4-1. *Table and Class Name Conventions*

Table	Class
events	Event
people	Person
categories	Category
order_items	OrderItem

All tables are assumed to have a unique identity column named id. This column should be the table's *primary key* (a value used to uniquely identify a table's row). This is a fairly common convention in database design. (For more on primary keys in database design, the Wikipedia entry has a wealth of useful information and links: http://en.wikipedia.org/wiki/Primary_key.)

The belief in convention over configuration is firmly entrenched in the Rails philosophy, so it should come as no surprise that there are more conventions at work than those listed here. You'll likely find that they all make good sense, and you'll be able to use them without paying much attention.

Introducing the Console

Ruby comes with a great little tool: an interactive interpreter. It's called irb (for Interactive Ruby). Most of the time, you'll invoke irb using the console program that ships with Rails, but you can start up an irb session whenever you want by typing irb at the command prompt. The advantage of the console is that it enjoys the special privilege of being integrated with your project's environment. This means it has access and knowledge of your models (and subsequently, your database).

We'll be using the console as a means to get inside the world of our Event model and to work with it in the exact same way as our Rails application would. As you'll see in a minute, this is a great way to showcase the capabilities of Active Record interactively.

You can execute any arbitrary Ruby code in irb and do anything you might otherwise do inside your Ruby programs: set variables, evaluate conditions, and inspect objects. The only essential difference between an interactive session and a regular old Ruby program is that irb will echo the return value of everything it executes. This saves you from having to explicitly print the results of an evaluation. Just run the code, and irb will print the result.

You'll be able to tell whenever you're inside an irb session by looking for the double greater-than signs (>>), which indicate the irb prompt, and the arrow symbol (=>), which indicates the response.

As you continue to progress with both Ruby and Rails, you'll find that irb is an essential tool. Using irb, you can play around with code and make sure it works as you expect before you write it into your programs.

Let's load it and start to experiment with our Event model. Make sure you're inside the event manager application directory, and then type ./script/console on your command line. This will cause the irb console to load with the *development* environment and leave you at a simple prompt, waiting for you to enter some code.

```
$ ./script/console
Loading development environment.
>>
```

If you've been following along with the previous chapters, then you should have a model called Event (in app/models/event.rb), and you probably already entered some sample data when playing with scaffolding in the previous chapter. If not, make sure you get up to speed by reading Chapter 3 before moving on.

From the console, we can interrogate our Event model for information. For instance, we might ask it for its column names.

```
>> Event.column_names
=> ["id", "title", "location", "occurs_on", "url", "description"]
```

Look at that! All our columns are presented as a Ruby array (which we can tell by the fact that they are surrounded by square brackets). We got the `column_names` class method courtesy of the `ActiveRecord::Base` class from which our `Event` class inherits. Actually, we get a lot of methods courtesy of `ActiveRecord::Base`. To see just how many, we can ask.

```
>> Event.methods.size
=> 396
```

That's a lot of methods! Don't worry—you don't need to memorize all 396 of them, and most of them are private to Active Record and are used internally, so you'll never even use them. Still, it's important, if for no other reason than to get a sense of what you get for free just by subclassing Active Record. Even though in this case, `ActiveRecord::Base` is considered the *superclass*, it sure makes our lowly `Event` class super, doesn't it? (Sorry, enough bad humor.)

A CRASH COURSE IN RUBY CLASS DESIGN

Object-oriented programming is all about objects. You create classes that encapsulate all the logic required to create an object, along with its properties and attributes, and use the class to produce new objects, each of which is a unique instance, distinct from other objects of the same class. That might sound a little abstract (and with good reason—*abstraction*, after all, is the name of the game), but if it helps, you can think of a class as being an object factory.

The obvious example is that of a car factory. Contained within a car factory are all the resources, tools, workers, and processes that are required to produce a shiny new car. Each car that comes off the assembly line is unique. The cars may vary in size, color, and shape, or they may not vary from each other much at all. The point is that even if two cars share the exact same attributes, they are not the same car. You certainly wouldn't expect a change to the color of one car to affect all the others, would you? Well, in object-oriented programming, it's not much different. The class is the factory that produces objects, which are called *instances* of a class. From a single factory, an infinite number of objects can be produced.

```
class Car
end

car1 = Car.new
car2 = Car.new
```

car1 is a Car object, which is to say, it's an instance of the class Car. Each car is a different object, created by the same factory. Each object knows which class it belongs to (which factory created it), so if you're ever in doubt, you can ask it:

```
car2.class #=> Car
```

Our `Car` class doesn't really do anything that useful—it has no attributes. So, let's give it some. We'll start off by giving it a `make`. This would be something like Toyota or Nissan. Of course, we need to define a way to read and write these attributes. We do this by creating aptly named *reader* and *writer* methods. Some object-oriented languages refer to these as *getters* and *setters*. The two sets of terms are pretty much interchangeable, but Ruby favors the former. Let's go ahead and add a reader and writer for the `make` attribute now.

```
class Car
  # A writer method. Sets the value of the @make attribute
  def make=(text)
    @make = text
  end

  # A reader method. Returns the value of the @make attribute
  def make
    @make
  end
end
```

The methods we just defined (`make()` and `make=()`) are instance methods. This is because they can be used only on instances of the class, which is to say, the individual objects that have been created from the class. To create a new instance of the `Car` class, we use the `new` constructor.

```
my_car = Car.new
```

That's all that's required to create a new instance of the class `Car` in a local variable called `my_car`. The variable `my_car` can now be considered a `Car` object. Although we have a new `Car` object, we haven't yet given it a `make`. If we use the reader method we created to ask our car what its make is, we'll see that it's `nil`.

```
my_car.make #=> nil
```

Apparently, if we want our car to have a make, we'll have to set it. This is where the writer method comes in handy.

```
my_car.make = 'Toyota'
```

This sets the value of the `make` attribute for our car to `Toyota`. If we had other `Car` objects, their makes would remain unchanged. We're setting the attribute only on the `my_car` object. Now when we use the reader method, it confirms that the `make` attribute has been updated.

```
my_car.make #=> 'Toyota'
```

Of course, you can change the value any time you want.

```
my_car.make = 'Mazda'
```

And again, if you ask your `Car` object its make, it will tell you.

```
my_car.make #=> 'Mazda'
```

That's a simple example, but it illustrates a couple of very important points: Classes are used to create objects and objects have attributes. Every object has a unique set of attributes, different from other objects of the same class.

The reason for this crash course in Ruby class design is to illustrate the point that modeling with Active Record is a lot like modeling with standard Ruby classes. In fact, if you decided to think of Active Record as being an extension to standard Ruby classes, you wouldn't be very far off. In practice, this fact makes using Active Record in Ruby quite natural. And since Active Record can reflect on your tables to determine which fields to map automatically, you need to define your attributes in only one place: the database. That's DRY!

Active Record Basics: CRUD

Active Record is a big topic, so we're going to start with the basics. We already alluded to the so-called big four earlier, but here they are again: create, read, update, and delete, affectionately known as CRUD. In one way or another, most of what you do with Active Record in particular, and with databases in general, relates to CRUD. Rails has really embraced CRUD as a design technique and as a way to simplify the modeling process. It's no surprise then that we're going to take an in-depth look at how to do CRUD with Active Record.

We'll build on the events application we started in the previous chapter. Although our application doesn't do very much yet, it's at a stage where it will be easy to demonstrate these concepts in a more concrete fashion.

We'll be doing this whole section on the console, so keep it open as you work, and feel free to experiment as much as you want. The more experimentation you do, the deeper your understanding will be.

Creating New Records

We're going to start by creating a new event in the database so we have something to work with. There are a few different ways to create new model objects, but they're all variations on the same theme. We'll show you how each of them works and explain the often subtle differences between them as we go.

Using the new Constructor

The most basic way to create a new model object is with the new constructor. If you read the crash-course sidebar on Ruby classes, you're sure to recognize it. If you didn't, then it's enough that you know new is the usual way to create new objects of any type. Active Record classes are no different. Let's try it now.

```
>> event = Event.new
=> #<Event:0x23a98e8 @new_record=true, @attributes={"title"=>nil, "url"=>nil,
"occurs_on"=>nil, "description"=>nil, "location"=>nil}>
```

All we're doing here is creating a new Event object and storing it in the local variable, event. True to form, the console responds with the return value of method, which, in this case, is a *string* representation of the model object. It may look a little funny, but this is what all Ruby objects look like when we inspect them. You can see from the response that there are a couple instance variables set: @new_record, which tells us that this is a new object that has not yet been persisted to the database, and @attributes, which contains a hash of the attributes that Active Record garnered by reflecting on the columns in the table. Of course, we can confirm either of these by asking the object.

```
>> event.new_record?
=> true
>> event.attributes
=> {"title"=>nil, "url"=>nil, "occurs_on"=>nil, "description"=>nil, "location"=>nil}
```

Here, we're using *reader* methods, which read and return the value of the attribute in question. Since this is a brand-new record and we haven't given it any information, all our attributes are nil, which means they have no values. Let's remedy that now using (what else?) *writer* methods.

```
>> event.title = 'RailsConf'
=> "RailsConf"

>> event.location = 'Portland, Oregon'
=> "Portland, Oregon"

>> event.occurs_on = '2007-05-17'
=> "2007-05-17"

>> event.url = 'http://railsconf.org'
=> "http://railsconf.org"
```

```
>> event.description = "An awesome gay 'ole time with other Rails programmers."
=> "An awesome gay 'ole time with other Rails programmers."
```

■**Note** A return of `nil` always represents "nothing." It is a helpful little object that stands in the place of nothingness. If we ask an object for something and it returns `false`, then false is *something* so it's not a helpful representation. As a nerdy fact, in logics, false and true are equal and opposite values, but they are values in the end. The same is true of zero (0). The number 0 is not truly "nothing." It is an actual representation of an abstract nothing, but it is still something. That's why in programming we have `nil` (or `null` in other languages).

Now when we inspect our `Event` object, we can see that it has attributes.

```
>> event
=> #<Event:0x23a98e8 @new_record=true, @attributes={"title"=>"RailsConf",
 "url"=>"http://railsconf.com", "occurs_on"=>"2007-05-17", "description"=>"An
awesome gay 'ole time with other Rails programmers.",  "location"=>"Portland,
Oregon"}>
```

We still haven't written a new record. If you were to look at the `events` table in the database, it would still be empty. (If you squint really hard at the preceding object inspection string, you'll notice the `@new_record` variable is still `true`, and that no `id` has been assigned yet.) That's because we haven't yet saved the object to the database. Fortunately, saving an Active Record object couldn't be any easier.

```
>> event.save
=> true
```

When you save a new record, a SQL `INSERT` statement is constructed behind the scenes. If the `INSERT` was successful, the `save` operation returns `true`; if it fails, `save` returns `false`. We can ask for a `count` of the number of rows in the table just to be sure that a record was created.

```
>> Event.count
=> 1
```

Sure enough, we have our first event! You've got to admit, that was pretty easy. (Now, you might have created some events already during the scaffolding session. If so, don't be surprised if you have more than one event already.) Additionally, if we ask the event whether or not it is a `new_record?`, it will respond with `false`. Since it's saved, it's not "new" anymore.

```
>> event.new_record?
=> false
```

Let's create another event. This time we'll omit all the chatter from the console so you can get a better sense of how the process plays out. We create a new object and place it in a variable, we set the object's attributes, and finally, we save the record. Note that while we're using the local variable `event` to hold our object, it can be anything you want. Usually, you'll use a variable that indicates the type of object you're creating, like `event`, or if you prefer shorthand, just `e`.

```
>> event = Event.new

>> event.title       = "Jeff's Birthday Party"
>> event.location    = "Flaming Moe's"
>> event.url         = 'http://quotedprintable.com'
>> event.description = "Bring gifts to *me*!"
>> event.occurs_on   = '2007-10-13'

>> event.save
```

Note While writer methods look like assignments, they're really methods in disguise. `event.title = 'something'` is the functional equivalent of `event.title=('something')`, where `title=()` is the method. Ruby provides a little syntactic sugar to make writers look more natural.

Now we're rolling! We've already created two events and haven't had to write a lick of SQL. Given how easy this is, you might be surprised that we can do it in even fewer steps, but we can. Instead of setting each attribute on its own line, we can pass all of them to `new` at once. Here's how we could rewrite the preceding process of creating a new record in fewer lines of code:

```
event = Event.new(:title       => "Jeff's Birthday Party",
                  :location    => "Flaming Moe's")
                  :url         => "http://quotedprintable.com",
                  :description => "Bring gifts to *me*!",
                  :occurs_on   => "2007-10-13",
event.save
```

Not bad, but we can do even better. The new constructor creates a new object, but it's our responsibility to save it. If we forget to save the object, it will never get written to the database.

Using the create Constructor

When you want to create an object and save it in one fell swoop, you can use the create constructor. We'll use it now to create our third event.

```
>> Event.create(:title => "RuPy Conference",
                 :location => "Poznan, Poland",
                 :url => 'http://rupy.wmid.amu.edu.pl',
                 :description => "See, we can all get along!")
                 :occurs_on => '2007-04-14',

=> #<Event:0x2284648...>
```

Instead of returning true or false, the create constructor returns the object it created—in this case, an Event object. We're actually passing a hash of attributes to the create constructor. While hashes are normally surrounded by curly braces, *when a hash is the only argument to a Ruby method, the braces are optional.* In fact, we could just have easily created the attributes hash first, and then given that to create.

```
>> attributes = { :title       => "Jeff's Birthday Party",
                  :location    => "Flaming Moe's" }
                  :url         => "http://quotedprintable.com",
                  :description => "Bring gifts to *me*!",
                  :occurs_on   =>" 2007-04-14",

>> Event.create(attributes)
=> #<Event:0x2325610...>
```

And let's now see how many events we've created by doing a count.

```
>> Event.count
=> 4
```

You're getting the hang of this now. To summarize, when you want to create a new object and save it manually, use the new constructor; when you want to create and save in one operation, use create. We've already created three new records, which are plenty for now, so let's move on to the next step: finding records.

Reading (Finding) Records

Now that we have a few events to play with, it's time to practice finding them. Every model class understands the find method. We've already touched on it briefly, but find is actually quite versatile and accepts a number of options that modify its behavior.

Let's start with the basics. find is a class method. That means you use it on the model class rather than an object of that class, just as we did for the new and create constructors. Just like new and create, a find operation, if successful, returns a new object.

There are actually three ways to call find:

- find(:id): Finds a single record by its unique id.

- find(:first): Finds the first record.

- find(:all): Finds all records in the table.

You can also pass in a hash of options in addition to :id, :first, or :all. These options include :order and :conditions, among others. We'll go through the different ways to call find in turn and explain how to use each.

Finding a Single Record Using an ID

The :id and :first options always return a single record at most. The :id option is specific; you use it when you're looking for a specific record and you know its unique id. If you give it a single id, it will either return the corresponding record (if there is one) or raise an exception (if there isn't). The :first option is a little more forgiving; it returns the first record in the table, or nil if the table is empty, as explained in the next section.

You can find a single record using its unique id using find(:id). Here's how it works:

```
>> Event.find(1)
=> #<Event:0x2250e10 @attributes={"title"=>"Tiki Party", "url"=>nil,
"occurs_on"=>"2007-09-02", "id"=>"1", "description"=>nil, "location"=>"Hampton's
Apartment"}>
```

As you can see, we found the event with the id of 1. (This is our event 1. Your result will show whichever event you entered first.) If we wanted to take a closer look at what was returned, we could store the result in a local variable.

```
>> event = Event.find(1)
=> #<Event:0x2555340...>
>> event.id
=> 1
>> event.location
=> "Hampton's Apartment"
```

Here, we stored the object that `find` returned in the local variable `event`. Then we were able to interrogate it and ask for its attributes.

Now, all this worked because an event with the id 1 *actually exists*. If instead we had searched for a record that we know doesn't exist (say, 1037), Active Record would have raised an exception.

```
>> Event.find(1037)
Active Record::RecordNotFound: Couldn't find Event with ID=1037
        from active_record/base.rb:1035:in `find_one'
        from active_record/base.rb:1018:in `find_from_ids'
        from active_record/base.rb:419:in `find'
        from (irb):5
```

Active Record raises a `RecordNotFound` exception and tells us it couldn't find any events with the `id` of 1037. Of course it couldn't. We know that no such record exists. The lesson here is that you use `find(:id)` when you're looking for a specific record that you expect to exist. If the record doesn't exist, it's probably an error you want to know about; therefore, Active Record raises `RecordNotFound`.

RECOVERING FROM RECORDNOTFOUND ERRORS

When you use `find` with a single `id`, you expect the record to exist. But often you're not in control of the input, such as when it comes from a URL. While the path `/events/show/1` might happily return a result, what's stopping Joe User from changing the parameters (say, to `/events/show/1037`) in an attempt to mess with your application? You probably don't want to raise an exception every time something like this happens. You want to recover gracefully.

So, how can you recover gracefully from a `RecordNotFound` exception should you need to? You can use Ruby's facility for error handling: `begin` and `rescue`. Here's how this works:

```
begin
  Event.find(1037)
rescue ActiveRecord::RecordNotFound
  puts "We couldn't find that record"
end
```

First, we open a `begin` block. Then, we cause a `RecordNotFound` error by deliberately searching for a record that we know doesn't exist. When the error occurs, Ruby runs the code we put inside the `rescue` part of the body, which prints a friendly message.

Finding a Single Record Using :first

You can find the first record the database returns using find(:first). This will always return exactly one item, unless the table is empty, in which case, nil is returned.

```
>> Event.find(:first)
=> #<Event:0x2247874 @attributes={"title"=>"Tiki Party", "url"=>nil,
"occurs_on"=>"2007-09-02", "id"=>"1", "description"=>nil, "location"=>"Hampton's
Apartment"}>
```

Keep in mind that this isn't necessarily the first record in the table. It actually depends on the database software you're using. It's the equivalent of saying SELECT * FROM table LIMIT 1 in SQL. If you ever need to find a record and don't particularly care which record it is, find(:first) can come in handy. Note that find(:first) doesn't raise an exception if the record can't be found.

Finding All Records

So far, we've looked at finding a single record. In each case, find returned a single Event object. But what if you want to find more than one event? In our application, we'll want to display all the events on the homepage.

If you provide find with the symbol :all, it returns all records for that class.

```
>> events = Event.find(:all)
=> [#<Event:0x223aad4>, #<Event:0x223aa98>, #<Event:0x223aa0c>, #<Event:0x223a980>]
```

The square brackets in the response indicate that find has returned an array. We can confirm this by asking the events variable what its class is.

```
>> events.class
=> Array
```

Sure enough, events tells us it's an Array. To be precise, it's an array of Event objects. Like all Ruby arrays, we can ask for its size.

```
>> events.size
=> 4
```

Since events is an array, we can access the individual elements it contains by using its *index*, which is numeric, starting at 0.

```
>> events[0]
=> #<Event:0x223aad4 @attributes={"title"=>"Tiki Party", "url"=>nil,
"occurs_on"=>"2007-09-02", "id"=>"1", "description"=>nil, "location"=>"Hampton's
Apartment"}>
```

And once we've isolated a single Event object, we can get at its attributes.

```
>> events[0].title
=> "Tiki Party"
```

What's happening here is that find(:all) produced an array, and we accessed the object at the 0 index and called the title method. We can also use the first method, which all arrays respond to, and get the same result, but with a little more natural syntax.

```
>> events.first.title
=> "Tiki Party"
```

If we wanted to iterate over the collection, we could use the each method, which, again, works with all arrays. Here, we'll loop over the array, extract each item into a variable called event, and print its location attribute using the puts command.

```
>> events.each {|event| puts event.location }
Hampton's Apartment
Portland, Oregon
Flaming Moe's
Poznan, Poland
```

Sometimes you want your results ordered. For example, if you're listing all your events, you probably want them listed chronologically. The find method also accepts an argument that defines on which column or columns to order the results. It's called :order, and for you SQL heroes, it corresponds to the SQL ORDER clause.

```
>> events = Event.find(:all, :order => 'occurs_on')
=> [#<Event:0x250b7e0...>, #<Event:0x250b27c...>, #<Event:0x250a804...>]
>> events.each {|event| puts event.occurs_on }
2007-04-14
2007-05-17
2007-09-02
2007-10-13
```

By default, any column that is ordered is in ascending order (for example, 1–10, or a–z). If you want to reverse this to get descending order, use the DESC modifier (the same way you would in SQL, since the value of :order is really just a SQL fragment).

```
>> events = Event.find(:all, :order => 'occurs_on DESC')
=> [#<Event:0x24dfdd4...>, #<Event:0x24dfdac...>, #<Event:0x24dfd84...>]
>> events.each {|event| puts event.occurs_on }
2007-10-13
2007-09-02
2007-05-17
2007-04-14
```

Finding with Conditions

While finding a record by its primary key is useful, it requires that you know the id to begin with, which isn't always the case. Sometimes you want to find records based on other criteria. This is where conditions come in to play. Conditions correspond to the SQL WHERE clause. If you want to find a record by its title, you pass a hash of options to find with a key of :conditions and a value that contains either a hash of conditions or a SQL fragment.

Here, we'll use a hash of conditions to indicate we want the first event with the title of RailsConf.

```
>> Event.find(:first, :conditions => {:title => 'RailsConf'})
=> #<Event:0x25974c0 @attributes={"title"=>"RailsConf"...}>
```

Because we used find(:first), we'll get only one record (the first one in the result set, even if there is more than one result). If we instead use find(:all), we'll get back a collection, even if the collection has only one item in it.

```
>> Event.find(:all, :conditions => "starts_at > '2007-01-01'")
=> [#<Event:0x24bbde4.>, #<Event:0x24bbde5.>, #<Event:0x24bbde6.>]
```

Notice the square brackets and remember that they indicate an array. More often than not, when you're doing a find(:all) operation, you're expecting more than one record in return. But find(:all) will always produce an array, even if that array is empty.

```
>> Event.find(:all, :conditions => {:title => 'Nonexistent'})
=> []
```

Using Dynamic Finders

It doesn't get any easier than dynamic finders. We call these finders *dynamic* because they use Ruby's method_missing functionality to automatically create methods that don't exist until runtime. Using dynamic finders, you can include the attribute you're looking for directly in the method name. This will make more sense when you see it in action.

```
>> Event.find_by_title('RailsConf')
=> #<Event:0x2592b64 @attributes={"title"=>"RailsConf", ...}>
```

```
>> Event.find_by_occurs_on('2007-10-13')
=> #<Event:0x2554e90 @attributes={"occurs_on"=>"2007-10-13", ...}>
```

There are several variations of dynamic finders, which are summarized in the Table 4-2.

Table 4-2. *Dynamic Finders*

Finder	Example
find_by_*(cond)	find_by_title('RailsConf') # => Event
find_all_by_*(cond)	find_all_by_location('Canada') # => Array
find_by_*_and_*(cond1, cond2)	find_by_title_and_location('Party', 'Canada') # => Event
find_all_by_*_and_*(cond1, cond2)	find_all_by_title_and_location('Party', 'Canada') # => Array

Updating Records

Updating a record is a lot like creating a record. You can update attributes one at a time and then save the result, or you can update attributes in one fell swoop. When you update a record, a SQL UPDATE statement is constructed behind the scenes. First, we use a find operation to retrieve the record we want to update; next, we modify its attributes; and finally, we save it back to the database.

```
>> event = Event.find(1)
>> event.title = "Birthday Fest"
>> event.url    = "http://quotedprintable.com"
>> event.save
=> true
```

This should be looking pretty familiar by now. The only real difference between this process and the process of creating a new record is that instead of creating a brand-new row, we fetch an existing row. We update the attributes in the exact same way, and we save the record in the same way. Just as when you're creating a new record, when save operates on an existing record, it returns true or false, depending on whether or not the operation was successful.

When you want to update an object's attributes and save it in a single operation, you use the update_attributes method. Unlike when creating a new record with create, because you're updating a record, you need to have fetched that record first. That's where the other subtle difference lies. Unlike create, which is a class method (it operates on the class, not on an object), update_attributes is an instance method. Instance methods work on objects, or instances of a class. Here's an example:

```
>> event = Event.find(3)
>> event.update_attributes(:title => "A Boring Name", :location => "A Boring
Location")
=> true
```

Deleting Records

We're finally at the last component of CRUD: delete. When you're working with databases, you inevitably need to delete records. If a user cancels her order, or if a book goes out of stock, or even if you have an error in a given row, you might want to delete it. Sometimes you need to delete all rows in an entire table, and sometimes you want just to delete a specific row. Active Record makes deleting rows every bit as easy as creating them.

There are two styles of row deletion: `destroy` and `delete`. The `destroy` style works on the *instance*. It instantiates the object, which means that it finds a single row first, and then deletes it from the database. The `delete` style operates on the *class*, which is to say it operates on the table rather than a given row from that table.

Using destroy

The easiest and most common way to remove a record is to use the `destroy` method, which means the first thing we need to do is find the record we want to destroy.

```
>> event = Event.find(1)
>> event.destroy
```

For those interested, the SQL that Active Record generates in response to the `destroy` operation is as follows.

```
DELETE FROM events WHERE id = 1;
```

As a result, the event with the `id` of 1 is permanently destroyed. But we still have the object hanging around in the variable `event`, so how can it really be gone? The answer is that while the object remains hydrated (which is to say that it retains all its attributes), it's *frozen*. You can still access its attributes, but you can't modify them. Let's see what happens if we try to change the location.

```
>> event.location = 'foobar'
TypeError: can't modify frozen hash
```

So, it appears that the now deleted `event` is a frozen hash. While the object remains, it is read-only, so we can't modify it. Given this fact, if we're just going to be deleting the record, we don't really need to create an explicit `Event` object after all. We can do the `destroy` in a one-line operation.

```
>> Event.find(1).destroy
```

Here, the object instantiation is implicit. We're still calling the `destroy` instance method, but we're not storing an `Event` object in a local variable first.

We can still do better. We can use the class method `destroy`, which does a `find` automatically. Just like `find` and `create`, you can use `destroy` directly on the class (that is, you don't create an object first). Since it operates on the table and not the row, you need to help it out by telling it which row or rows you want to target. Here's how we would delete the event with the id 1:

```
>> Event.destroy(1)
```

Sometimes you want to destroy more that one record. Just as with `find`, you can give `destroy` an array of primary keys whose rows you want to remove. You use the square brackets ([ ]) to indicate that you're passing an array.

```
>> Event.destroy([1,2,3])
```

Even though `ActiveRecord::Base.destroy` is a class method, it does, in fact, instantiate each object before destroying it. We can tell this by looking at its source.

```
def destroy(id)
  id.is_a?(Array) ? id.each {|id| destroy(id) } : find(id).destroy
end
```

Here, we can see that if the received argument is an array, `destroy` will iterate over the array and call the same `destroy` method once for each item in the array. This will effectively cause it to take the `else` path of the conditional, which performs a `find` first (instantiating the object), and then calls the instance version of `destroy`. Neat, huh? That pretty much covers `destroy`.

Using delete

The second style of row deletion is `delete`. Every Active Record class has class methods called `delete` and `delete_all`. The `delete` family of methods differ from `destroy` in that they don't instantiate or perform callbacks on the object they're deleting. They remove the row immediately from the database.

Just like `find` and `create`, you use `delete` and `delete_all` directly on the class (that is, you don't create an object first). Since it operates on the table and not the row, you need to help it out by telling it which row or rows you want to target. Here's how it looks:

```
>> Event.delete(1)
=> 1
```

Here, we specified a single primary key for the event we wanted to delete. The operation responded with the number of records that were removed. Since a primary key uniquely identifies a single record, only one record was deleted.

Just as with `find`, you can give `delete` an array of primary keys whose rows you want to delete. You use the square brackets (`[]`) to indicate that you're passing an array.

```
>> Event.delete([1,2,3])
=> 3
```

> **Note** Unlike `find`, which is capable of collecting any arguments it receives into an array automatically, `delete` must be supplied with an array object explicitly. So, while `Model.find(1,2,3)` will work, `Model.delete(1,2,3)` will fail with an argument error (because it's really receiving three arguments). To delete multiple rows by primary key, you must pass an actual array object. The following will work, since it's a single array (containing three items), and thus, a single argument: `Model.delete([1,2,3])`.

Deleting with Conditions

You can delete all rows that match a given condition with the `delete_all` class method. The following will delete all events before a certain date.

```
>> Event.delete_all("ends_at < '2007-01-01'")
>> 5
```

The return value of `delete_all` is the number of records that were deleted.

> **Caution** If you use `delete` without any arguments, it will delete all rows in the table, so be careful! Most of the time, you'll pass it a string of conditions.

When Good Models Go Bad

So far, we've been very nice to our models and have been making them happy by providing them with just the information that they need. But we know that in the previous chapter, we provided *validations* that were preventing us from saving bad records to the database. Specifically, we told the `Event` model that it should never allow itself to be saved to the database if it isn't provided a `title` and `location`. Taking a look at the `Event` model, shown in Listing 4-1, you can recall how validations are specified.

Listing 4-1. *The app/models/event.rb File*

```
class Event < ActiveRecord::Base
  belongs_to :user
  validates_presence_of :title, :location
end
```

You may have noticed in our generated scaffolding that we use a helper method called error_messages_for(:event) to print out a helpful little error message. That helper isn't black magic; it's simply a bit of code that asks the model for its list of errors (also referred to as the *errors collection*), and returns a nicely formatted block of HTML to show the user.

■**Note** You may have noticed that we call methods in Ruby with the dot (.) For instance, we would say @user.errors to get the error collection back. However, there is an idiomatic convention in Ruby documentation of using the # symbol, along with the class name, to let the reader know that there is a method it can call on an object. For example, on our Event class, we could use the method @event.title as Event#title, because it's something that acts upon a particular @event, but not the Event class itself. You have also seen that we can write the code Event.count, because we don't need to know about a particular @event, but only Event objects in general. Keep this convention in mind when you're reading Ruby documentation.

The secret to this is that every Active Record object has an automatic attribute added to it called errors. To get started, let's create a fresh new Event object.

```
>> event = Event.new
=> #<Event:0x2536f30 @new_record=true, @attributes={"title"=>nil, "url"=>nil,
"occurs_on"=>nil, "description"=>nil, "location"=>nil}>
>> event.errors.any?
=> false
```

This seems odd because we know that this new event should have errors because it's invalid. We didn't give it a title or a location. It turns out that this is because we haven't triggered the validations yet. We can cause them to occur a couple of ways. The most obvious way is to attempt to save the object.

```
>> event.save
=> false
```

Every time we've used save before, the model has happily chirped true back to us. But this time, save returns false. This is because before the model would allow itself to be saved, it ran through its gauntlet of validations, and one or more of those validations failed.

You would be right to guess that if we tried `event.errors.any?` again, it would return true.

```
>> event.errors.any?
=> true
```

Let's interrogate the errors collection a little closer with the `full_messages` method.

```
>> event.errors.full_messages
=> ["Title can't be blank", "Location can't be blank"]
```

Voilà! Look how helpful the model is being. It's passing back an array of error messages.

If there is just one attribute that we care about, we can also ask the errors collection for a particular attribute's errors.

```
>> event.errors.on(:title)
=> "can't be blank"
```

Notice that since we told it which attribute we were looking for, the message returned a slightly different result than before. What if we ask for an attribute that doesn't exist or doesn't have errors?

```
>> event.errors.on(:nonexistent)
=> nil
```

We get back `nil`, which lets us know that we didn't find anything.

Another helpful method is `size`, which as your saw earlier, works with all arrays.

```
>> event.errors.size
=> 2
```

Saving isn't the only way that we can cause our validations to run. We can actually just ask a model object if it's `valid?`.

```
>> event.valid?
=> false
```

If you try that on a new object, the errors collection will magically fill up with your nice pretty errors.

Summary

In this chapter, you've become familiar with using the console to work with your models. You've learned how to create, read, update, and destroy model objects. Also, we've briefly looked into how to see the simple errors caused by the validations that we set up on our model in the previous chapter.

In the next chapter, we're going to discuss how to create relationships (called *associations*) between our models, and you'll really start to see how Active Record helps you work with your data in extremely powerful ways. We'll also expand on the concept of validations and show you how you can do a lot more than just `validates_presence_of`. You'll see that Rails provides a whole bevy of prewritten validators and even an easy way to write your own customized validators.

CHAPTER 5

■ ■ ■

Advanced Active Record: Enhancing Your Models

In the previous chapter, we introduced the basics of Active Record and how to use it. In this chapter, we're going to delve more deeply into Active Record and teach you how to enhance your models.

Model enhancement is a rather general term. It refers to endowing your models with attributes and capabilities that go beyond what you get from simply subclassing `ActiveRecord::Base`. A model contains all the logic that governs its citizenship in the world of your application. In the model, you can define how it interacts with other models, what a model should accept as a minimum amount of information for it to be considered valid, and other abilities and responsibilities.

Models need to relate to each other. In the real world, bank accounts have transactions, books belong to authors, and products have categories. We refer to these relationships as *associations*, and Active Record makes them easy to work with. Models also have requirements. For instance, you can't have a transaction without an amount—it might break your system if someone tried to have an empty transaction. So, Active Record gives you easy ways to tell a model what it should expect in order to be saved to the database.

This chapter will teach you how to programmatically enhance your models, so that they're more than just simple maps of your tables. To demonstrate the concepts, we'll be building on the events application you started in Chapter 3, so keep it handy if you want to follow along with the examples.

Adding Methods

Let's begin with a brief review of the Active Record basics. At the simplest level, Active Record works by automatically wrapping database tables whose names match the plural, underscored version of any classes that inherit from `ActiveRecord::Base`. For example,

if you wanted to wrap the users table, you would simply create a subclass of
ActiveRecord::Base called User, like this:

```
class User < ActiveRecord::Base
end
```

That's all you really need to have Active Record map the users table and get all the
basic CRUD functionality we described in Chapter 4. But few models are actually this
bare.

So far, we've been leaving our models classes unchanged. That's a good thing, and it
speaks to the power and simplicity of Active Record. However, it leaves something to be
desired. Most of the time, your models will need to do a lot more than just wrap a table.

■Note If you're familiar with SQL, you're probably feeling that Active Record provides you with only
simple-case solutions and it can't handle complicated cases. That's entirely untrue. While SQL is useful for
highly customized database queries, most Rails projects rarely need to touch SQL, thanks to some clever
tricks in Active Record.

The primary way in which we enhance models is by adding methods to them. This is
what's referred to as adding domain logic. With Active Record, all the logic for a particular
table is contained in one place: the model. This is why the model is said to encapsulate
all the domain logic. This logic includes access rules, validations, relationships, and, well,
just about anything else you feel like adding.

In addition to all the column-based reader and writer methods you get by wrapping
a table, you're free to define your own methods on the class. In fact, an Active Record subclass isn't much different from a regular Ruby class. About the only difference is that you
need to make sure you don't unintentionally overwrite any of Active Record's methods
(find, save, or destroy, for example). For the most part, though, this isn't a problem.

Let's look at a simple example. We're often faced with the problem of having to format
data, rather than accessing a model attribute in its raw form. In our events application, we
would like to be able to produce a formatted, long title that includes the name of the event,
its location, and its date. To accomplish this, all we need to do is define a new instance
method that performs the concatenation of those attributes and produces a formatted
string. We'll call the method long_title. Add the code shown in Listing 5-1 just before the
last end statement in the app/models/event.rb file.

Listing 5-1. *Custom long_title Method, in app/models/event.rb*

```
class Event < ActiveRecord::Base
  #...

  def long_title
    "#{title} - #{location} - #{occurs_on}"
  end

end
```

We've just created an instance method on the model; that is, we've told the Event model that it's now endowed with a new attribute called long_title. We can address long_title in the same way as we would any other method on the class. Let's open an irb session and try this on the console. From your terminal window, start up the Rails console with the following command:

```
$ ./script/console
```

This should drop you at a simple irb prompt with two right arrows and a blinking cursor. From here, we'll find an event and call the long_title method.

```
>> Event.find(:first).long_title
=> "Tiki Party - Hampton's Apartment - 2007-09-02"
```

So you see, there is no difference between the methods that Active Record creates and those we define ourselves. Here, instead of just asking the model for one of the attributes garnered from the database column names, we've defined our *own* method called long_title, which does a bit more than the standard title method.

The methods you add to your models can be as simple as returning true or false, or as complicated as doing major calculations and formatting on the object. The full power of Ruby is in your hands to do with as you please.

Don't worry if you don't feel comfortable adding your own methods to models just yet. The important part to note from this first section is that Active Record models are regular Ruby objects that can be augmented, modified, played with, poked, and turned inside out with sufficient Ruby-fu. Knowing this will be extremely helpful in being able to pull back the curtain and understand the advanced features of Active Record.

FAT MODELS

Some people might be made nervous by the `long_title` method we just created. They might see it as a violation of the MVC paradigm. They might ask, "Isn't formatting code supposed to be in the view?" In general, the answer is yes. However, it often helps to have models that act as intelligent objects. If you ask a model for some information about itself, it's natural to assume that it can give you a decent answer that doesn't require a large amount of work later on to figure out what it meant. So, small formatted strings and basic data types that faithfully represent the data in the model are good things to have in your code.

An intelligent model like this is often called "fat." This means that instead of performing model-related logic in other places (that is, in controllers or views), you keep it in the model, thus making it fat. This makes your models easier to work with and will help your code stay DRY.

A basic rule of thumb while trying to stay DRY is that if you find yourself copying and pasting a bit of code, then it might be worth your time to take a moment and figure out if there is a better way to approach the problem. For instance, if we had kept the `Event#long_title` formatting outside the model, we may have needed to repeat the same basic string-formatting procedure every time we wanted a human-friendly representation of an event's title. Then again, creating that method is a waste of time if we're going to use it in only one place in the application and never again.

This is where programmer experience comes in. As you learn and mature in your Rails programming, you will find it easier and easier to figure out where stuff is supposed to go. If you are always aiming for a goal of having the most maintainable and beautiful code you can possibly write, your projects will naturally become easier to maintain.

Next, we will look at another common form of model enhancement: associations. Active Record's associations give you the ability to define in simple terms how models relate to and interact with each other.

Using Associations

It's a lowly application that has only one table. Most applications will have many tables, and these tables will typically need to relate to each other in one way or another. *Associations* are a common model enhancement that let you relate tables to each other.

Associations are quite natural constructs that we encounter all the time in the real world: articles have comments, stores have products, magazines have subscriptions, and so on. In a relational database system like MySQL, you relate tables using a *foreign key reference* in one table to the *primary key* of another table.

Let's take the example of articles and comments. In a situation where a given article can have any number of comments attached to it, we say that each comment *belongs to* a particular article. Figure 5-1 demonstrates the association from the database's point of view.

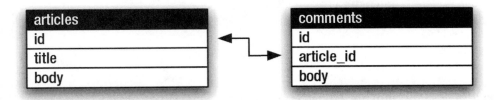

Figure 5-1. *The relationship between the articles and comments tables*

In the example in Figure 5-1, we use a column named article_id in the comments table to identify the related article in the articles table. In database-speak, we say that comments holds a *foreign key reference* to articles.

By Rails convention, the foreign key column is the singular, lowercase name of the target class with _id appended. So, for products that belong to a particular store, the foreign key would be named store_id; for subscriptions that belong to magazines, the foreign key would be named magazine_id; and so on. Here's the pattern:

#{*singular_name_of_parent_class*}_id

Table 5-1 shows a few more examples just to drive this concept home.

Table 5-1. *Sample Foreign Key References*

Model	Table	Foreign Key to Reference This Table
Article	articles	article_id
Person	people	person_id
Friend	friends	friend_id
Category	categories	category_id
Book	books	book_id

Whenever you need one table to reference another table, just remember to create the foreign key column in the table doing the referencing. That's all your table needs before you can put Active Record's associations to work.

Declaring Associations

As you've probably come to expect by now, Active Record makes working with associations easy. You don't need to get down to the bare metal of the database very often. As long as you understand the concept of primary and foreign keys, and how to create basic relationships in your tables, Active Record will do the proverbial heavy lifting, converting foreign key relationships into rich object associations. This means you get to access associated objects cleanly and naturally using Ruby:

```
article.comments
store.products
magazine.subscriptions
```

Once the relationships are defined in your database tables, you use a set of macro-like class methods in your models to create associations. They look like this:

- has_one

- has_many

- belongs_to

- has_and_belongs_to_many

Here's a quick example. The Message model declares a has_many relationship with Attachment; Attachment returns the favor by declaring that each of its objects belongs to a particular Message:

```
class Message < ActiveRecord::Base
  has_many :attachments
end

class Attachment < ActiveRecord::Base
  belongs_to :message
end
```

Given these instructions, Active Record will expect to find a table called attachments that has a field in it called message_id (the foreign key reference). It will use this association to let you say things like Message.find(1).attachments and get an array (or a *collection*) of Attachment objects that belong to the Message with an id of 1. Moreover, you can work with your associations in both directions. So, you can say `Attachment.find(1).message` to access the `Message` to which the `Attachment` with an `id` of 1 belongs. It sounds like a mouthful, but once you get the hang of it, you'll find it's quite intuitive.

Whenever you declare an association, Active Record will automatically add a set of methods to your model that make dealing with the association easier. This is a lot like the way in which Active Record creates methods based on your column names. Once it notices that you've declared an association, it dynamically creates methods that enable you to work with that association. We'll go through each different type of association and describe how to work with them. We'll also talk a little about the various options you can use to fine-tune your associations.

Creating One-to-One Associations

One-to-one associations describe a pattern where *a row in one table is related to exactly one row in another table.*

Suppose we have an application with employees and addresses, and each employee has exactly one address. Assume we have `Employee` and `Address` models, and the corresponding `users` and `profiles` tables have the appropriate columns. We can tell our `Employee` model that it *has one* `Address` and our `Address` model that it *belongs to* an `Employee`. Active Record will take care of the rest. The `has_one` and `belongs_to` macros are designed to read like regular English, so they sound natural in conversation and are easy to remember. Each represents a different side of the equation, working in tandem to make the association complete.

■**Note** Part of the Rails philosophy on development is that the gap between programmers and other project stakeholders should be bridged. Using natural language, such as *has one* and *belongs to*, in describing programmatic concepts helps bridge this gap, providing a construct that everyone can understand.

Consider the following (simplistic) schema definitions and model implementations for `Employee` and `Address`, respectively.

```
create_table :employees do |t|
  t.column :name, :string
end

create_table :addresses do |t|
  t.column :employee_id, :integer
  t.column :street,      :string
end
```

Notice the existence of the foreign key `employee_id` in the `addresses` schema. Also recall that we don't need to specify primary keys in migrations since they're created automatically. We declare the one-to-one association on the `Employee` and `Address` models as follows:

```
class Employee < ActiveRecord::Base
  has_one :address
end

class Address < ActiveRecord::Base
  belongs_to :employee
end
```

■**Note** While we've shown them together here, each of these classes would typically be in their own file in the `app/models` directory.

The `has_one` declaration on the `Employee` model tells Active Record that it can expect to find at least one record in the `addresses` table that has an `employee_id` matching the primary key of a row in the `employees` table. The `Address` model, in turn, declares that each of its records `belongs_to` a particular `Employee`.

Telling the `Address` model that it `belongs_to :employee` is saying, in effect, that each `Address` object references a particular `Employee`. We could even go so far as to say that `Employee` is the parent and `Address` is the child. The child model is dependent on the parent and therefore references it. Figure 5-2 demonstrates the `has_one` relationship.

has_one

Employee :has_one Address
Address :belongs_to Employee

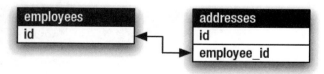

Figure 5-2. *The one-to-one relationship between employees and addresses*

Let's get inside a console session (./script/console) and see how this comes together. You'll be able to follow along as we create objects and relate them to one another. First, we'll create an employee and an address, as follows:

```
>> employee = Employee.create(:name => 'Dwight Schrute')
=> #<Employee:0x210dcb5>
>> address = Profile.create(:street => '1725 Slough Avenue')
=> #<Address:0x230dbb4>
```

Although we've successfully created a new employee and a new address, we haven't yet associated them with each other. If we ask the Employee object for its address, it will respond with nil.

```
>> employee.address
=> nil
```

To make the association happen, we specify it like any regular assignment on the Employee object, and then call save, like so:

```
>> employee.address = address
=> #<Address:0x230dbb4>
>> employee.save
=> true
```

Assignment is assignment—whether it's a name attribute to which you're assigning the value Joe or an association method to which you're assigning an object. Now when we ask the Employee object for its address, it will happily respond with one.

```
>> employee.address
=> #<Address:0x230dbb4>
```

That's all there is to it. While this is pretty good, we can actually do a bit better. We can create and save the address in one shot, and have it perform the association automatically, like this:

```
>> employee.create_address(:street => '1725 Slough Avenue ')
=> #<Address:0x210cbc2>
```

Using the create_address method for creating a new address will initialize the Address object, set its foreign key, and save it to the database. This works for any has_one association, no matter what it's named. Active Record automatically generates the create_#{association_name} method for you. So, if you had a User model set up with an association like has_one :account, you would get the create_account method automatically.

These alternatives for doing the same thing might seem confusing, but they're really just variations on the same theme. In all cases, you are creating two objects (the parent and the child) and telling them about one another. Whether you choose to do this in a multistep operation or all on one line is entirely up to you.

Earlier we said that declaring a has_one association causes Active Record to automatically add a suite of methods to make working with the association easier. Table 5-2 shows a summary of the methods that are added when we declare a has_one and belongs_to relationship between Employee and Address, where @employee is an Employee instance.

Table 5-2. *Methods Added by the has_one Association in the Employee/Address Example*

Method	Description
@employee.address	Returns the associated (Address) object; nil is returned if none is found
@employee.address=(address)	Assigns the associated (Address) object, extracts the primary key, and sets it as the foreign key
@employee.address.nil?	Returns true if there is no associated Address object
@employee.build_address(attributes={})	Returns a new Address object that has been instantiated with attributes and linked to @employee through a foreign key but has not yet been saved
@employee.create_address(attributes={})	Returns a new Address object that has been instantiated with attributes and linked to @employee through a foreign key and that has already been saved

While we're using the Employee.has_one :address example here, the rules work for any object associated to another using has_one. Here are some examples, along with sample return values:

```
@user.profile #=> #<Profile:0x130dcb1>
@user.profile.nil? #=> false
@user.build_profile(:bio => 'eats trees and leaves') #=> #<Profile:0x130dcb1>
@user.create_profile(:bio => 'eats trees and leaves') #=> #<Profile:0x130dcb1>
```

The has_one declaration can also include an options hash to specialize its behavior if necessary. Table 5-3 lists the most common options. For a complete list of all options, consult the Rails API documentation (http://api.rubyonrails.org/classes/ActiveRecord/Associations/ClassMethods.html).

Table 5-3. *Common has_one Options*

Option	Description	Example
:class_name	Specifies the class name of the association. Used when the class name can't be inferred from the association name.	has_one :location, :class_name => 'Address'
:conditions	Specifies the conditions that the associated object must meet in order to be included as a WHERE SQL fragment.	has_one :address, :conditions => "active = 1"
:foreign_key	Specifies the foreign key used for the association in the event that it doesn't adhere to convention of being the lowercase, singular name of target class with _id appended.	has_one :address, :foreign_key => 'location_id'
:order	Specifies the order from which the associated object will be picked as an "ORDER BY" SQL fragment.	has_one :address, :order => "created_at DESC"
:dependent	Specifies that the associated object should be removed when this object is. If set to :destroy, the associated object is deleted using the destroy method. If set to :delete, the associated object is deleted without calling its destroy method. If set to :nullify, the associated object's foreign key is set to NULL.	has_one :address, :dependent => :destroy

Creating One-to-Many Associations

One-to-many associations describe a pattern where *a row in one table is related to one or more rows in another table.* Examples would be an Email that has many Recipients, or a Magazine that has many Subscriptions. It's time to say good-bye to contrived examples and put these principles to work in our events application.

Adding the User Model

When we first started the events application, we decided to let anyone create new events. This worked fine when there was only one person using the system, but we want this to

be a multiple-user application and let different people sign up, sign in, and start managing their own events, separately from one another.

Up until now, our events have been orphaned—they don't belong to anyone. We're
going to remedy that now by creating a User model and associating users with events. In
our system, each event is going to belong to a user, and a user may have many events.
Figure 5-3 illustrates this association.

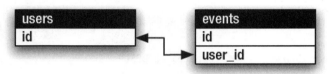

Figure 5-3. *The one-to-many relationship between users and events*

Let's fire up the generator and create the User model now.

```
$ ./script/generate model User
```

Just as you saw in the previous chapter, the model generator creates, among other
things, a model file in app/models and a migration in db/migrate. Open db/migrate/
003_create_users.rb and give it the schema definition shown in Listing 5-2 (add the
following code to the file).

Listing 5-2. *Migration to Create the users Table, db/migrations/003_create_users.rb*

```
class CreateUsers < ActiveRecord::Migration
  def self.up
    create_table :users do |t|
      t.column :login,         :string
      t.column :email,         :string
      t.column :password, :string
    end

    # Add a foreign key reference to users in the events table
    add_column :events, :user_id, :integer
  end
```

```
  def self.down
    drop_table :users
    remove_column :events, :user_id
  end
end
```

This is standard migration fare. In the `self.up` definition, we used the `create_table` method to create a new `users` table. The new table object is *yielded* to the block in the variable, `t`, on which we call the `column` method to create each row. Along with the standard `login` and `email` fields, we're specifying a `hashed_password` field, which we'll use for authentication, as we'll explain in the "Reviewing the Updated Models" section later in this chapter. The primary key, `id`, will be created automatically, so there's no need to specify it here. Pay particular attention to the `user_id` column in the `self.up` section. It's the foreign key reference column we've been talking so much about. Also note that its type is `:integer`. That's important, because it's referring to a numeric `id`.

Now all we need to do is run the migration and create the table using the `db:migrate` Rake task. Run the migration with the following command:

```
$ rake db:migrate
```

```
== CreateUsers: migrating ========================================================
-- create_table(:users)
   -> 0.0035s
-- add_column(:events, :user_id, :integer)
   -> 0.0065s
== CreateUsers: migrated (0.0103s) ==============================================
```

With the table and foreign keys in place, Listings 5-3 and 5-4 show how we declare the one-to-many association in our `Event` and `User` models. Add these to the relevant models now.

Listing 5-3. *belongs_to Declaration in app/models/event.rb*

```
class Event < ActiveRecord::Base
  belongs_to :user
end
```

Listing 5-4. *has_many Declaration in app/models/user.rb*

```
class User < ActiveRecord::Base
  has_many :events
end
```

That's all there is to it. This bit of code has endowed our `Event` and `User` models with a lot of functionality.

■**Note** All associations (except for `has_and_belongs_to_many`, which we'll cover shortly) need to declare a `belongs_to` on at least one side of the association. The rule of thumb is that the `belongs_to` declaration always goes in the class with the foreign key.

Creating a New Associated Object

Our associations are in place, but we don't have any data in the database with which to test them. We'll remedy that now by creating a new `User` object and attaching some events to it. We'll do this exercise on the console.

First, let's create a new user. We'll use the `create` constructor and pass in all the attributes directly as a hash. (If you need a quick review on how to create new records using Active Record, refer to Chapter 4.)

```
>> user = User.create(:login => 'mary',
                      :email => 'mary@example.com',
                      :password => 'secret')
=> #<User:0x2515ad0>
```

Now that we have a user, we can test whether the association between users and events is set up correctly. If it is, we should be able to ask the `User` object for its associated events, and it will respond with a collection. Even though we have haven't created any events for this user yet, it should still work, returning an empty collection.

```
>> user.events
=> nil
```

Great! The `has_many` association is working correctly and `User` instances now have an events method, which was created automatically by Active Record when it noticed the `has_many` declaration.

Let's give this user some events. Enter the following commands:

```
>> user.events << Event.find(:first)
=> [#<Event:0x2585c18>]
>> user.events.size
=> 1
>> User.find(1).events
=> [#<Event:0x25279b0>]
```

By using the << (append) operator, we were able to attach an Event onto our User. Now, what did that do exactly? Let's look into the event and find out:

```
>> Event.find(1).user_id
=> 1
```

See how this event now has a user_id in it that points to the user with an id of 1? This means we have successfully related the two objects. In fact, we can even ask an Event instance for its User.

```
>> Event.find(1).user
=> #<User:0x2515ad0>
```

Voilà! Our models can really start to express things now. What's happening here is that the has_many and belongs_to declarations are just creating more methods, as we did earlier with the long_title method. Let's look at what else these happy little helpers brought along to the party. Table 5-4 shows a summary of the methods that are added when we declare a has_many and belongs_to relationship between User and Event. (@user represents a User instance.)

Table 5-4. *Methods Added by the has_many Association in the User and Event Models*

Method	Description
@user.events	Returns an array of all the associated events. An empty array is returned if no events are found.
@user.events=(events)	Replaces the events collection with the one supplied.
@user.events << event	Adds one or more events to the collection and saves their foreign keys.
@user.events.delete(events)	Removes one or more events from the collection by setting their foreign keys to NULL.
@user.events.clear	Removes every Event object from the collection without deleting them from the database.
@user.events.empty?	Returns true if there are no associated Event objects for this @user.

Continued

Table 5-4. *Continued*

Method	Description
@user.events.size	Returns the number of associated Event objects for this @user.
@user.event_ids	Returns an array of associated event ids.
@user.events.clear	Clears all associated objects from the association by setting their foreign keys to NULL.
@user.events.find	A find that is automatically "scoped" off the association; that is, it will find only within items that would be returned with a find(:all). Here's an example: @user.events.find(:first, :title => 'Hoedown').
@user.events.build(attributes={})	Returns a new Event object that has been instantiated with attributes and linked to @user through a foreign key but has not yet been saved. Here's an example: @user.events.build(:title => 'Hoedown').
@user.events.create(attributes={})	Returns a new Event object that has been instantiated with attributes and linked to @user through a foreign key and has already been saved. Here's an example: @user.events.create(:title => 'Hoedown').

We're using the User.has_many :events example here, but the rules work for any object associated with another using has_many. Here are some examples, along with sample return values:

```
@employee.tasks
  #=> [#<Task:0x230dbb4>,#<Task:0x230dbb5>]
@employee.tasks << Task.new
  #=> [#<Task:0x230dbb4>,#<Task:0x230dbb5>,#<Task:0x230dbb6>]
@employee.task_ids #=> [1,2,3]
@employee.tasks.clear #=> []
@employee.tasks.find(:first) #=> #<Task:0x230dbb4>
@employee.tasks.create(:name => 'Refactor') #=> #<Task:0x230dbb9>
```

You can also pass in options to your association declaration to affect the way that you work with those associations. Table 5-5 lists some of the most common options.

Table 5-5. *Common has_many Options*

Option	Description	Example
:class_name	Specifies the class name of the association. Used when the class name can't be inferred from the association name.	has_many :registered_users, :class_name => 'User'
:conditions	Specifies the conditions that the associated objects must meet in order to be included as a WHERE SQL fragment.	has_many :events, :conditions => "active = 1"
:foreign_key	Specifies the foreign key used for the association in the event that it doesn't adhere to convention of being the lowercase, singular name of target class with _id appended.	has_many :events, :foreign_key => 'activity_id'
:order	Specifies the order in which the associated objects are returned as an ORDER BY SQL fragment.	has_many :events, :order => "occurs_on DESC"
:dependent	Specifies that the associated objects should be removed when this object is. If set to :destroy, the associated objects are deleted using the destroy method. If set to :delete, the associated objects are deleted without calling their destroy method. If set to :nullify, the associated objects' foreign keys are set to NULL.	has_many :events, :dependent => :destroy

There's much more to has_many associations than we can possibly hope to cover here, so be sure to check out the Rails API documentation (http://api.rubyonrails.org/ classes/ActiveRecord/Associations/ClassMethods.html) for the full scoop.

Applying Association Options

It's time to apply what you've learned to our domain model. Specifically, we'll use the :order option to apply a default order to the User.has_many :events declaration, and use the :dependent option to make sure that when we delete a user, all their events are deleted as well.

Specifying a Default Order

When we access a user's events, we want to make sure that they come back in the *order* in which they will occur. Specifically, we want the oldest to be at the bottom and the furthest in the future to be at the top of the list. We can do this by configuring our has_many association with a default order using the :order option. Add the :order option to the has_many :events declaration, as shown in Listing 5-5.

Listing 5-5. *:order Option Added to has_many*

```
has_many :events,
         :order => "occurs_on DESC"
```

We give the name of the field that we want to order by, and then we say either ASC (ascending) or DESC (descending) to indicate the order in which the results should be returned. Since time moves forward (to bigger numbers), we want to make sure that we are going back in time, so we use the DESC keyword here.

■**Note** ASC and DESC are SQL keywords. We're actually specifying a *SQL fragment* here, which we'll discuss in the "Building Conditions for Advanced Finding" section later in this chapter.

We can also specify a secondary order by adding a comma in between arguments. Let's say we wanted to sort by the title of the event *after* we sort by the date. So, if two events occur on the same day, they will be ordered first by the date, and then by the lexical order of the title. Listing 5-6 shows the event title added to the :order option.

Listing 5-6. *Adding the Title to the :order Option for has_many*

```
has_many :events,
         :order => "occurs_on DESC, title ASC"
```

You'll notice that we use ASC for ordering on the title. This is because as letters go up in the alphabet, their value goes up. So, to sort alphabetically, use the ASC keyword.

Specifying Dependencies

Frequently, you'll have dependencies between your models. For instance, in our events application, if we delete users, we want to make sure they don't have events in the system. Said another way, an Event is dependent on its User. We can let Active Record take care of this for us automatically by specifying the `:dependent` option to our association. Listing 5-7 shows all the options to `has_many :events`, including the `:dependent` option.

Listing 5-7. *:dependent Option Added to has_many*

```
has_many :events,
         :order => "occurs_on DESC, title ASC",
         :dependent => :destroy
```

By passing in the symbol `:destroy`, we are saying that not only are events dependent, but also that when the owner is deleted, we want to call the `destroy` method on every related event. This ensures that any `*_destroy` callbacks on the event instances will be called (we'll talk about callbacks later in this chapter, in the "Making Callbacks" section). If we wanted to skip the callbacks, we could use the `:delete` option in place of `:destroy`, which will delete the records directly via SQL.

Let's say we just wanted to set the foreign key column (`user_id`) to `NULL` in the `events` table, instead of completely destroying the event. This would essentially orphan the events. We can do this by using the `:nullify` option in place of `:destroy`.

```
has_many :events,
         :order => "occurs_on DESC, title ASC",
         :dependent => :nullify
```

So, if we did that and deleted a user, Active Record would automatically update the events and break all the foreign key references. If we didn't do this, we might have `events.user_id = 1037` when there is no `User` with an `id` of 1037. For our application, we want to keep it as `:destroy`.

Creating Many-to-Many Associations

Often, the relationship between two models is many-to-many. This describes a pattern where *two tables are connected to multiple rows on both sides*. We'll use this in our events application to add categories to events. If we wanted to allow only one category to be selected for a given event, we could use `has_many`. But we want to be able to apply multiple categories.

Think about this for a minute: an event can have many categories, and a category can have many events—where would the `belongs_to` go in this situation? Neither model belongs to the other in the traditional sense. In Active Record-speak, we refer to this kind of association as `has_and_belongs_to_many` (often referred to as `habtm` for short).

The `has_and_belongs_to_many` association works by relying on a join table that keeps a reference to the foreign keys involved in the relationship. The join table sits between the tables we want to join: `categories` and `events`. Not surprisingly, then, the join table in this case will be called `categories_events`. Pay particular attention to the table name. It's formed from the names of each table in alphabetical order, separated by an underscore. In our case, the `c` in categories comes before the `e` in events, hence, `categories_events`. Figure 5-4 illustrates this relationship.

has_and_belongs_to_many

Event :has_and_belongs_to_many Categories
Category :has_and_belongs_to_many Events

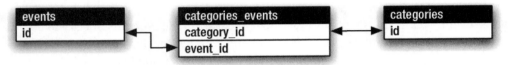

Figure 5-4. *The many-to-many relationship between events and categories*

Let's start by adding the `Category` model. This is a simple matter of generating the model. Since the category schema definition is so simple (consisting of just a `name` column), we'll let the generator fill in the migration for us by passing field arguments directly to the generator. Run the following command inside your application root:

```
./script/generate model Category name:string
```

You'll notice that we generated this model a bit differently than the others. We added `name:string` onto the end of the `generate` method. This is a shortcut to have your migrations automatically generated with the *field_name:type* that you specify. This is a handy trick when you're generating simple schemas. Let's look at that migration and see what was generated, as shown in Listing 5-8.

Listing 5-8. *The db/migrate/004_create_categories.rb File*

```ruby
class CreateCategories < ActiveRecord::Migration
  def self.up
    create_table :categories do |t|
      t.column :name, :string
    end
  end

  def self.down
    drop_table :categories
  end
end
```

We need another migration to create the join table. Let's do that now by running the following command:

```
$ ./script/generate migration create_categories_events
```

Listing 5-9 shows the result.

Listing 5-9. *The db/migrate/005_create_categories_events.rb File*

```
class CreateCategoriesEvents < ActiveRecord::Migration
  def self.up
    create_table :categories_events, :id => false do |t|
      t.column :event_id,    :integer
      t.column :category_id, :integer
    end
  end

  def self.down
    drop_table :categories_events
  end
end
```

Remember that when using `create_table`, you don't need to specify the primary key, as it will be created automatically. Well, in the case of a join table, we actually don't want a primary key. This is because the join table isn't a first-class entity in its own right. Since creating tables without primary keys is the exception and not the rule, we need to explicitly tell `create_table` that we don't want to create an `id`. Take a close look at the call to `create_table` in Listing 5-9. We pass in the option `:id => false`. This prevents `create_table` from creating the primary key.

Go ahead and run this migration:

```
$ rake db:migrate
```

```
== CreateCategories: migrating ================================================
-- create_table(:categories)
   -> 0.0033s
== CreateCategories: migrated (0.0034s) =======================================

== CreateCategoriesEvents: migrating ==========================================
-- create_table(:categories_events, {:id=>false})
   -> 0.0034s
== CreateCategoriesEvents: migrated (0.0035s) =================================
```

With the Category model and the join table in place, we're ready to let Active Record in on our association. Open the Event and Category models and add the has_and_belongs_to_many declarations to them, as shown in Listings 5-10 and 5-11.

Listing 5-10. *has_and_belongs_to_many Declaration in app/models/event.rb*

```
class Event < ActiveRecord::Base
  belongs_to :user
  has_and_belongs_to_many :categories
end
```

Listing 5-11. *has_and_belongs_to_many Declaration in app/models/category.rb*

```
class Category < ActiveRecord::Base
  has_and_belongs_to_many :events
end
```

We should also create a few categories to work with. We like to do this with fixtures. *Fixtures* are textual representations of database records. They can be used to populate your database with data, and they're a great place to keep so-called seed data. Using fixtures, we'll kill two birds with one stone: fixtures are easy to load into the database any time we wish, and they'll be useful later on, when we're testing our application in Chapter 9. The model generator created an empty categories fixture in test/fixtures/categories.yml. Open it and add a few categories so that it looks like Listing 5-12.

Listing 5-12. *The test/fixtures/categories.yml File*

```
conferences:
  id: 1
  name: Conferences

parties:
  id: 2
  name: Parties

concerts:
  id: 3
  name: Concerts
```

```
readings:
  id: 4
  name: Readings

movies:
  id: 5
  name: Readings
```

That should do nicely. You can load fixtures using the Rake task db:fixtures:load, specifying the fixtures you want to load using the FIXTURES variable.

```
$ rake db:fixtures:load FIXTURES=categories
```

If you need to add more categories later, you can just append them to the fixture file and reload it. We'll talk more about fixtures in Chapter 9, but this first look should give you an idea of how they work.

Let's give this a test run now. Get your console ready and run the following commands.

```
>> event = Event.find(:first)
=> #<Event:0x268157c>
>> category = Category.find_by_name('parties')
=> #<Category:0x26388b8 @attributes={"name"=>"Parties", "id"=>"2"}>
>> event.categories << category
=> [#<Category:0x26388b8 @attributes={"name"=>"Parties", "id"=>"2"}>]
>> event.categories.any?
=> true
>> event.categories.size
=> 1
```

Here, we automatically associate a category with an event using the << operator. In this case, when you use << with has_and_belongs_to_many, it automatically saves the new association. Some things in Active Record don't happen until you say save, but this is one of the examples where that part is done automatically,

We can even do this from the category's side of the association. Try the following:

```
>> category.events.empty?
=> false
>> category.events.size
=> 1
>> category.events.find(:first).title
=> "Tiki Party"
```

We just did the opposite of the previous test. We said that has_and_belongs_to_many works in both directions, right? So, we simply found our new category and asked it for its first event, which we can see is now Tiki Party, because that's what we associated in the other direction, too.

Using has_and_belongs_to_many is a very simple way to approach many-to-many associations. However, it has its limitations. Before you're tempted to use it for associating users with events they would like to attend (activities), we should point out that it has no way of storing additional information on the join. What if we wanted to know *when* someone decided to attend an event, or how many people the attendee is going to bring along? This kind of data fits naturally in the *join table*. Rails includes another type of association called has_many :through, which allows us to create rich joins like this.

Creating Rich Many-to-Many Associations

Sometimes when you're modeling a many-to-many association, you need to put additional data on the join model. But, since Active Record's has_and_belongs_to_many uses a join table (for which there is no associated model), there's no model on which to operate. For this type of situation, you can create "rich" many-to-many associations using has_many :through. This is really a combination of techniques that end up performing a similar but more robust version of has_and_belongs_to_many.

The basic idea is that you build a full model to represent the join table. In our application, we will build a model called a Registration. You could say that users have many registrations that belong to an event, or users have many events through registrations. Figure 5-5 illustrates this relationship.

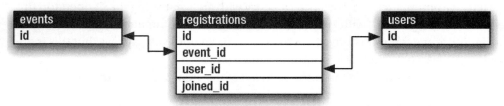

Figure 5-5. *The rich many-to-many relationship between events and users, through registrations*

Let's generate the model and migration for the `registrations` table now.

```
$ ./script/generate model registrations
```

Listing 5-13 shows the result.

Listing 5-13. *The db/migrate/006_create_registrations File*

```
class CreateRegistrations < ActiveRecord::Migration
  def self.up
    create_table :registrations do |t|
      t.column :user_id,    :integer
      t.column :event_id,   :integer
      t.column :note,       :string,  :length => 400
      t.column :created_at, :datetime
    end
  end

  def self.down
    drop_table :registrations
  end
end
```

To keep things simple, we're just going to allow people to add a note whenever they want to attend an event. For instance, someone might want to say "Can't wait to be there! I'm so excited!" or "Is packagethief coming?"

Let's update our models with what we need. Add the code snippets shown in Listings 5-14, 5-15, and 5-16 to the relevant models.

Listing 5-14. *belongs_to Declarations in app/models/registration.rb*

```
class Registration < ActiveRecord::Base
  belongs_to :user
  belongs_to :event
end
```

Listing 5-15. *belongs_to, has_many, and has_and_belongs_to_many Declarations in app/models/event.rb*

```
class Event < ActiveRecord::Base
  belongs_to :user
```

```
  has_many :registrations
  has_many :attendees, :through => :registrations, :source => :user
  has_and_belongs_to_many :categories
end
```

Listing 5-16. *has_many Declarations in app/models/user.rb*

```
class User < ActiveRecord::Base
  has_many :events
  has_many :registrations
  has_many :activities, :through => :registrations, :source => :event
end
```

You'll notice that we reworked how we are naming associations. One aspect of the Rails philosophy is that we should always be questioning and refactoring our code to work with best practices. So, in this incarnation, events that we are attending as a user are called `activities`, and `events` are events that we are hosting.

So, as an added benefit, `has_many :through` allows us to easily have nice names on our associations. The `:source` option lets us define the source name of the association. In this case, the activity in question is an event, so we set the `:source` option accordingly. The `through` associations let us pretend that the middle table (`registrations`) doesn't exist.

Let's play with this on the console to see how it works. We'll start by finding any event and creating a brand-new user that can register for the event:

```
>> event = Event.find(:first)
=> #<Event:0x3258d2c>
>> user = User.create(:login => 'simon', :email => 'simon@example.com', :password ➥
=> 'secret')
=> #<User:0x3251b1c>
```

Because this user is brand new, it won't have any registrations or activities at this point, nor will the event have any attendees. We can confirm this fact by asking:

```
>> user.registrations.any?
=> false
>> user.activities.any?
=> false
>> event.attendees.any?
=> false
```

To register this user for an event, we simply create a new registration object like we would any association, and pass in the event we want to register for. We do this using `registrations.create`.

```
>> user.registrations.create(:event => event)
=> #<Registration:0x323ffe8>
```

Let's reload the user object and interrogate it again. This time around, you'll see that we have a registration.

```
>> user.reload
=> #<User:0x3251b1c>
>> user.registrations.any?
=> true
```

Activities are what we're calling events that a user has registered for. Again, if we ask whether the user object has any activities, it will respond with true.

```
>> user.activities.any?
=> true
```

The activities method returns an array of events (remember that when we declared the activities association, we specified that the :source was :event):

```
>> user.activities
=> [#<Event:0x3231ee8]
```

The event will now have an attendee. Let's reload the event object and take a look:

```
>> event.reload
=> #<Event:0x3258d2c>
>> event.attendees.any?
=> true
>> event.attendees.include?(user)
=> true
```

Building Conditions for Advanced Finding

In Chapter 4, we covered using the find class method in Active Record, along with most of its options. Now we are going to expand on different ways to build conditions for your find operations. Building conditions is one of the most important things you do with your models.

Using a Conditions Hash

The most basic condition style is the hash syntax. Active Record takes the Hash passed into the conditions option, and turns the keys into column names and the values into parameters to match. The hash syntax is useful only if you are trying to find an exact match.

Run the following commands to try out the hash syntax.

```
>> Event.find(
      :all,
      :conditions => {:location => '174 Spadina',
                      :occurs_on => '2007-01-01'}
   )
=> [] # no results
```

The hash syntax works well for straightforward find operations where you use only ANDs to join together the conditions (that is, all conditions must match). However, sometimes you need more flexibility than exact matches.

Using a SQL Fragment

To specify conditions, you can pass in a SQL fragment as a string that is sent directly to the query. You need to have a pretty decent knowledge of SQL to use this kind of syntax, but it does provide a lot of flexibility, and you can create arbitrarily complex SQL fragments if you're a SQL-ninja.

Let's try the same find operation as in the previous section, but using a pure SQL condition fragment.

```
>> Event.find(:all, :conditions => "occurs_on = '2007-09-02'")
=> [#<Event:0xb73f63b4 @attributes={..."occurs_on"=>"2007-09-02"...}>]
```

Now let's try something more complicated that only SQL is able to do.

```
Event.find(
  :all,
  :conditions => "occurs_on < '23-03-2007' OR location NOT LIKE '%Hampton%'"
)
```

Instead of using the = sign, we are using the less-than (<) symbol to make sure that the date occurs after March 23, 2007. This is followed by the SQL OR operator, which says "if this first part isn't a match, then try the left-hand side and give it a second chance at matching." Therefore, we check the right-hand side only if the left-hand side fails. If an item fails the occurs_on match, we check to see if the location is NOT LIKE Hampton. You can think of OR as a more permissive joining operator. It only cares that one of the conditions is a match. OR has a sister named AND, which requires that both conditions are true.

```
Event.find(
  :all,
  :conditions => "occurs_on < '23-03-2007' AND location NOT LIKE '%Hampton%'"
)
```

We are also using the SQL LIKE (modified using NOT, for negation) operator, which allows us to make partial matches. Normally, when using =, SQL requires that the string matches *perfectly*. However, LIKE is more permissive and allows partial matches when used with the % wildcard. Allow us to explain: The % symbols are SQL wildcard characters that apply in LIKE clauses. A % at the beginning of pattern says that the pattern must match at the end of the field (the beginning can be any sequence of characters); a % at the end means that the pattern must match at the beginning, where the end can be any sequence of characters. Using a % on both sides of the pattern means that it must match anywhere in the field. Using %Hampton% means that the word Hampton must occur somewhere (anywhere) in the description. Therefore, a party with the name "Big Hampton's Birthday Party" would be accepted as a match.

As you can see, this usage has all the flexibility of SQL, but it also has SQL's natural limitations. For instance, you may need to find information based on what the user passes into the application via the request parameters in your application (we'll cover request parameters in the next chapter). If you aren't careful, that data can be very dangerous to your application, because it's open to SQL injection attacks. This is when a user submits malicious code that will trick your database server into doing far more than you intended. For more information about SQL injection, check out the Wikipedia article at http://en.wikipedia.org/wiki/SQL_injection. Fortunately, Rails gives us a way to avoid such threats—using the array condition syntax, which performs correctly quoted replacements.

Using an Array

The array condition syntax gives you the ability to specify conditions on your database calls in a safer way than using SQL syntax. Also, you don't need to worry so much about SQL specifics like quoting and other concerns, since it does automatic conversions for you on the inputs you give it. This is how it protects against SQL injection—it ensures that the substituted values are safely quoted, thereby preventing malicious users from injecting arbitrary SQL into your queries.

The following example requires the use of a nice little Ruby method called Date.today. Basically, it returns a Date object that is set to the current date. Let's see if we can find all of the events that occur on this particular day.

```
>> Event.find(:all, :conditions => ["occurs_on = ?", Date.today]).size
=> 0
```

It doesn't look like much is going on today. However, if we had any events that matched today, they would have been returned. Instead of writing in the date, we simply put a ? in the spot where we would normally write the value we want to find. It took the second element in the array and replaced it where the first ? appeared. Additionally, the array syntax automatically took our date and converted it into something that our database would like. In fact, we can spy on our `log/development.log` file and see the conversation.

```
Event Load (0.113583)   SELECT * FROM events WHERE (occurs_on = '2007-03-22')
```

We gave it a `Date` object and it turned it into the nice format that pleases our database. If we had passed it a string, it wouldn't have converted at all. We can even pass it some information from another model.

```
Event.find(
  :all,
  :conditions => ["occurs_on = ?", Event.find(:first).occurs_on]
)
```

That condition will return all of the events that occur on the same day as the event that we found first. You can pass as many conditions as you want, as long as they occur in the same order as the question marks.

```
Event.find(
  :all,
  :conditions => ["occurs_on = ? or title like ?", Date.today, "%Tiki%"]
)
```

MONITORING THE LOGS

In the example in this section, we checked the `log/development.log` file to see what had happened. It's often useful to monitor what the server is doing. You may have already noticed that when you run `./script/server`, it is telling you information about what is going on in your application. However, different web servers (depending on what you have installed) will give you different outputs, some more descriptive than others.

Fortunately, Rails prints all of its activities to a log file. If you look in your `log` directory, you will notice `log/development.log`. This is the file where all of the activities of your server are output. If you are running in production mode, the log file will be `log/production.log`.

This file is being written to live by your server. Sometimes it is useful (especially on a live server) to monitor the events occurring on your server. If you're on a UNIX system, you can run the command `tail -f log/development.log` to get a live feed from your logs. If you're on a Windows system, you can find several applications that behave like `tail` with a quick Google search.

During debugging, it can be useful to output messages to the log to see what's going on with your application. Almost anywhere in your application, you can do this.

```
logger.debug "This will only show in development"
logger.warn "This will show in all environments"
```

Both of these messages will print directly to the `log` file and can be extremely useful for figuring out what is going on with your server.

The main disadvantage with the array syntax is that it can become confusing to remember the order of the elements you are passing in for the conditions.

Instead of simply adding a list of things at the end of the array, you can also pass in a hash and change the question marks to actual named replacements. This can help you keep the order of your arguments straight.

```
Event.find(
  :all,
  :conditions => [ "title like :search or description like :search",
                  {:search => "%Tiki%"}]
)
```

As you can see, we are able to reuse the same term multiple places in our condition. If we were using the regular array syntax, we would have to create them. This is especially useful if you have many, many conditions.

Using Association Proxies

Association proxy is a fancy term for the ability to "chain" together multiple calls to Active Record. We've been using this technique throughout the entire book, but haven't given it any special mention. Here is a basic example of association proxies:

```
Event.find(:first).registrations.find(:all)
```

This will return all of the registrations for the first event returned. The second `find` (off registrations), will be automatically scoped to the event, which is to say, it will find registrations that belong to that event. If you remember, `registrations` is a `has_many` relationship on the `Event` model. The cool part is that this isn't two queries to the database. It does all of this in one request to the database.

Scoped finders are also more secure. Imagine a multiple-user system where data owned by one user shouldn't be accessible by another user. Simply finding an associated object, say, a document, by its `id` wouldn't restrict it to documents owned by a particular user. You could pass in the `document_id` and the `user_id` as conditions, but that's sloppy and error-prone. The correct way to do this would be to scope all find operations off the user in question. For example, assuming you had a `User` object stored in the variable `current_user`, `current_user.documents.find(1)` would ensure that the document with id 1 would be returned only if it belonged to the `current_user`.

Anyone who has done database work will realize that this incredibly simple syntax is far easier than the SQL queries that need to be created to achieve similar results. If you play around with these chains, you can check out the log to see the SQL that was generated—you'll be happy that you didn't have to write that yourself!

This technique doesn't just apply to finding. It can be used to automatically assign ownership with `build` and `create` constructors by setting the appropriate foreign keys. Consider the following example where we're creating a new document for the `current_user`. This will automatically set the document's `user_id` to that of the current user.

```
current_user.documents.create(:name => 'Private')
```

This is much better than the alternative, which would be to go through the `Document` model directly and set the `user_id` as an attribute (`Document.create(:user_id => current_user.id`). As a rule, whenever you need to restrict find operations to an owner, or if you are assigning ownership, you should use the power of the association proxy.

■**Tip** The association proxy is one of the most commonly underused elements of Active Record. Rails core team members, Jamis Buck and Michael Koziarski, have written a great article on this topic, in which they describe several anti-patterns you should avoid. We highly recommend you read this article in full. You can find it at `http://therailsway.com/2007/3/26/association-proxies-are-your-friend`.

Applying Validations

It's probably a safe bet that you don't want every field in your tables to be optional. Certain fields need to be required, terms of service agreements need to be accepted, and passwords need to be confirmed. That's just the way it is when you're building web applications, and Rails understands this. Consider this example of a `User` model:

```
class User < ActiveRecord::Base
  validates_presence_of     :username
  validates_confirmation_of :password
  validates_acceptance_of   :terms_of_service
end
```

Like associations, validations are a set of high-level macros that let you selectively apply common validation requirements to your model's attributes. In this section, we'll create a full set of validations for our events application, and you'll see first-hand how easy it is to perform basic validations with Active Record. We're going to start by building a couple custom validation methods, and then we will apply some of the built-in validations.

Building Custom Validation Methods

In our events application, we would like to make sure that no one creates an event that happens in the past. First, we need to create a method so that we can ask an Event if its occurs_on field is in the past. This method is useful outside validations, because we might want to indicate on the interface later when an event has happened. Let's add that method now and call it is_in_the_past?. Add the code shown in Listing 5-17 to the Event model.

Listing 5-17. *is_in_the past? Method, in app/models/event.rb*

```
def is_in_the_past?
  occurs_on < Date.today
end
```

This gets us a step closer to our goal. When building validations, Active Record gives us a nice object to use called errors. Whenever we want to add a validation error to the list of errors, we just say event.add(column_name, error_message). So, lets implement a method called has_not_occurred that uses this functionality, as shown in Listing 5-18.

Listing 5-18. *has_not_occurred Method, in app/models/event.rb*

```
def has_not_occurred
  errors.add("occurs_on", "is in the past") if occurs_on && is_in_the_past?
end
```

This will check if we should apply the error by evaluating the if statement. If that if statement is true, we want to add an error into the errors object. Note that before we test to see if it's in the past, we make sure that occurs_on is not nil. This is so that our test won't throw an error. If occurs_on is nil, that will be handled by another validator.

So, how do we tell Active Record that this method should be run before a save? We use the validate class method and pass it a symbol with the name of the method. At the top of our Event class, add the code shown in Listing 5-19.

Listing 5-19. *validate Method, in app/models/event.rb*

```
class Event < ActiveRecord::Base
  #...
  validate :has_not_occurred
  #...
end
```

This just lets Active Record know to pay attention to our new `has_not_occurred` method. Later, we'll write tests to make sure that this is working. But you can also go to the console and try to create an invalid object to see if it will report back errors for you. The easiest way to get to errors in an Active Record object is with `events.errors.full_messages`. After you do that, let's look through the built-in validations.

Using Built-in Validations

Rails has a myriad of built-in validators. We're going to cover a few of them here, as we apply them to our events application. Check the API for details on all the Rails validators (`http://api.rubyonrails.com/classes/ActiveRecord/Validations/ClassMethods.html`).

Just as a reference as we get started, there are two common options that you can pass into any built-in validator. These are described in Table 5-6.

Table 5-6. *Default Options for All Validators*

Option	Description	Example
:message	Specifies the error message shown if validation fails.	:message => "too long"
:on	Specifies when this validation happens. The default is :save. Other options are :create and :update.	:on => :create

Validating That a Value Has Been Entered

You can use `validates_presence_of` to make sure that a user has entered *something* into a field. This is very useful in many cases. In fact, we are going to add this validator to our `Event` model, as shown in Listing 5-20.

Listing 5-20. *validates_presence_of Method, in app/models/event.rb*

```
class Event < ActiveRecord::Base
  validates_presence_of :title, :location
end
```

The default message is "can't be blank."

Validating That a Value Is Unique

Often, you will want to make sure that a certain field is unique. The validates_uniqueness_of method validates whether the value of the specified attributes are unique across the system. We will use this method in our User model to make sure that each login name is unique, as shown in Listing 5-21.

Listing 5-21. *validates_uniqueness_of Method, in app/models/user.rb*

```
class User < ActiveRecord::Base
  validates_uniqueness_of :login
end
```

When the record is created, a check is performed to make sure that no record exists in the database with the given value for the specified attribute (that maps to a column). When the record is updated, the same check is made but disregarding the record itself. The default error message is "#{name} has already been taken."

The validates_uniqueness_of method can also validate whether the value of the specified attributes are unique based on multiple scope parameters. For example, you could use it to make sure that a teacher can be on the schedule only once per semester for a particular class.

```
class Schedule < ActiveRecord::Base
  validates_uniqueness_of :teacher_id, :scope => [:semester_id, :class_id]
end
```

Validating the Length or Size

Sometimes you want to validate the length, or size, of a field entry. You can do this by using the validates_length_of method. We'll use this method in our User model to specify a valid range of characters for a login name, as shown in Listing 5-22. The option for specifying a range of values is :within.

Listing 5-22. *validates_length_of Method, in app/models/user.rb*

```
class User < ActiveRecord::Base
  validates_length_of :login, :within => 4..40
end
```

If you want to ensure only the minimum or maximum, you can use the :minimum or :maximum attributes. Table 5-7 lists the validates_length_of method options.

Table 5-7. *Options for validates_length_of*

Option	Description
:minimum	Specifies the minimum size of the attribute
:maximum	Specifies the maximum size of the attribute
:is	Specifies the exact size of the attribute
:within	Specifies the valid range (as a Ruby Range object) of values acceptable for the attribute
:allow_nil	Specifies that the attribute may be nil; if so, the validation will be skipped
:too_long	Specifies the error message to add if the attribute exceeds the maximum
:too_short	Specifies the error message to add if the attribute is below the minimum
:wrong_length	Specifies the error message to add if the attribute is of the wrong size
:message	Specifies the error message to add if :minimum, :maximum, or :is is violated

Validating the Format of an Attribute

The validates_format_of method checks whether a value is in the correct format. Using this method requires familiarity with regular expressions (regex) or being able to steal other people's regular expressions. The classic example (and the one we need) is email. Add the method shown in Listing 5-23 to our User model.

Listing 5-23. *validates_format_of Method, in app/models/user.rb*

```
class User < ActiveRecord::Base
  validates_format_of :email, :with => /^[^@][\w.-]+@[\w.-]+[.][a-z]{2,4}$/i
end
```

Don't be put off by how complicated this looks. We simply pass in the `:with` option and a regex object to say what patterns we want to match.

■**Tip** If you want to learn more about using regular expressions, you will find many tutorials and books on the subject. One good reference is *Regular Expression Recipes* (Apress, 2004).

Validating Confirmation

Whenever a user changes an important piece of data (especially the password), you may want the user to confirm that entry by typing it again. This is the purpose of the `validates_confirmation_of` method. When you use this helper, you create a new virtual attribute called `#{field_name}_confirmation`. Let's add this to our `User` model for password confirmation, as shown in Listing 5-24.

Listing 5-24. *validates_confirmation_of Method, in app/models/user.rb*

```
class User < ActiveRecord::Base
  validates_confirmation_of :password
end
```

The `password` attribute is a column in the `users` table, but the `password_confirmation` attribute is virtual. It exists only as an in-memory variable for validating the password. This check is performed only if `password_confirmation` is not `nil` and runs whenever the user saves the object.

Making Callbacks

You will often want to have things happen during the life cycle of the model. Certain actions need to happen during certain events pertaining to a particular model. For instance, what if you wanted to send out an email to your administrator whenever someone canceled her account? Or perhaps you want to make sure to create a new model because some other model was also created. These are just a couple of examples of when you want certain actions in the life of a model to generate some associated actions.

To implement this, Active Record has *callbacks*. Six callbacks are commonly used in Active Record models:

- `before_create`

- `after_create`

- before_save

- after_save

- before_destroy

- after_destroy

As you can see, the names of the Rails callbacks describe their purpose. When you create a method with any of these names in your model, the method will be called automatically by the model during the time that the name suggests. For instance, if you make a before_save method, that method will be called every time the model object is saved.

Any callback that starts with before_ can stop the execution chain if it returns false. For instance, if you were to define the following before_create, you would ensure that this model object would *never* be created.

```
def before_create
  false
end
```

This can be a "gotcha" later if you are doing something like an assignment of false to a variable. If you're ever confused why a model won't save, check your before filters.

In our events application, we would like to make sure that when a user creates an event, that user automatically become an attendee. To set this up, we will add an after_create method to the Event class that will automatically make the user join the list of attendees when that user creates an event. Add the method shown in Listing 5-25 to the Event model.

Listing 5-25. *after_create Method, in app/models/event.rb*

```
def after_create
  attendees << user
end
```

We used the shortcut << method to simply throw the model's user into the list of attendees. Note that << automatically saves if the parent object is saved. This is nice and simple, but we should probably use the pattern as we did for validate in Listing 5-19, where we passed in a symbol that references the method to run when the validation was performed. This helps keep the code readable and easier to augment in the future, since we can supply an arbitrary number of methods to run on a callback, separated by a comma. We'll name the method ensure_owner_attends and tell Active Record to run it after a record is created, as shown in Listing 5-26.

Listing 5-26. *ensure_owner_attends Method Specified As an after_create Callback, in app/models/event.rb*

```
after_create :ensure_owner_attends

def ensure_owner_attends
  attendees << user
end
```

We're doing a bit more error checking this time and making sure that the user isn't already attending. This is so we can use this method more than once without breaking anything. Then we simply tell `after_create` on which method to call back.

Active Record provides many more callbacks than we've mentioned here, but those listed at the beginning of this section are the ones that we find ourselves using often. Some of the others are used in extremely rare cases (for instance, `after_initialize`, which is called after an object is initialized). These callbacks can help you with just about anything you need to do during the life cycle of a model. They are part of "smart" models, which know how to deal with their own birth, life, and death.

Reviewing the Updated Models

We've made a lot of changes to our models, so let's make sure we're on the same page before we move on. First, take a look at the `Event` model in Listing 5-27 and make sure that yours matches.

Listing 5-27. *Current Event Model, in /app/models/event.rb*

```
class Event < ActiveRecord::Base
  belongs_to :user
  has_many :registrations
  has_many :attendees, :through => :registrations, :source => :user
  has_and_belongs_to_many :categories

  validates_presence_of :title, :location

  after_create :ensure_owner_attends
  validate     :has_not_occurred

  def is_in_the_past?
    occurs_on < Date.today
  end
```

```
  def long_title
    "#{title} - #{location} - #{occurs_on}"
  end

  protected
    def ensure_owner_attends
      unless attendees.include? user
        attendees << user
      end
    end

    def has_not_occurred
      errors.add("occurs_on", "is in the past") if occurs_on && is_in_the_past?
    end
end
```

Updating the User Model

Our Event model is nicely filled out, but we still need to do a little bit of work on our User model. We'll be applying a lot of the techniques we described in this chapter, such as custom methods to allow us to perform user authentication, and validation methods to make sure our data stays clean.

When we created the user migration (Listing 5-2), we added a field called password. This field stored a plain-text password, which if you think about it, isn't very secure. It's always a good idea to encrypt any sensitive data so it can't be easily read by would-be intruders. We'll deal with the encryption in the User model itself, but the first thing we'll do is rename the field in the database from password to hashed_password. This is so we can create a custom accessor called password with which we can set the password while maintaining a field to store the encrypted version in the database. The plain-text password will never be saved.

To accomplish this, we'll create a migration. From the terminal, issue the following command to create the new migration:

```
$ ./script/generate migration rename_password_to_hashed_password
```

Next, fill in the migration as shown in Listing 5-28.

Listing 5-28. *Migration to Rename password to hashed_password in db/migrate/ 007_ rename_ password_to_hashed_password.rb*

```
class RenamePasswordToHashedPassword < ActiveRecord::Migration
  def self.up
    rename_column :users, :password, :hashed_password
  end

  def self.down
    rename_column :users, :hashed_password, :password
  end
end
```

Run the migration using the rake db:migrate command as follows:

```
$ rake db:migrate
```

Next, update your User model so that it looks like Listing 5-29. In Listing 5-29, we've programmed all the user authentication methods we'll need for allowing users to log in. Let's take a look at the code first, and then we'll describe in detail what we've done.

Listing 5-29. *Current User Model, in app/models/user.rb*

```
require 'digest/sha1'

class User < ActiveRecord::Base
  attr_accessor :password

  has_many :events,
           :dependent => :destroy
  has_many :registrations,
           :dependent => :destroy
  has_many :activities, :through => :registrations, :source => :event

  validates_presence_of    :login
  validates_length_of      :login, :within => 3..40
  validates_uniqueness_of  :login, :case_sensitive => false
  validates_format_of      :login, :with => /^[\w\.-]+$/i

  validates_presence_of    :email
  validates_format_of      :email, :with => /^[^@][\w.-]+@[\w.-]+[.][a-z]{2,4}$/i

  validates_presence_of    :password,                    :if => :password_required?
  validates_length_of      :password, :within => 4..40, :if => :password_required?
```

```ruby
  validates_confirmation_of :password,                    :if => :password_required?

  before_save :encrypt_new_password

  def self.authenticate(login, password)
    user = find_by_login(login)
    return user if user && user.authenticated?(password)
  end

  def authenticated?(password)
    hashed_password == encrypt(password)
  end

  protected
    def encrypt_new_password
      return if password.blank?
      self.hashed_password = encrypt(password)
    end

    def password_required?
      hashed_password.blank? || !password.blank?
    end

    def encrypt(string)
      Digest::SHA1.hexdigest(string)
    end
end
```

Whenever you're storing something sensitive, like a password, you want to encrypt it. To encrypt the password in our User model, we use a simple algorithm called a hash that will create a random-looking string from the provided input. This hashed output cannot be turned back into the original string easily, so even if someone steals your database, he will have a prohibitively difficult time discovering your users' passwords. Ruby has a built-in library called Digest, which includes many hashing algorithms.

Let's go through the additions to our User model:

- require 'digest/sha1': We start by requiring the Digest library we will use for encrypting the passwords. This loads the needed library and makes it available to work with in our class.

- `attr_accessor :password`: This defines an accessor attribute, `password`, at the top of the class body. This tells Ruby to create reader and writer methods for `password`. Since the password column doesn't actually exist in our table anymore, a `password` method won't be created automatically by Active Record. Still, we need a way to set the password before it's encrypted, so we make our own attribute to use. This will work just like any model attribute, except that it won't be persisted to the database when the model is saved.

- `before_save :encrypt_new_password`: This `before_save` callback tells Active Record to run the `encrypt_new_password` method before it saves a record. That means it will apply to all operations that trigger a save, including `create` and `update`.

- `encrypt_new_password`: This method should perform encryption only if the `password` attribute contains a value, since we wouldn't want it to happen unless a user is changing her password. So, if the `password` attribute is blank, we return from the method and the `hash_password` value is never set. If the `password` value is not blank, we have some work to do. We set the `hashed_password` attribute to the encrypted version of the password by laundering it through the `encrypt` method.

- `encrypt`: This method is fairly simple. It leverages Ruby's `Digest` library that we included on the first line to create an SHA1 digest of whatever we pass it. Since methods in Ruby always return the last thing evaluated, `encrypt` will return the encrypted string.

- `password_required?`: When we're performing our validations, we want to make sure we're validating the presence, length, and confirmation of the password only if validation is required. And it's required only if this is a new record (the `hashed_password` attribute is blank) or if the `password` accessor we created has been used to set a new password (`!password.blank?`). To make this easy, we've created the `password_required?` predicate method, which returns `true` if a password is required, or `false` if it's not. We then apply this method as an `:if` condition on all our password validators.

- `self.authenticate`: You can tell this is a class method because it's prefixed with `self` (it's defined on the class *itself*). That means you don't access it via an instance; you access it directly off the class, just as you would with `find`, `new`, or `create` (`User.authenticate`, not `@user = User.new; @user.authenticate`). The `authenticate` method accepts a login and an unencrypted password. It uses a dynamic finder (`find_by_login`) to fetch the user with a matching login. If the user was found, the user variable will contain a `User` object; if not, it will be `nil`. Knowing this, we can return the value of user if, and only if, it is not `nil` and the `authenticated?` method returns `true` for the given password (`user && user.authenticated?(password)`).

- authenticated?: This is a simple predicate method that checks to make sure the stored hashed_password matches the given password after it has been encrypted (via encrypt). If it matches, true is returned.

Let's play with these new methods from the console so you can get a better idea of how this comes together.

```
>> User.authenticate("eugene", "secret")
=> #<User:0xb74197d8>
>> User.authenticate("eugene", "secret2")
=> nil
```

So, when we ask the User model to authenticate someone, we pass in the login and the plain-text password. The authenticate method hashes the given password and then compares it to the stored (hashed) password in the database. If the passwords match, the User object is returned and authentication was successful. When we try to use an incorrect password, nil is returned. In Chapter 6, we'll write code in our controller to use these model methods and actually allow users to log in to the site. But for now, we have a properly built and secure back end for how users will authenticate.

Summary

After reading this chapter, you should have a complete understanding of Active Record models. We've covered associations, conditions, validations, and callbacks at breakneck speed. Now the fun part starts. In the next chapter you will get to use all the groundwork that we established in this chapter to produce the web interface for the data structures we have created here. This is when you really get to reap the benefits of your hard work.

CHAPTER 6

■ ■ ■

Action Pack: Working with the View and the Controller

When you type a URL into your browser's address bar and click enter, a few things happen behind the scenes. First, the URL is translated into a unique address by which the server that hosts the application can be identified. The request is then sent to that server, which begins a chain of events that culminates in a response. The response is usually, but not always, in the form of an HTML document, which is essentially a text document full of special codes that your browser understands and can render visually on your screen. At this point, the request cycle is complete, and the browser waits for further input from you. If you click a link somewhere on the page, or type a new URL in the address bar, the cycle begins all over again: the request is sent, the server processes it, and the server sends back the response.

When you make a request to a Rails application, this request cycle is the responsibility of a component of Rails called Action Pack. The Action Pack library is an integral component of the Rails framework and one that you'll need to get quite familiar with if you intend to master Rails.

In this chapter, we'll begin with an overview of Action Pack, and then get to work using it in our sample events application.

Action Pack Components

We already discussed the MVC pattern, but in case you need a refresher, here it is. The model is your application's world, most often represented by database objects, like articles, comments, or subscribers. The controller is the grand orchestrator, dealing with requests and issuing responses. The view is the code that contains instructions for rendering visual output for a browser, like HTML.

Armed with this refresher, you might be able to guess what roles are played by the Action Pack. Since this isn't a test, we'll give away the answer: Action Pack is the controller and the view. The controller performs the logic, and the view renders the template that is given back to the requesting browser. Not surprisingly, the two modules that make up Action Pack are named accordingly: Action Controller and Action View.

At this point, you might be wondering why the view and the controller are wrapped up in a single library, unlike models, which have a library of their own. The answer is subtle and succinct: controllers and views are very closely related. In the pages that follow, we'll paint a more complete picture of both the role and the relationship of controllers and views, how they work, and how they work together to create and control the interface of a Rails application.

Action Controller

Controllers orchestrate your application's flow. Every time a user requests a page, submits a form, or clicks a link, that request is handled—in one way or another—by a controller. When you're programming your application, you spend a lot of your time building controllers and giving them instructions on how to handle requests.

The concept of controllers can sometimes be difficult for newcomers to grasp. Even if you've built web applications before, say in ASP or PHP, you might not be used to this form of separation, where the mechanics of flow are controlled by a separate entity and not embedded in the pages themselves.

Let's look at the example of the CD player in your car to illustrate the concept of controllers. The player is required to respond to certain events, such as pressing the Play button, fast forwarding, or rewinding a track. When you push a button, you expect something to happen—you've made a request, and you wait for the subsequent response.

If your CD player were a Rails application, the instructions for what to do when a certain event takes place, such as the pressing of the Eject button, would be contained in a controller. If you were to sketch it out on paper, it might look something like this:

- CD Player

    - Play

    - Stop

    - Fast-forward

    - Rewind

    - Eject

These events, or actions, describe what the player should be capable of *doing*. Obviously, each of these actions would need to be programmed to do something with the disc that's inside the player. When someone presses Eject, you would first call on the stop action (if the disc is playing), and then arrange for the player to spit out the disc. You would code all the instructions for dealing with an eject event into the controller—specifically, inside the eject action. The same would apply for play, fast-forward, and rewind.

It's worth noting that this type of logic has nothing to do with the CD itself, nor does it have anything to do with the music on the CD. If this were a Rails application, the CD would be the model. It can be used independently of the player. In fact, it can be used in all sorts of players, not just the one in your car.

The stereo in your car is probably capable of more than just playing CDs. Most have a radio receiver built in as well. The radio would have its own set of events that would likewise need to be handled. These actions might include things like changing stations, setting presets, and switching between AM and FM. To keep things well organized, you would probably want to group these actions inside their own controller, separate from the CD controller. After all, the radio and the CD player do different things.

When you're dealing with a Rails application, it's not much different. You separate the things that you need your application to do with an object from the object itself. Even when you're not dealing directly with an object (adjusting the volume on your car stereo has little to do with either the CD in the player or the station on the radio), you still handle the event inside a controller.

Each controller in Rails is designed as a Ruby class. Without getting too technical, here's how the CD player example would look if it were a Ruby class:

```
class CDPlayer
  def play
  end

  def stop
  end

  def fast_forward
  end

  def rewind
  end

  def eject
  end
end
```

Inside the CDPlayer class, we've defined a method for each action, or each thing we want our CD player to be able to do. So, if we were to send the message "play" to an instance of the CDPlayer class, it would know how to handle it (of course, since the play method is empty in our example, nothing would happen). On the other hand, if we sent the message "pause," Ruby would raise an exception and tell us that the method was not found. If we wanted `CDPlayer` objects to respond to that message, we would need to add a method called (you guessed it) `pause`.

All the methods in this class are public, which means that they can be invoked by anyone. We don't need to do anything special to a method to make it public. *Unless otherwise declared, all methods in a Ruby class are public by default.* If we were to mark an action as private, though, it could be used only internally by the class. For example, if the `stop` method were private, it would raise a `NoMethodError` if we called it from outside the `CDPlayer` class. However, the `eject` method is free to call on `stop`, because it does so internally. While the usefulness of this feature will become apparent as you continue to learn about controllers, consider this: if your CD player needed to display the time remaining for a given track, it might need to perform a few calculations to figure that out. You might create a method for doing these internal calculations, but would you want that method to be accessible from the outside? Would you have a button called Calculate on your player?

It's time for a working definition: *Action Controllers are Ruby classes containing one or more public methods known as actions.* Each action is responsible for responding to a request to perform some task. A typical controller is most often a collection of actions that relate to a specific area of concern. For example, consider the events application we've been building in the previous chapters. The controller that manages events has the class name `EventsController` and has action methods for listing, creating, reading, updating, and deleting events.

While our example of the CD player worked well to illustrate the basic concept of controllers, it won't take us much further when dealing with web applications. If we were really dealing with a CD player, we would press Play, the disc would start playing, and that would be the end of it. But since Rails was specifically designed for building web applications, it makes a fair number of assumptions about what we want our actions to do when they're finished firing. Chief among these is the rendering of a view.

Imagine that you're reading a list of posts on someone's blog. You click the title of a post, and you expect to be taken to a new screen that shows you just that post. You requested an action (show), and in response, you've received a new screen. This happens all the time in the world of web applications: when you click a link, you expect to go to a new page.

In Rails, it is the general case that when actions have completed their work, they respond by rendering a view. In fact, the concept of actions rendering views is so common that Rails has internalized it as a convention: *unless otherwise stated, when an action is finished firing, it renders a view.* How does Rails know what view to render if you don't tell it? It looks for a view whose name matches that of the requested action. This should give you some insight as to why Action Controller and Action View are bundled together in Action Pack. Because of the way controller actions relate to views, a few other mechanisms facilitate their communication, all of which we'll cover shortly.

Action View

The Action View library is the second half of Action Pack. Given that controllers are responsible for handling the request and issuing a response, views are responsible for rendering the output of a response in a way a browser (or any other user agent) can understand. Let's say you requested the index action from the EventsController. After performing the logic to retrieve a list of events, the controller hands off to the view, which formats the list of events to make them look pretty. The controller then collects the results of the render, and the HTML is sent back to the browser, thus completing the request cycle.

While the controller and the view are separate entities, they need to communicate with each other. The primary mechanism by which they do this is through shared variables. These shared variables are called *instance variables* and are easy to spot in Ruby because they are prefixed with the @ symbol. Keep this in mind as you look at the following view example in which we use an instance variable called @events to produce an event listing:

```
<html>
  <body>
    <ul>
      <% for event in @events %>
        <li><%= event.title %></li>
      <% end %>
    <ul>
  </body>
</html>
```

Even without knowing any Ruby, you should be able to guess what this code does: it iterates over the collection of events stored in the variable @events and prints the title for each between HTML list-item (<li>) tags. If @events contained three events whose titles were One, Two, and Three, respectively, the preceding code would be compiled to the following:

```
<html>
  <body>
    <ul>
      <li>One</li>
      <li>Two</li>
      <li>Three</li>
    <ul>
  </body>
</html>
```

At this point, you might be wondering where the variable @events came into being. If you guessed in the controller, you would be right. The controller sets up instance variables that the view can access. In this case, the controller created a variable called @events and the view was given automatic access to it. Notice that the view doesn't perform any logic to fetch the list of events; it simply relies on the controller to have set up the variable and performs the display logic necessary to turn the collection into a browser-ready HTML list.

Embedded Ruby

The codes you see mixed into the HTML markup are actually Ruby. Since templates that are capable of dealing only with static HTML wouldn't be very useful, Action View templates have the benefit of being able to use Embedded Ruby (ERb) to programmatically enhance them.

Using ERb, you can embed Ruby into your templates and give them the ability to deal with data from the controller to produce well-formed HTML representations. ERb is included in the Ruby standard library, and Rails makes extensive use of it. You trigger ERb by using embeddings such as <% %> and <%= %> in your template files to evaluate or print Ruby code, respectively. If you've ever worked with ASP, JSP, or PHP, this style of embedding should be familiar to you.

In the example in the preceding section, the loop is constructed within *evaluation embedding* tags (<% %>), and the event's title is printed using *output embedding* tags (<%= %>). Pay close attention to the subtle difference between the two embedding types: output embedding includes an equal sign; regular embedding does not. When you use output embedding, you're effectively saying *print the results of the Ruby code when it's evaluated*. Regular embedding does not print results; it simply evaluates whatever is in between the tags and goes on its merry way. If you mistakenly omitted the equal sign, no errors would be raised, but nothing would be printed either. You would have a set of empty list tags.

Helpers

The terms of the MVC are fairly strict in the way they advocate the separation of components. Controllers really shouldn't concern themselves with the generation of view code, and views shouldn't concern themselves with anything but the simplest of logic. While it's possible to use ERb to execute arbitrary Ruby code inside a view, and while controllers are certainly capable of generating markup, it's generally considered in violation of the MVC pattern to do so. This is where helpers come in to play.

Action Pack's *helpers* do exactly what their name implies: they help views by providing a convenient location to encapsulate code that would otherwise clutter the view and violate the terms of the MVC. They offer a middle ground between controllers and views and help to keep your application organized and easy to maintain.

If you think about it, ERb tags really aren't the best place for performing complex logic, and templates can quickly become unwieldy when creating markup programmatically. For this reason, Action Pack includes a large suite of built-in helpers for generating all sorts of HTML fragments—from creating forms and formatting dates, to making hyperlinks and image tags. And when the built-in helpers aren't enough, you can write your own. Each controller gets its own helper module that's mixed in automatically, ready to lend your templates a hand when they need it.

Routing

All the information pertaining to which controller and action to call on comes in the form of the request URL. Action Pack includes a specialized component called *routing*, which is responsible for dissecting the incoming URL and delegating control to the appropriate controller and action.

Every request that comes into your web application originates in the form of a URL. The routing system allows you to write the rules that govern how each URL is picked apart and handled.

A traditional URL contains the path to a file on the server, relative to the server's home directory. Here's an example:

```
http://example.com/articles/show.asp?id=1037
```

We can tell a lot from this URL. First, we know that the server technology being used is Microsoft's ASP. Given that, we also know that this URL resolves to the show.asp script, which is inside the /articles directory. In this case, there is no URL rewriting going on; the mapping of the URL to the script that handles it is one to one.

The problem with this kind of mapping is that the developer has no control over the URL. The URL is coupled to the script. What if you wanted to invoke the show.asp script, but wanted the URL to read articles/detail.asp instead of show.asp? Or better yet, what if you didn't want to expose the underlying script implementation (ASP) at all and use just articles/detail? There would be no way. The lack of flexibility in this kind of URL mapping is a problem. If you ever need to change the name of the script being invoked, you instantly break all the URL references. This can be a major pain if you need to update all your code, and especially if your pages are indexed by search engines.

Action Pack's routing solves this problem by decoupling the URL from the underlying program implementation. In Rails, the URL is related to the specific resource being requested, and it can be formatted to correctly identify that resource without having to conform to the name of script that does the handling. When thought of in this way, URLs become part of the interface of an application, unrelated to the files that are ultimately invoked to process a request.

There are a myriad of reasons why a routing system is a good idea. Here are just a few of them:

- Decoupled URLs can convey meaning, becoming part of the interface.

- Clean, readable URLs are more user-friendly and easier to remember.

- URLs can be changed without affecting the underlying implementation.

The routing pattern used by Rails is actually quite simple and intuitive, and is well demonstrated by the default route:

```
map.connect ':controller/:action/:id'
```

The first segment of the URL identifies the controller, the second segment identifies the action, and the third identifies a parameter called id, which will be made available to the controller when the request is handled. Given a URL like the following, we can determine everything we need to know about where in our application the request will be handled:

```
http://localhost:3000/events/show/1
```

This URL will be translated into a request for the show action on the events controller and be furnished with a single parameter, id, which presumably identifies the event to show. This is a common pattern in web application design, hence its default designation by Rails.

Of course, like most things in Rails, this pattern is open to configuration, and one of the great benefits of routes is that since they are decoupled, they can be customized to create meaningful URLs without much effort. This chapter will teach you how to build and customize routes for your application, how to create named routes, and how to use routes when creating links and redirects in your code.

The Action Pack Request Cycle

We refer to the entire request-to-response process as the Action Pack *request cycle*. The request cycle consists of the following steps:

1. Rails receives a request from the outside world (usually a browser).

2. Routing picks apart the request to determine the controller and action to invoke.

3. A new controller object is instantiated and an action method is called.

4. The controller interacts with the model (usually performing a CRUD operation).

5. A response is sent back to the browser, either in the form of a render or a redirect.

Figure 6-1 illustrates the process.

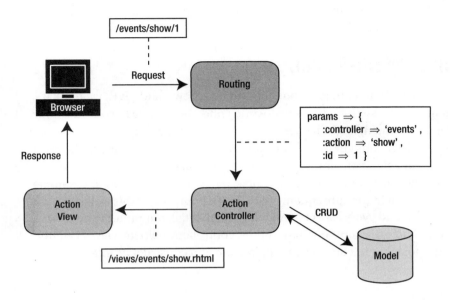

Figure 6-1. *The Action Pack request cycle*

Not too long ago (and to be sure, today still), developers used to construct so-called "server pages." Such a page would have a bunch of code at the top of an otherwise static page, just above the opening HTML tag. The markup would be littered with all sorts of code, and it wouldn't be at all unusual to see the database being accessed, forms being processed, sessions being set, and all manner of logic being performed in-line. The web server would be responsible for controlling the application—one page redirecting to another, running the code, and then dumping the results to the screen.

We won't get into the multitude of reasons why this is a bad idea, except to say that it presents the problem of coupling. In this scenario, the business logic and the view are all mashed together, making things more difficult to maintain and debug. ASP and PHP pages are notable offenders, and if you're coming from either of these camps, the concept of separating concerns might be foreign at first. Here's a way to think about it that might help. Imagine taking all that code and logic from the top of each page and sticking it in one place, leaving only the HTML behind. Then instead of using the web server to invoke each page as you would with a static site, have the web server call on a single dispatcher that finds the code you want to execute and calls it. The code it would invoke—the file that contains all your processing logic extracted from the server page—would be called the controller. Instead of dividing logic among "pages," it would be divided into actions.

The single biggest advantage of this pattern is that the processing logic is decoupled from the view and safely contained in one place. As you'll see, it's a lot easier to work this way. The interplay between actions is considerably easier to visualize and understand when it is not spread out over a host of locations. Your server pages become lightweight views, left to handle only the simplest of instructions, if any at all.

A Controller Walk-Through

Instead of boring you with more theory about controllers, views, and MVC, we think it's best to dig right in and start writing some real-world code. We're going to continue building our events application, highlighting the finer points and describing the places where convention wins out over configuration. Along the way, we'll touch on some of the most essential controller and view concepts. By the end of this walk-through, you'll have a complete grasp of how the Rails request cycle works, and you'll have a working example to refer to and expand on in the subsequent chapters. The purpose of this walk-through is not to examine each and every aspect of Action Pack in detail, but rather to give you a practical overview of how the components—routes, controllers, helpers, views, layouts, and partials—work together to control your application and construct its interface.

Setting Up Routes

Links and URLs are important in web applications. They serve as the entry point to the application and contain all the information required to route an incoming request to the controller and action that will handle it. Before we get into the meat of creating controllers and defining actions, we need to spend a few minutes talking about how we get from request to response. As we explained earlier, it all starts with routing.

Routing Basics

In Rails, all the rules for mapping URLs to controllers are a matter of configuration. You'll find the `routes.rb` file in the `config` directory. If you open that file in your editor now and examine it, you'll see the default route defined last. We've already introduced it, but it bears repeating:

```
map.connect ':controller/:action/:id'
```

Routes work based on pattern matching and can include variables to set directly within the pattern. Here, the pattern is a three-segment string partitioned by slashes (/) and containing variables to set, where the variables are prefixed by a colon (:). The first segment sets the `:controller` variable, the second the `:action` variable, and the third the `:id` variable. These variables will be used to determine the controller and action to invoke, and the parameters to send along. The pattern is matched from left to right, and the variables are optional. If the `:id` variable is empty, only the controller and action will be set. If the `:action` variable is empty, only the `:controller` variable will be set, and so on.

Routing priority is based on the order in which routes exist in `routes.rb`, so that the first route defined has the highest priority. If an incoming URL matches the first route defined, the request will be sent along and no other routes will be examined. It's for this reason that we place the default route last.

Routes are defined using the `connect` method. The first argument to `connect` is the pattern to match. The second argument is the request parameters to initialize in the form of a Ruby hash.

Here's an example where we're matching a specific pattern and setting a hash of parameters in response:

```
map.connect '/albums/list', :controller => 'albums', :action => 'list'
```

This route will match a URL like `http://example.com/albums/list` and route the request to the `list` action on the `albums` controller. We can also set arbitrary parameters when using the route. For example, let's say we wanted to set a parameter called `query` that we could access and use in our controller.

```
map.connect '/products/search/:query',
  :controller => 'products', :action => 'search'
```

This route will match a URL like `http://example.com/products/search/ipod`, routing the request to the `products` controller and the `search` action. The third segment in the URL will be assigned to the `:query` parameter because we specified `:query` as an in-line variable.

Routes can get quite complex, and it's possible to apply conditions and other forms of logic to them. For the most part though, you'll get a lot of mileage from the general cases we've outlined here. The Rails API documentation (`http://api.rubyonrails.org/classes/ActionController/Routing.html`) contains details on using the more complex routing features.

Named Routes

One of the coolest things about routing in Rails is a feature known as *named routes*. You can assign a name to a given route to make referring to it in code easier. Instead of defining a route with `map.connect`, you replace the `connect` part with the name you want to give to the route.

For example, let's take the `albums` route we defined in the previous section and turn it into a named route.

```
map.albums '/albums/list', :controller => 'albums', :action => 'list'
```

With this definition in place, Rails will create methods that allow us to reference this particular route using its name: `albums_url` and `albums_path`. The *_url variant returns a full URL including the protocol and hostname (`http://example.com/albums/list`), whereas the `*_path` variant returns just the path (`/albums/list`).

We'll cover redirection methods and hyperlink generation helpers later in this chapter, but we'll point out now that you can use them with named routes:

```
link_to "Albums", albums_url #=> <a href="/albums/list">Albums</a>
```

This is more succinct than the alternative, which would involve specifying the parameters to identify the controller and action manually:

```
link_to "Albums", :controller => 'albums', :action => 'list'
  #=> <a href="/albums/list">Albums</a>
```

As you can see, the result is identical. However, the named route is shorter, DRYer, and impervious to changes made at the routing level. So, if you were to change the controller name from `albums` to `records`, you wouldn't need to update your links that use the named route; for the unnamed version, you would.

Configuring Routes for the Event Manager

Let's configure the routes we're going to be using in our events application. We haven't built all the controllers and actions yet (we'll do that next), but that shouldn't stop us from getting the routes in place. Open `config/routes.rb` in your editor. Start with the section that reads:

```
# Allow downloading Web Service WSDL as a file with an extension
# instead of a file named 'wsdl'
map.connect ':controller/service.wsdl', :action => 'wsdl'
```

We're not using the Web Service WSDL in our application, so you can safely delete these lines. In the cutting-edge version of Rails, this definition has become extinct, so don't be surprised if you don't see it in the file you're editing. Next, add the following routes, making sure they're above the default route (the very last one in the file):

```
map.login  'login',  :controller => 'users', :action => 'login'
map.logout 'logout', :controller => 'users', :action => 'logout'
map.signup 'signup', :controller => 'users', :action => 'new'

map.events     'events',          :controller => 'events'
map.new_event  'events/new',      :controller => 'events', :action => 'new'
map.edit_event 'events/edit/:id', :controller => 'events', :action => 'edit'
map.event      'events/show/:id', :controller => 'events', :action => 'show'
```

Take a minute to examine these definitions. They're pretty straightforward. There's a route to match the login URL, which will look like /login, as well as the /logout route, the /signup route, and so on. When a URL comes in that matches any of these patterns, we're forwarding it along to a specific controller and action. If the incoming URL matches none of these patterns, it will fall through to the default route (:controller/:action/:id), which will hand it off to the controller and action specified by the positional arguments in the URL, if they exist. If no controller or action that matches the URL exists, an error will be generated.

You can handle an empty request for the root of your application's domain using map.root and specifying an empty pattern to match. In our events application, we want the root URL (http://localhost:3000) to connect to the list of events. To accomplish this, we'll add a route like the following and make it the first route:

```
map.root '', :controller => 'events', :action => 'index'
```

■**Caution** In edge-Rails, map.root receives a special designation and works without the empty pattern to match (""). If you get an error when using map.root, remove the empty pattern so the route looks like map.root :controller => 'events', :action => 'index'.

The :action => 'index' parameter is actually redundant; taking a hint from most web servers, Rails assumes the index action if none is specified. Speaking of web servers, since the server looks for matching "static" files located in the /public directory before ever invoking Rails, and since there's a default index.html file there (it's the Rails welcome page you saw in Chapter 2), we'll need to delete it before our default route will take effect.

Static files, like those located in /public, are served by the web server independently of Rails. This means images, style sheets, and JavaScript files are all served in this manner, without any server-side processing, (which, by the way, is why we call them static).

So, go ahead and delete public/index.html now.

Listing 6-1 shows our final routes file, minus some of the comment clutter. Make sure yours looks just like this before you move on.

Listing 6-1. *The config/routes.rb File*

```
ActionController::Routing::Routes.draw do |map|
  map.root, '', :controller => 'events'

  map.login  'login',  :controller => 'users', :action => 'login'
  map.logout 'logout', :controller => 'users', :action => 'logout'
  map.signup 'signup', :controller => 'users', :action => 'new'
```

```
  map.events      'events',              :controller => 'events'
  map.new_event   'events/new',          :controller => 'events', :action => 'new'
  map.edit_event  'events/edit/:id'      :controller => 'events', :action => 'edit'
  map.event       'events/show/:id',     :controller => 'events', :action => 'show'

  # Install the default route as the lowest priority.
  map.connect ':controller/:action/:id'
end
```

Now that we have some routes defined, let's move on to creating the controllers and actions that will ultimately respond to these routes. Ready? Let's go!

Generating a Controller

It's time to create our first controller from scratch. If you haven't noticed already, Rails ships with generators for most common tasks, and controllers are no exception. The syntax for the controller generator is as follows:

```
$ ./script/generate controller ControllerName [actions] [options]
```

As a minimum, the controller generator takes the name of the controller as an argument, which you can specify using either CamelCase (sometimes called MixedCase) or underscore_case. The generator also takes an optional list of actions to generate. For every action you specify, you'll get an empty method stub in the controller and a template in app/views/#{controller_name}. To see a list of all available options, you can run the generator without arguments.

Tip The help output for the controller generator contains sample usage and options that you're sure to find interesting. All of the generators (and most UNIX commands, for that matter) respond to the --help argument (or variations thereof), so you're encouraged to try it whenever you're issuing a system command.

Generate the Users controller using the following command:

```
$ ./script/generate controller Users
```

```
exists  app/controllers/
exists  app/helpers/
create  app/views/users
exists  test/functional/
```

```
create  app/controllers/users_controller.rb
create  test/functional/users_controller_test.rb
create  app/helpers/users_helper.rb
```

Take the time to read the output of the generator so you get a sense of all the files that were just created. Notice where the templates are located: in the app/views directory, inside a subdirectory named for controller. In this case, since our controller is called users, our templates go inside app/views/users. Let's open the newly minted controller file and have a look:

```
class UsersController < ApplicationController
end
```

Tip It's a convention in Rails that controller names should always be plural.

As you can see, all the generator gives us is an empty stub. If we want our users controller to do anything useful, we'll need to add an action and give it something to do. Let's create the first action on the controller now. Edit users_controller.rb so that it looks like Listing 6-2.

Listing 6-2. *Updated app/controllers/users_controller.rb*

```
class UsersController < ApplicationController
  def new
    @user = User.new
  end
end
```

Before our action renders a view, we arrange for it to set an instance variable that the view can use. Just to refresh your memory, an instance variable is a special kind of Ruby variable that is unique to a given instance of a class, serving as a way for an object to maintain its state. Since views are, in essence, an extension of the controller object, they can access its instance variables directly (though not without some behind-the-scenes Ruby magic that Rails takes care of for you). For all intents and purposes, however, you can consider instance variables shared between controllers and views.

You can store any Ruby object in an instance variable, including strings, integers, models, hashes, and arrays. Since we want to initialize a new user, we've created an instance variable called @user and hydrated it with a new instance of the User model. If you recall from the Chapter 4, the new method returns a new, unsaved object.

WHAT MAKES A CLASS AN ACTION CONTROLLER?

If you're the curious sort (and, of course, you are), you might be wondering how the UsersController, a seemingly normal Ruby class, becomes a full-fledged Action Controller. Well, if you look closely, you'll notice that UsersController inherits from another class: ApplicationController. In order to get a better picture of what's going on, let's take a peek at the ApplicationController class in app/controllers/application.rb.

```ruby
class ApplicationController < ActionController::Base
end
```

The mystery is quickly solved. Our simple controller becomes an Action Controller by subclassing the ApplicationController class, itself a subclass of ActionController::Base. This is an example of inheritance and is common in object-oriented programming. When one class subclasses another, it inherits all the behavior and methods of the parent. In the case of our users controller, it inherits all the capabilities of the application controller. Likewise, ApplicationController inherits all the capabilities of *its* parent, ActionController::Base. It's the ActionController::Base class that effectively endows our users controller with its special abilities.

The application controller is the base from which all the controllers you make will inherit. Since it's the parent of all controllers in your application, it's a great place to put methods that you want accessible in every controller.

Creating a Template

Our next step is to create a template for our action to render. Create a new file in app/views/users called new.rhtml and edit it so it looks like this:

```
<h2>I am the new template!</h2>
```

Make sure your local web server is running (./script/server), and open http://localhost:3000 in your browser. Assuming everything is firing correctly, you'll see your new page:

```
I am the new template!
```

It's not very pretty, but it works. And it demonstrates the most basic of Action Pack's conventions at work: *templates are organized by controller name, and a template with the same name as the action being invoked will be rendered automatically.* You didn't need to wire up anything. Merely by requesting the new action on the users controller, Rails rendered the new template in the app/views/users directory.

After determining which controller to invoke, Rails proceeds to instantiate it and call its `new` method. Its default response after running the `new` action is to perform a render. Rails looks for a template named `new.rhtml` in the `app/views/users` directory and loads it.

At this point, the request cycle, while not very eventful from the browser's perspective, is complete. If you refresh your browser, the cycle begins anew and the same result is rendered. Notice how all the internals are already taken care of for you. All you need to do is create an appropriately named controller, action, and view, stick them in the right place, and request the URL in your browser. Rails takes care of making sure everything gets knitted together properly.

■**Note** In edge-Rails, the `.rhtml` extension is deprecated in favor of `.erb` (for Embedded Ruby, or ERb). This isn't the case for the most recent stable version of Rails at the time of this writing (1.2.3), but it's something to keep an eye out for in the future. The `.rhtml` extension will still be supported for a long while and isn't scheduled to officially disappear until Rails 2.0.

While we're kicking the tires, let's see what happens if we comment out the `new` action, like this:

```
class UsersController < ApplicationController
  #def new
  #  @user = User.new
  #end
end
```

If you refresh your browser, you'll notice that nothing has changed. No, that's not because the web server needs to be restarted, nor is it because the page is cached. As it turns out, even if an action is missing, Rails will still look to see if it can find a template named for the sought-after action and render it if found. After all, sometimes you need to render a template but you don't have any logic to perform.

Before we go any further, use your browser's view source command to see the HTML that was produced. Now, if you know anything about HTML (and chances are you do), you'll quickly realize that we're lacking something here: the `<html>` tags. Sure, you see your content, but where's the layout? Most web pages have headers, footers, sidebars, and other page elements that, when styled, make the page look pretty. Fortunately, Rails has a built-in facility for dealing with page layouts.

Working with Layouts

Rails uses layouts to interpolate the output of an individual template into a larger whole—a reversal of the common pattern of including a shared header and footer on every page (which if you've done any work in other languages like PHP or ASP will be all too familiar). The scaffold generator we ran in Chapter 3 created a layout file and placed it in app/views/layouts/events.rhtml. It's named after the controller we generated (events), and will be applied automatically *to that controller only*. That's the way it works in Rails. Just as an action tries to render itself using a view that matches its name, so does a controller attempt to use a layout that matches its name. However, we'd like our layout to apply to *all* our controllers, including the one we're working on now.

To have it apply to all our controllers, we can rename it to application.rhtml. Go ahead and do that now, and when you're finished, open it in your editor. You should see something like the file shown in Listing 6-3.

Listing 6-3. *The app/views/layouts/application.rhtml File*

```
<!DOCTYPE html PUBLIC "-//W3C//DTD XHTML 1.0 Transitional//EN"
  "http://www.w3.org/TR/xhtml1/DTD/xhtml1-transitional.dtd">

<html xmlns="http://www.w3.org/1999/xhtml" xml:lang="en" lang="en">
  <head>
    <meta http-equiv="content-type" content="text/html;charset=UTF-8" />
    <title>Events: <%= controller.action_name %></title>
    <%= stylesheet_link_tag 'scaffold' %>
  </head>
  <body>

    <p style="color: green"><%= flash[:notice] %></p>
    <%= yield %>
  </body>
</html>
```

At rendering time, the layout will yield the results of the template fragment's execution in place. See the <%= yield %> bit that we've highlighted in bold? That's the important part. Wherever you put the yield keyword is where your content will go.

One more thing to note here: Rails is all about convention over configuration. Here, the convention is that a layout with the name application.rhtml is automatically applied to all templates unless an alternate is specified in the controller. This means that if you were to change the name of the layout as it stands, it wouldn't be automatically applied. If you wanted to apply a different layout to a given controller, you could specify it in the controller itself using the class method, layout.

```
class ExampleController < ApplicationController
  layout 'my_layout' # Will look for a layout in app/views/layouts/my_layout.rhtml
end
```

COMMON LAYOUT CONVENTIONS

A few conventions apply to working with layouts:

- A layout named `application.rhtml` will be applied automatically unless a more specific candidate exists or is explicitly specified in the controller.

- A layout that matches the name of a controller will be automatically applied if present. Controller-specific layouts take precedence over the application-level layout.

- You can use the `layout` directive at the class level in any controller (that is, not inside an action) to set the layout for the entire controller: `layout 'my_layout'`.

- You can include a layout for a specific action with an explicit call to render inside the action: `render :layout => 'my_layout'`.

- Sometimes you want to render an action without a layout. In that case, you can pass `false` in place of the layout name: `render :layout => false`.

In practice, we usually just use `application.rhtml` and rarely take advantage of the controller-specific layout functionality. On the occasions when we need to use a different layout for a particular controller, we use the `layout` directive.

Creating a Registration Form

Enough tire-kicking. Let's add some real code to the `new` template so you can see it in action. The `new` action has a single purpose: to initialize and display the form for creating a new user. The actual creation of a new `User` object is the responsibility of the `User` model (remember our discussions of the model back to Chapters 4 and 5), but it's orchestrated by the controller. Moreover, it needs data (like a login and password), which it must procure from somewhere. We're going to extract this information from HTML form elements, which we'll place in the template and handle in the controller. Let's design the form now. Edit `new.rhtml` so that it looks like Listing 6-4.

Listing 6-4. *Updated app/views/users/new.rhtml*

```
<h2>User Registration</h2>

<% form_tag :action => 'create' do %>
  <p><label>Login:<br />
  <%= text_field :user, :login %></label></p>
```

```
  <p><label>Email:<br />
  <%= text_field :user, :email %></label></p>

  <p><label>Password:<br />
  <%= password_field :user, :password %></label></p>

  <p><label>Password confirmation:<br />
  <%= password_field :user, :password_confirmation %></label></p>

  <p><%= submit_tag 'Sign up!' %></p>
<% end %>
```

We're using form helpers here for each of our fields. Refresh your browser again, and you'll see they function to produce a nicely formatted HTML form. Use your browser's view source command to look at the HTML that was generated.

```
<h2>User Registration</h2>

<form action="/users/create" method="post">
  <p><label>Login:<br />
  <input id="user_login" name="user[login]" size="30" type="text" /></label></p>

  <p><label>Email:<br />
  <input id="user_email" name="user[email]" size="30" type="text" /></label></p>

  <p><label>Password:<br />
  <input id="user_password" name="user[password]" size="30"
   type="password" /></label></p>

  <p><label>Password confirmation:<br />
  <input id="user_password_confirmation" name="user[password_confirmation]"
   size="30" type="password" /></label></p>

  <p><input name="commit" type="submit" value="Sign up!" /></p>
</form>
```

Here, you can see the generated HTML. Note the way in which Rails formats the name attribute of each form element: *model[attribute]*. This helps when it comes to parsing the parameters from the form, which you'll see shortly. If you were to manually create your form elements (which you need to do sometimes), you could use this naming convention to make sure your form values are easy to parse in the controller. Most of the time, though, you'll use form helpers when working with forms, especially when dealing with Active Record objects. Let's spend some time discussing form helpers now.

Using Form Helpers

One of the best things about working with templates in Rails is the presence of helpers. Rails comes with a bunch of helper methods for taking the tedium out of generating those bits of HTML that your views need. And let's face it, nothing is more of a drag to build than HTML forms. Fortunately, Rails understands the plight of the web developer all too well, and provides a suite of easy ways to build forms.

Two basic varieties of form helpers are available:

- `FormHelper`: Active Record-aware tag helpers for creating forms that hook into models.

- `FormTagHelper`: Helpers that just output tags. They are not integrated with Active Record. The names of these helpers are suffixed with _tag.

The `FormHelper` type is aware of Active Record objects assigned to the template; the `FormTagHelper` (note the `Tag`) type is not. The advantage of the Active Record-aware, `FormHelper`, helpers is that they know how to populate themselves with data and can automatically be highlighted in the event of validation errors from the model. But not every form element you'll make corresponds directly to a model attribute. That's where the `FormTagHelper` group comes in handy. These have no special relationship with Active Record; they just output form tags.

In our registration form (Listing 6-3) we used four helpers: `form_tag`, `text_field`, `password_field`, and `submit_tag`.

The `form_tag` helper is of the `FormTagHelper` variety. It simply creates an HTML form tag and places everything in the `do..end` block inside the resulting form. By default, forms use the HTTP `POST` method. If you want to use a different method, you need to specify it manually using the `:method` option (for example, `:method => :get`).

GET VS. POST

The HTTP protocol defines several request methods, the most popular of which are GET and POST. Both are methods for requesting a web page; the difference is in how the request is sent. GET is the simpler of the two. It includes all the information about the request as part of the URL. POST sends information invisibly, which is to say, as part of the request header and not part of the URL. So, you can't type a POST request into your browser's location bar. Every time you request a web page via the location bar in your browser, you're using GET. When you submit a form, say to register on a web site, the form is submitted via a POST.

So, how do you know when to use which? The best way to think of this is to consider GET a read method. It should never do anything "destructive," as in modifying a database record. POST, on the other hand, can be thought of as a write method. When you need to update or delete data, use POST.

Remember that you should never put a state-changing action behind a GET request. For more information, see www.w3.org/2001/tag/doc/whenToUseGet.html.

The `text_field` helper is of the `FormHelper` variety, meaning that it corresponds to Active Record objects. It creates an HTML `input` tag whose type is set to `"text"` and assigns it a name and an ID that match the given object and method (`user` and `login` in our example). Here's what the rendered output looks like:

```
<input id="user_login" name="user[login]" size="30" type="text" />
```

The `password_field` helper is also of the `FormHelper` variety. It is the same as `text_field`, except its type is set to `"password"`. The `password` type ensures that the input is masked (replaced by asterisks) to prevent anyone from seeing the password as it's entered. Here's what the HTML output looks like:

```
<input id="user_password" name="user[password]" size="30" type="password" />
```

The `submit_tag` helper is a `FormTagHelper` that creates an `input` element whose type is set to `"submit"`. It accepts the name of the submit button as its first argument. Since this is a `FormTagHelper`, it doesn't hook into Active Record. It just spits out a tag.

All these helpers (and to be sure, most helpers in Rails) accept a hash of options as their last argument to customize the resulting HTML. For example, if we wanted to give our login field a class of `large`, we would write the following:

```
text_field :user, :login, :class => 'large'
```

which would add the `class` attribute to the output:

```
<input class="large" id="user_login" name="user[login]" size="30" type="text" />
```

You can pass arbitrary options in this way, all of which will end up as attributes on the resulting tag. For example, if you wanted to apply an in-line `style` attribute, you could use `:style => 'background: #fab444'`. Here's a list of some of the most common `FormHelper` helpers:

- `text_field`

- `hidden_field`

- `password_field`

- `file_field`

- `text_area`

- `check_box`

- `radio_button`

All these methods can be suffixed with _tag to create standard HTML tags (with no Active Record integration).

For a full list of `FormHelper` and `FormTagHelper` methods, consult the Rails API, where you'll find a complete reference along with usage examples:

- http://api.rubyonrails.org/classes/ActionView/Helpers/FormHelper.html

- http://api.rubyonrails.org/classes/ActionView/Helpers/FormTagHelper.html

Now, back to our form. Let's see what happens when you submit it. (Make sure your server is still running.) Go ahead and click the Sign up! button. You'll see the following message displayed on your screen:

```
Unknown action
No action responded to create
```

So, what happened here? Well, just as the message says, Rails wasn't able to find an action called `create` on the `users` controller. Of course it couldn't—we haven't created one yet. If you look at the output from your server running on the console, you'll see what happened:

```
Processing UsersController#create (for 127.0.0.1 at 2007-02-24 19:21:29) [POST]
  Session ID: 6b21a8f9a3efecb12f52bfc286984378
  Parameters: {"user"=>{"login"=>"",
                        "email"=>"",
                        "password"=>"",
                        "password_confirmation"=>""},
              "commit"=>"Sign up!",
              "action"=>"create",
              "controller"=>"users"}
```

See the section titled `Parameters`? You might recognize this as a Ruby hash (we've formatted it prettily to make it easier to read). This hash contains all the form values we just submitted. Notice that there's an entry for the controller (`users`) and the action we submitted to (`create`). The `user` portion of the hash looks like this:

```
"user" => { "login" => "",
            "email" => "",
            "password" => "",
            "password_confirmation" => "" }
```

If you're thinking this looks a lot like the options hashes you were passing to the `User` objects when you were working with Active Record on the console, you're right. Rails automatically turns form elements into a convenient hash that you can pass into your models to create and update their attributes. We'll put this feature to use in our next action, create, which we'll get to in a minute. First, let's take a deeper look at params.

Processing Request Parameters

Request parameters—whether they originate from requests of the GET or POST variety—are accessible via the params hash. To be specific, params is really a method that returns a Hash object so you can access it using hash semantics. Hashes in Ruby are similar to arrays, but indexed by arbitrary keys, unlike arrays which are indexed (and ordered) by number. (If you need a quick review of the Hash object, flip to Appendix A for a Ruby primer.)

The value of any request variable can be retrieved by its symbolized key. So, if there's a variable called id in the request parameters, you can access it with params[:id]. Likewise, both the controller and the action name are also request parameters, stored in the params hash by the routing component when it picked apart the request. You can get their values by using params[:controller] and params[:action].

Just to drive this concept home, let's look at a sample URL and display the params hash that it would populate.

```
http://localhost:3000/users/index?name=arthur&number=1037
```

```
params #=> { :controller => 'users',
             :action      => 'index',
             :name        => 'arthur',
             :number      => '1037' }
```

Writing a Create Action

With an understanding of params under your belt, let's continue developing our controller. The create action is the target of the form submission. As you saw in the error message you just triggered, you'll need to write this action if you expect anything worthwhile to happen. Let's do that now. Add the method shown in Listing 6-5 to your users controller, just under the new method:

Listing 6-5. *Create Action Added to app/controllers/users_controller.rb*

```
def create
  @user = User.new(params[:user])
  if @user.save
    flash[:notice] = 'Thanks for signing up!'
    redirect_to :controller => 'events', :action => 'index'
```

```
  else
    render :action => 'new'
  end
end
```

Let's walk through this. First, we initialize a new User object with whatever attributes come in via the params hash, storing it the @user instance variable. Then we try to save it.

If the save is successful, we use a facility that Rails provides called the flash to set a message before redirecting to the index action on the events controller. The flash is a special kind of storage mechanism provided by Rails for convenience. It encapsulates the pattern of wanting to set a message on one action and have that message persist to the next, only to disappear after that action is rendered. This is useful for providing user feedback, as we're doing here to say "Thanks for signing up." If you look back to your layout file in app/views/layouts/application.rhtml, you'll see where the flash message is displayed:

```
<p style="color: green"><%= flash[:notice] %></p>
```

The flash message we set will be available to the controller and action we redirect to (the index action on the events controller). Just like params, the flash is implemented as a Ruby hash. You store values in it based on a key. The key can be anything you like, but here we're using the symbol :notice, which is a Rails convention. When rendering a flash message that contains an error, we usually use the :error key.

If the save fails, we render the new action again so that any errors can be corrected.

Rendering Responses

You already know that, by default, when an action has completed, it will attempt to render a template of the same name. Sometimes you want to render a different template, though.

In the create action we just created, if the @user.save succeeds, we want to set a friendly flash message and redirect. However, if the save fails, we want to render the new template. If we didn't explicitly render new, the action would fall through to its default behavior and attempt to render a template named create, which, of course, doesn't exist.

The render method takes several options for its first argument: :text, :nothing, :inline, and :update.

Note The :update response is fairly specialized. You use it when you're rendering Ajax responses, as you'll learn in Chapter 7.

Redirecting

It might not sound like it, but a redirection is a response. Redirects don't really happen on the server side. Instead, a response is sent to your browser that tells it to perform a redirection to another URL. The specifics of issuing a redirect aren't something you need to worry about, though, since Rails provides a specialized method to take care of the internals. That method is called `redirect_to`, and it's one you'll find yourself using a lot, so it's a good idea to get familiar with it.

As you can see from the example in the `create` action, `redirect_to` takes a hash of options. Most of the time, you'll specify the name of a controller, action, or both. The current controller is presumed unless a controller value is given, so in our case, Rails will redirect to the `index` action in the `users` controller. You can also pass around parameters when redirecting; any key/value pairs you append to the redirect will be parameterized and become part of the `params` hash.

Displaying Error Messages in Templates

Let's try submitting the form again. Make sure you leave the form empty so you can see whether the validations are working as expected. Sure enough, the form doesn't save. In fact, you'll notice that you're still on the same screen and that the form elements are highlighted in red, as shown in Figure 6-2.

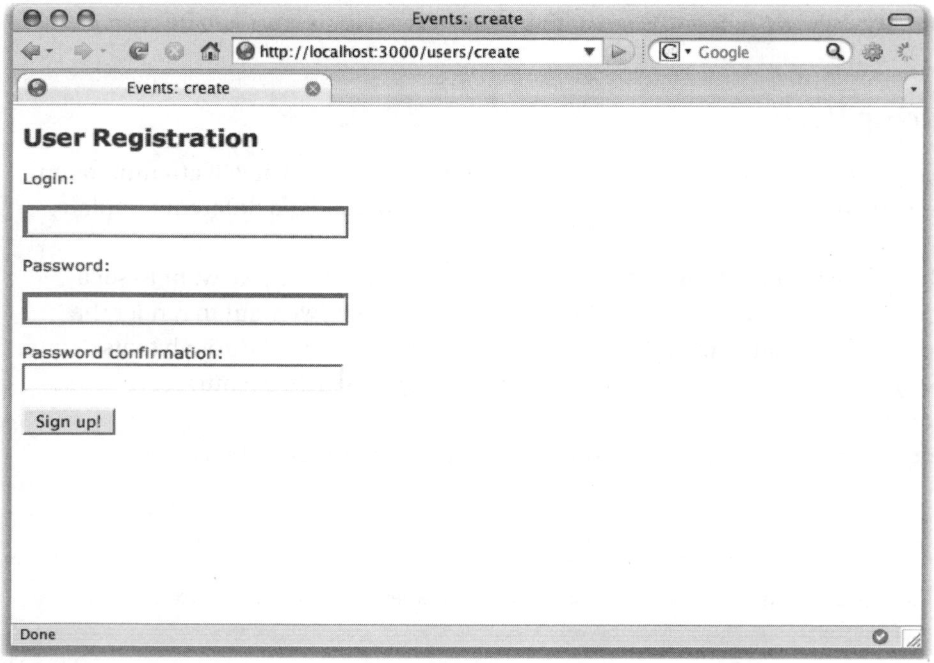

Figure 6-2. *Fields that fail validation are highlighted in red.*

If you look at the HTML source, you'll see that the input tags are surrounded by div elements with the class name fieldWithErrors:

```
<div class="fieldWithErrors">
  <input class="large" id="user_login" name="user[login]" size="30"
  type="text"  value="" />
</div>
```

Rails does this automatically for any fields that failed validation, and you can use these classes to style invalid elements.

■**Note** The style rules that turn the invalid fields red are generated by the scaffold generator and are in public/stylesheets/scaffold.css. All static files, such as stylesheets and images, are located in the public directory.

But wait a minute. Where is the formatted list of errors that we got with our invalid events? Well, the scaffold generator added the helper that displays these, but if we want them to show up here, we'll have to do it ourselves. We'll use the error_messages_for helper and tell it the name of the model whose errors we want to see—in this case, User. Add the following to the top of the new template in app/views/users/new.rhtml:

```
<%= error_messages_for :user %>
```

Now submit the form one more time, again with empty fields. You should see the error messages, as shown in Figure 6-3.

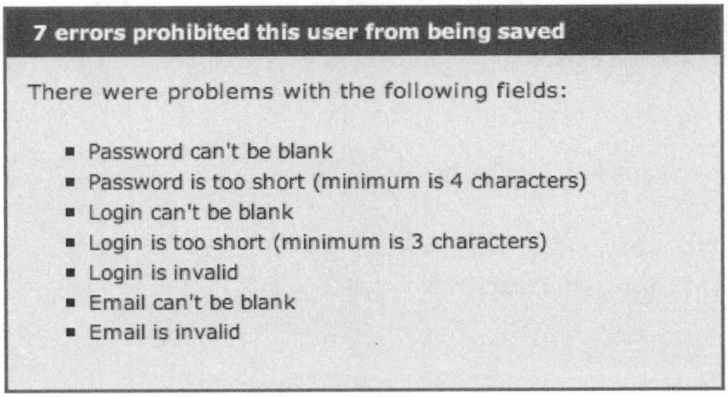

7 errors prohibited this user from being saved

There were problems with the following fields:

- Password can't be blank
- Password is too short (minimum is 4 characters)
- Login can't be blank
- Login is too short (minimum is 3 characters)
- Login is invalid
- Email can't be blank
- Email is invalid

Figure 6-3. *Error messages for invalid events*

With all the plumbing in place, let's submit the form with valid data. If all goes according to plan, the new user should be created, and you'll be redirected to the events controller, where you'll see the friendly flash message we set. Notice that if you refresh the page using your browser's refresh button, the flash message will disappear.

Adding the Edit Form

The next step is to add the edit and update actions to the controller. We'll also need an edit template. Create a new action called edit, as shown in Listing 6-6 (it looks a lot like the new action).

Listing 6-6. *Edit Action Added to app/controllers/users_controller.rb*

```
def edit
  @user = User.find(params[:id])
end
```

Next, create the edit template in app/views/users/edit.rhtml as shown in Listing 6-7.

Listing 6-7. *The app/views/users/edit.rhtml Template*

```
<h2>Edit User</h2>

<% form_tag :action => 'update' do %>
  <p><label>Login:<br />
  <%= text_field :user, :login %></label></p>

  <p><label>Email:<br />
  <%= text_field :user, :email %></label></p>

  <p><label>Password:<br />
  <%= password_field :user, :password %></label></p>

  <p><label>Password confirmation:<br />
  <%= password_field :user, :password_confirmation %></label></p>

  <p><%= submit_tag 'Save Changes' %></p>
<% end %>
```

As you can see from the form_tag method, this form will submit to the update action on the events controller. We need to add the update method to our controller, so let's do that now, as shown in Listing 6-8.

Listing 6-8. *Update Action Added to app/controllers/users_controller.rb*

```
def update
  @user = User.find(params[:id])
  if current_user.update_attributes(params[:user])
    flash[:notice] = 'Information updated'
    redirect_to :action => 'show', :id => @user.id
  else
    render :action => 'edit'
  end
end
```

The update action looks almost identical to the create action. The main difference is that instead of instantiating a new User object, we're fetching an existing one. We use Active Record's update_attributes method to update all the User attributes with those from the params hash and save it in one shot. If the update fails, update_attributes will return false, and our if statement will take the else path.

You can't help but notice that the new and edit templates look essentially the same. Given Rails' emphasis on DRY, as you would expect, there's a way to clean this up, and that's what we'll look at next.

Staying DRY with Partials

A typical web application is rife with view code and often suffers from a lot of needless duplication. Our HTML forms for adding and modifying users are good examples of forms that are very similar. Wouldn't it be nice if there was a way to reuse the common elements from one form in more than one place? That's where partial templates come in.

Partial templates, usually referred to as just *partials*, are similar to regular templates, but they have a more refined set of capabilities. You'll see partials used quite often in a typical Rails application, because they help cut down on duplication and keep the code well organized. Partials follow the naming convention of being prefixed with an underscore, thus distinguishing them from standard templates (which are meant to be rendered on their own.

Rather than creating two separate forms, we'll keep our code DRY by using a single partial and include it from both the new and edit templates. First, let's take the form code from new.rhtml and put that code in its own file, as shown in Listing 6-9. We'll call this file _form.rhtml. Notice the leading underscore, which identifies it as a partial.

Listing 6-9. *The app/views/users/_form.rhtml File*

```
<%= error_messages_for :user %>

<p><label>Login:<br />
<%= text_field :user, :login %></label></p>

<p><label>Email:<br />
<%= text_field :user, :email %></label></p>

<p><label>Password:<br />
<%= password_field :user, :password %></label></p>

<p><label>Password confirmation:<br />
<%= password_field :user, :password_confirmation %></label></p>
```

Now we'll revise the template in new.rhtml by including the partial, as shown in Listing 6-10, and do the same for edit.rhtml, as shown in Listing 6-11. Notice that when referencing the partial in the render method, you don't include the leading underscore.

Listing 6-10. *The app/views/users/new.rhtml File*

```
<h2>User Registration</h2>

<% form_tag :action => 'create' do %>
  <%= render :partial => 'form' %>
  <p><%= submit_tag 'Sign up!' %></p>
<% end %>
```

Listing 6-11. *The app/views/users/edit.rhtml File*

```
<h2>Edit User</h2>

<% form_tag :action => 'update' do %>
  <%= render :partial => 'form' %>
  <p><%= submit_tag 'Save Changes' %></p>
<% end %>
```

Let's take a closer look at the render method.

```
<%= render :partial => 'form' %>
```

A single argument is passed to `render` in the form of hash. (Are you noticing yet that Rails is a big fan of the options hash?) The symbol `:partial` is the key, and the partial's name is the value. Upon seeing this, the `render` method searches the current directory for a file named `_form.rhtml`. Notice that we don't need to include the leading underscore or the file extension when specifying the partial's name; Rails knows to look for a file in the same directory as the calling template with a leading underscore. Let's take a brief detour here to explain a few things about partials.

One of the things that makes partials unique is special convenience: automatic local variable assignment by way of convention over configuration. That was a mouthful. Allow us to explain.

Automatic Local Variable Assignment in Partials

Partials are distinct by virtue of a convenience convention: the value of an instance variable with the same name as the partial will be available to the partial as a local variable. So, if you have a partial named `_albums` and an instance variable named `@albums`, you'll get a local variable called `albums` inside the partial.

Our form example doesn't do a very good job of illustrating this feature. Consider instead the following example, where we have all the necessary ingredients: an instance variable and a partial, both named `articles`.

```
class ArticlesController < ApplicationController
  def index
    @articles = Article.find(:all)
  end
end
```

Here's a `list` template (`app/views/articles/list.rhtml`) that renders the `_articles` partial:

```
<h1>Articles</h1>
<%= render :partial => 'articles' %>
```

And here's the `_articles` partial (`app/views/articles/_articles.rhtml`):

```
<ul>
  <% for article in articles %>
    <li><%= article.title %></li>
  <% end %>
</ul>
```

The `@articles` instance variable that was initialized in the `index` action is available in the partial as the local variable `articles` because the partial is named `articles`. See the pattern here?

This behavior might seem a little too magical for purists, but it's a great example of how Rails goes out of its way to save you the tedium of implementing common patterns. Still, for the purists among you, and for those rare occasions when you need to use configuration over convention, Rails makes it possible to explicitly set local template variables.

Explicit Local Variable Assignment in Partials

Automatic assignment is not the only way to assign local variables inside a partial template. The render method also accepts a hash of local variables identified by the :locals symbol. Imagine we have two instance variables: one containing a collection of articles and another one containing a collection of comments.

```
<%= render :partial => 'articles', :locals => { :comments => @comments } %>
```

Any number of local variables can be assigned in this way, and any object can be set as the value. In the preceding example, not only will the partial have access to the @articles collection through the automatically assigned articles variable, it will also have access to the contents of the @comments collection using the local variable comments.

Rendering a Collection of Partials

Our first example of rendering the articles partial can actually be improved a bit. Notice how we're iterating over the articles list inside the partial? Well, this is a common enough pattern that Rails has a better way of dealing with it. It's called *rendering a collection of partials*.

Here's how we would rewrite the list.rhtml file from the example:

```
<h1>Articles</h1>
<ul>
  <%= render :partial => 'article', :collection => @articles %>
</ul>
```

And here's how we would rewrite the _article.rhtml partial:

```
<li><%= article.title %></li>
```

Notice that we renamed the articles partial from the plural to the singular. Recalling what you know about automatic local variable assignment, this is because we want to deal with a single article. When you render using a collection, as we've done here, Rails will iterate over the given collection and yield the contents of the partial once for each iteration. The local variable article will become available inside the partial by virtue of the partial's name.

Adding the Login and Logout Actions

Our `users` controller needs to serve another important function: controlling the logging in and out of users. To accomplish this, we'll create two new actions: `login` and `logout`. The `login` action has an associated view template; the `logout` action does not. Listing 6-12 shows the new actions.

Listing 6-12. *Login and Logout Actions Added to app/controllers/users_controller.rb*

```ruby
def login
  if request.post?
    if user = User.authenticate(params[:login], params[:password])
      session[:user_id] = user.id
      redirect_to events_url
    else
      flash[:notice] = 'Invalid login/password combination'
    end
  end
end

def logout
  session[:user_id] = nil
  redirect_to login_url
end
```

We'll take a closer look at the `login` and `logout` actions soon, but before we go any further, we need to take a minute to talk about sessions.

Lying in State

Here's the thing: HTTP is stateless. In short, that means that each and every request you make across the HTTP protocol is autonomous. The web server has no idea that it has talked to your browser before; each request is like a blind date. Given this tidbit of information, you might be wondering how you can stay logged in to a given site. How can the application remember that you're logged in if HTTP is stateless? The answer is that we fake state.

You've no doubt heard of browser cookies. In order to simulate state atop HTTP, Rails uses cookies. When the first request comes in, Rails sets a cookie on the client browser. The browser remembers the cookie locally and sends it along with each subsequent request. The result is that Rails is able to match the cookie that comes along in the request with session data stored on the server.

Rails ships with a few different session storage mechanisms. You can choose to store session data directly on the application server via the file system (the current default), directly in the browser cookies (there is some controversy regarding the security of this approach), or in the database. We like the database approach the best, because it fits well with Rails' architectural principles.

The Shared-Nothing Architecture

Rails is built on the principle of a shared-nothing architecture. When we say *shared-nothing*, we mean that no piece of data is shared between the servers that host the application. Storing session data on the server would violate this principal.

Imagine that you were storing your session data on the file system of the server that runs your application. This would work fine as long as you were using only one server for your application. But what happens when your site becomes busy and you decide that you need multiple servers to keep up with the traffic? You would need to use a load balancer—a hardware or software layer that routes requests to one of several application servers to spread out the load. Say a request comes in to server 1, and you store some session data in the file system. Then server 1 gets busy, and the load balancer decides to send the next request to server 2. But the session data isn't on server 2; it's on server 1. This presents a dilemma. The shared-nothing architecture avoids this problem by keeping the state somewhere other than on the application server, like the database, as shown in Figure 6-4.

■**Note** David Heinemeier Hansson (the creator of Rails) has written about his thoughts on the shared-nothing architecture on his blog at `http://loudthinking.com/arc/000479.html`.

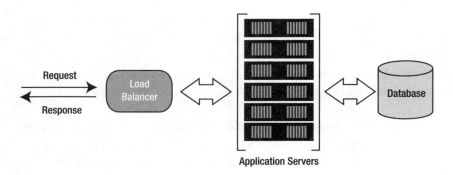

Application Servers

Figure 6-4. *Shared-nothing architecture*

■**Note** Purists will argue that this isn't really shared-*nothing*. After all, we're sharing the database server. But since a single database server can service dozens of application servers without a hitch, using it as a centralized storage location for session data is a worthy compromise.

Storing Sessions in the Database

The default file system session storage mechanism will "just work" with no configuration required. However, we feel that storing session data in the database is important enough that it's worth taking a brief detour to set up. Fortunately, Rails makes this an easy affair. There's a built-in Rake task called db:sessions:create that will make a migration to create the sessions table. To run it, enter the following from your application's directory on the command line:

```
$ rake db:sessions:create
```

```
exists   db/migrate
create   db/migrate/007_add_sessions.rb
```

This will create a migration to create the necessary sessions table in the database. All we need to do is run it.

```
$ rake db:migrate
```

Now that the sessions table has been created, we need to tell Rails that we want to use the database for session storage. This is matter of configuration, and is therefore specified in the config/environment.rb file. Open this file in your editor and you'll see the session configuration options are already there, though they're commented out.

```
# Use the database for sessions instead of the file system
# (create the session table with 'rake db:sessions:create')
# config.action_controller.session_store = :active_record_store
```

Remove the comment from the last line to activate the active_record_store option for sessions, as shown in Listing 6-13.

Listing 6-13. *Activating active_record_store in config/environment.rb*

```
# Use the database for sessions instead of the file system
# (create the session table with 'rake db:sessions:create')
config.action_controller.session_store = :active_record_store
```

You'll need to start and stop your web server for this change to take effect. Remember to use Ctrl+C to stop the server (and `./script/server` to start it up again).

Using the Session

Secure in the knowledge that Rails will take care of all the low-level details of sessions for us, using the `session` object couldn't be easier. The `session` is implemented as a hash, just like the `flash`. We should come clean here. The `flash` is, in fact, a `session` in disguise (you can think of it as a specialized session due to its auto-expiring properties). Not surprisingly, then, the `flash` and `session` interfaces are identical. We store values in the `session` according to a key.

```
session[:account_id] = @account.id
session[:account_id] # => 1

session['message'] = "Hello world!"
session['message'] # => "Hello world!"
```

Logging In a User

Now we can return to our new actions, starting with `login`. Here, you'll see the `session` object action (no pun intended).

```
def login
  if request.post?
    if user = User.authenticate(params[:login], params[:password])
      session[:user_id] = user.id
      redirect_to events_url
    else
      flash[:notice] = 'Invalid login/password combination'
    end
  end
end
```

First, we check to see if the request method is of the POST variety, which would indicate that the login form had been posted. If it's a GET, meaning no form data has been posted, we just want to render the `login` template, which will happen automatically since we're not sending any other response. If we have a POST, though, we use the `authenticate` class method from our `User` model to attempt a login (see Listing 5-28 in Chapter 5).

Remember that authenticate returns a User object if the authentication succeeds; otherwise it returns false. Therefore, we can perform our conditional and our assignment in one shot using if user = User.authenticate(params[:login], params[:password]). If the assignment takes place, we want to store a reference to this user so we can keep the user logged in—a perfect job for the session if there ever was one.

```
session[:user_id] = user.id
```

Notice that we don't need to store the entire User object in session. We store just a reference to the user's id. Why wouldn't we want to store the entire User object? Well, think about this for a minute: what if the user is stored in session and then that user later changes her login? The old login would remain in the session and would therefore be *stale*. This can cause further problems if the underlying User model changes. Your entire object could become stale, potentially causing a NoMethodError when accessing attributes that didn't exist on the model at the time it was placed in session. The best bet is to just store the id.

With a reference to the logged-in user safely stored in session, we can redirect to the events controller.

Logging Out a User

The logout action is fairly straightforward. We clear out the :user_id session by setting its value to nil, and then we redirect back to the login action.

```
def logout
  session[:user_id] = nil
  redirect_to login_url
end
```

This is a good way to clear out a specific session, but sometimes you want to clear the entire session without having to remember which keys to reset. Rails provides the method reset_session to do just that.

We've done a lot of work on the users controller so far. Listing 6-14 shows what it should look like at this stage.

Listing 6-14. *Actions Added in app/controllers/users_controller.rb*

```
class UsersController < ApplicationController
  def show
    @user = User.find(params[:id])
  end
```

```ruby
def new
  @user = User.new
end

def create
  @user = User.new(params[:user])
  if @user.save
    flash[:notice] = 'Thanks for signing up!'
    redirect_to :controller => 'events', :action => 'index'
  else
    render :action => 'new'
  end
end

def edit
  @user = User.find(params[:id])
end

def update
  @user = User.find(params[:id])
  if @user.update_attributes(params[:user])
    flash[:notice] = 'Information updated'
    redirect_to :action => 'show', :id => @user.id
  else
    render :action => 'edit'
  end
end

def login
  if request.post?
    if user = User.authenticate(params[:login], params[:password])
      session[:user_id] = user.id
      redirect_to :controller => 'events', :action => 'index'
    else
      flash[:notice] = 'Invalid login/password combination'
    end
  end
end
```

```
  def logout
    session[:user_id] = nil
    redirect_to :action => 'login'
  end
end
```

Improving the Events Controller and Templates

In walking through the construction of the users controller, we've covered generating controllers, creating templates and layouts, and DRYing up with partials. Now let's take that knowledge and apply it to the events controller (and templates).

Cleaning Up the Events Controller

Currently, our events controller is stock scaffolding. To be sure, scaffolding has its place; it served us quite well as a learning tool. But now it's time to rework the scaffolded version.

Open the events controller (app/controllers/events_controller.rb) in your editor. Notice how the scaffolder creates index and list actions. Take a close look, and you'll notice that the index action renders the list template. The two actions are pretty much identical, so there's no need for both of them. Let's make the index action render the list of events, as shown in Listing 6-15.

Listing 6-15. *Index Action Updated in app/controllers/events_controller.rb*

```
def index
  @event_pages, @events = paginate :events, :per_page => 10
end
```

Now delete the list action. This cuts down on the clutter. Also, using the index action as the "collection" action (wherein we display a list of resources) is a Rails convention not yet applied to the scaffold generator. We can apply another of the techniques you've learned—rendering a collection of partials—to further improve the code.

PROBLEM: PAGINATION

Pagination is the process of dividing up a result set into groups of pages, and you'll find examples of it all over the web. Google uses pagination to show you ten results per page for any query. Since it's so common in web development, Rails includes a pagination helper. Here's an example from the `index` action on the `events` controller.

```
@event_pages, @events = paginate :events, :per_page => 10
```

The `paginate` method returns a two-element array. In the preceding example, we're assigning each element to the `@events_pages` and `@events` instance variables, respectively. `@events_pages` contains the paginated object, and `@events` contains a collection of no more than the specified number of `Event` objects (in this case, 10). When it's time to display paginated results in a template, you can ask the current `@events_pages` object for its next and previous page and pass it to the controller via the `:page` parameter.

```
link_to('Previous', :page => @events_pages.current.previous)
link_to('Next', :page => @events_pages.current.next)
```

The pagination helper works well for simple cases, but can suffer from efficiency problems when used for very large result sets. Kevin Clark has written about the perils of pagination in an article titled "Things You Shouldn't Be Doing in Rails," which you can find at `http://glu.ttono.us/articles/2006/08/30/guide-things-you-shouldnt-be-doing-in-rails`.

For an alternative, more efficient approach, we like PJ Hyett and Chris Wanstrath's `will_paginate` plugin, which you can read about and download from `http://errtheblog.com/post/929`.

However, sometimes pagination isn't the best technique. One alternative proposed by Rails developer Pete Forde is endless scrolling. Read up on Pete's technique at `http://unspace.ca/discover/pageless`.

Using Partials in the Events Templates

As you learned when walking through the `users` controller, Rails includes a clever way of economizing on template code called partials. The pattern of rendering a collection of partials is particularly powerful. Let's rename the `list` template of our `events` controller to `index`, and then rewrite it to take advantage of partials. Listing 6-16 shows the modified version.

Listing 6-16. *Modified app/views/events/index.rhtml*

```
<h1>All Events</h1>

<%= render :partial => 'event', :collection => @events %>

<%= link_to 'Previous page', { :page => @event_pages.current.previous } ➥
    if @event_pages.current.previous %>
<%= link_to 'Next page', { :page => @event_pages.current.next } ➥
    if @event_pages.current.next %>
```

Listing 6-17 shows the _event partial.

Listing 6-17. *The app/views/events/_event.rhtml File*

```
<div class="event">
  <h2><%= event.title %></h2>
  <ul>
    <li><%= event.occurs_on %></li>
    <li><%= event.location %></li>
  </ul>
  <div class="description">
    <%= event.description %>
  </div>
</div>
```

When this template is rendered, Rails will automatically iterate over the collection and create a div element for each event.

Adding Categories to the Events Form

In Chapter 5, we added categories to the Event model, but neither our controller nor our templates know about this yet. Let's remedy that now, starting with the events form. Add the code shown in bold in Listing 6-18 to the form partial in app/views/events/_form.rhtml.

Listing 6-18. *Modified app/views/events/_form.rhtml*

```
<%= error_messages_for 'event' %>

<p><label for="event_title">Title</label><br/>
<%= text_field 'event', 'title' %></p>
```

```erb
<p><label for="categories">Categories</label><br/>
<%=
  select_tag(
    'categories[]',
    options_for_select(
      Category.find(:all).collect {|c| [c.name, c.id] },
      @event.category_ids
    ),
    :multiple => true
  )
%></p>

<p><label for="event_location">Location</label><br/>
<%= text_field 'event', 'location' %></p>

<p><label for="event_occurs_on">Occurs on</label><br/>
<%= date_select 'event', 'occurs_on' %></p>

<p><label for="event_url">Url</label><br/>
<%= text_field 'event', 'url' %></p>

<p><label for="event_description">Description</label><br/>
<%= text_area 'event', 'description', :rows => 5 %></p>
```

Note In order to fit within the page margins, we've reformatted the code for the `select_tag` method.
It looks a little unwieldy, but bear with us.

The `select_tag` method deserves a closer look.

```ruby
select_tag(
  'categories[]',
  options_for_select(
    Category.find(:all).collect {|c| [c.name, c.id] }, @event.category_ids
  ),
  :multiple => true
)
```

The `select_tag` method is another of Action View's form helpers. It creates a drop-down selection box, or if the `:multiple` option is set to `true` (as it is in our case), a multiple-choice selection box. By including a set of square brackets with the tag's name (`categories[]`), we're telling Rails to generate a collection of values in the `params` that are submitted.

It's important to note that `select_tag` generates only the HTML select tag. We need to generate the actual option tags ourselves. Again, Rails provides a helper to take care of the heavy lifting: `options_for_select`. The `options_for_select` helper accepts a collection and returns a string of option tags. Given a collection where the elements respond to `first` and `last` (such as a two-element array), the `firsts` serves as the option test, and the `lasts` serves as the option values. A second argument can be passed to `options_for_select` to specify any options that should be preselected. In our case, we're passing in all the `category_ids` for the given event so they will be preselected. This is easily the most advanced helper we've looked at so far, so it's okay to take it on faith a bit. Once we add the appropriate code to handle categories in the controller, everything should "just work."

You can find the full documentation for `select_tag` and `options_for_select` helpers in the Ruby API:

- `http://api.rubyonrails.org/classes/ActionView/Helpers/`
  `FormTagHelper.html#M000604`

- `http://api.rubyonrails.org/classes/ActionView/Helpers/`
  `FormOptionsHelper.html#M000510`

Handling Categories in the Events Controller

We need to let our controller know how to deal with categories. This is relatively easy. That said, it will likely be one of the most complex things you need to do in a typical controller, and to make it happen, we'll need to use a little Ruby-fu. Listing 6-19 shows how it's done. The new code is listed in bold.

Listing 6-19. *Create Action Modified in app/controllers/events_controller.rb*

```
def create
  @event = Event.new(params[:event])

  unless params[:categories].blank?
    @event.categories << Category.find(params[:categories])
  end
```

```
    if @event.save
      flash[:notice] = 'Event was successfully created.'
      redirect_to :action => 'index'
    else
      render :action => 'new'
    end
  end
end
```

First, we check whether a list of category id values was submitted in the params hash:

```
unless params[:categories].blank?
```

If there are categories in the params, we take advantage of the fact that
ActiveRecord::Base.find accepts an array of primary keys for record to find and returns
an array of the objects it finds. We further take advantage of the append operator, <<,
and use it to append the categories collection to the existing (empty) collection contained in @event.categories. The result is that we tack any selected categories on to the
@event.categories collection, and Active Record takes care of the rest. We can then
save our @event object as usual.

APPENDING TO ARRAYS

The append operator, <<, works with Ruby arrays. Here's a quick demonstration from irb (introduced
in Chapter 4):

```
> ary = [1,2,3]
=> [1, 2, 3]
> ary << 4
=> [1, 2, 3, 4]
> ary << 5
=> [1, 2, 3, 4, 5]
```

For more information about Ruby arrays, see Appendix A.

When we receive an update request, we need to handle things a little differently. We
can't just append new categories onto the existing collection, because some categories
may have been deleted. The easiest way to handle this is to reset all the @event's category
id values at once. When you use the has_and_belongs_to_many association, Active Record
automatically adds a method called #{collection}_ids to both sides of the relationship,
where #{collection} is the singular name of the collection. In the case of an Event that
has_and_belongs_to_many categories, the category_ids method is added to every Event

instance. When used, it replaces the existing collection with objects whose primary keys match those supplied. Listing 6-20 shows how this is handled, again with the modified code in bold.

Listing 6-20. *Update Action Modified in app/controllers/events_controller.rb*

```
def update
  @event = Event.find(params[:id])

  @event.attributes = params[:event]

  unless params[:categories].blank?
    @event.category_ids = params[:categories]
  end

  if @event.save
    flash[:notice] = 'Event was successfully updated.'
    redirect_to :action => 'show', :id => @event
  else
    render :action => 'edit'
  end
end
```

Instead of using the update_attributes method to update the Event object and save it in one fell swoop, we use attributes. The only difference between the two is that attributes doesn't automatically save the record. Since we want to avoid having to save twice (once to update the attributes via params and another time to update the categories), this makes sense. After the attributes have been set and the category_id values have been updated, we can save the record and respond accordingly to either success or failure.

Using Controller Filters

Filters provide a way for you to perform operations either before or after an action is invoked. There's even an around filter that can wrap the executing of an action. Of the three, the before filter is the most commonly used, so that's what we'll focus on here.

Here's how it works: all the code you place in a before_filter will be run before the action in question is called. Pretty simple, really. But there's a catch: if the before_ filter returns false, the action will not be executed. We often use this to protect certain actions that require a login. In our users controller, we want the new, create, login, and logout actions to remain open (anyone can access them), but we want to restrict all other actions to logged-in users. Here's how we can do that using filters:

```
class UsersController < ApplicationController
  before_filter :authenticate, :except => [:new, :create, :login, :logout]
end
```

This will cause the `authenticate` method to be run before every action except those listed. Assume the `authenticate` method is defined on the `application` controller and is therefore available to every other controller in the system. If the `authenticate` method returns false, the requested action will not be executed, thereby protecting it from unauthorized visitors.

You can also use the `:only` modifier to specify that the filter is to run for *only* the given actions. We could have written the preceding example more concisely as follows:

```
before_filter :authenticate, :only => :show
```

Without the `:only` or `:except` modifiers, the filter will run for all actions.

Controller inheritance hierarchies share filters downwards, but subclasses can also add or skip filters without affecting the superclass. Let's say you have applied a global filter to the `application_controller`, but you have a particular controller that you want to be exempt from filtration. You can use `skip_before_filter`, like this:

```
class ApplicationController < ActionController::Base
  before_filter :authenticate_with_token
end

class PublicController < ApplicationController
  # We don't want to check for a token on this controller
  skip_before_filter :authenticate_with_token
end
```

Filters are a fairly involved topic, and we've only scratched the surface here. Still, we've shown you the most common usage pattern: protecting actions. For more information about filters, including usage examples, check out the Rails API documentation at http://api.rubyonrails.com/classes/ActionController/Filters/ClassMethods.html.

Requiring Authentication with Filters

In our events application, we've decided that we want to protect event creation and modification, restricting access only to registered users. To do this, we'll use filters that call specific methods and check for the `user_id` session we set upon user login. Recall that any methods we add to the `application_controller` are available to all other controllers (since it's the superclass of all controllers).

Open the `application_controller` in app/controllers/application.rb and add the private methods that we'll use to enforce our authentication requirement, as shown in Listing 6-21.

Listing 6-21. *Modified app/controllers/application.rb*

```ruby
class ApplicationController < ActionController::Base

  protected
    # Returns the currently logged in user or nil if there isn't one
    def current_user
      return unless session[:user_id]
      @current_user ||= User.find_by_id(session[:user_id])
    end

    # Make current_user available in templates as a helper
    helper_method :current_user

    # Filter method to enforce a login requirement
    # Apply as a before_filter on any controller you want to protect
    def authenticate
      logged_in? ? true : access_denied
    end

    # Predicate method to test for a logged in user
    def logged_in?
      current_user.is_a? User
    end

    # Make logged_in? available in templates as a helper
    helper_method :logged_in?

    def access_denied
      flash[:notice] = "Please log in to continue"
      redirect_to login_url and return false
    end
end
```

The current_user method acts like an *accessor* for the currently logged-in user.
Since it returns a User object, we can call instance methods of User on it, such as
current_user.login. The authenticate method is our filter method (the one we'll call
from individual controllers). It checks whether there is a currently logged-in user via
logged_in? (which, in turn, checks that there is actually a User returned by current_user)
and calls access_denied, if there isn't. access_denied sets a message in the flash and redirects to the login action on the users controller.

We want two of these methods available in templates as well: logged_in? and
current_user. Having logged_in? available will allow us to make dynamic decisions about

whether or not a user is logged in. We can use this to show or hide administrative controls (such as adding or editing a given event). Having `current_user` around will also prove useful in templates, allowing us to access information about the users such as their login name or email address. Rails provides a handy way to extend the visibility of methods to templates by declaring them as helpers. You can use `helper_method` followed by a symbolic reference to the method in question, as we've done here. You can also pass an array of method references to `helper_method` if you want to declare them all at once.

Let's apply the filter to our `events` controller now. We'll also apply a filter to the `users` controller to restrict who can edit user profiles.

Applying Filters to Controllers

You apply filters using a declarative syntax. In this case, we want to check that a user is authenticated *before* we process a protected action, so we'll use the `before_filter`. Add the filter to the `events` controller, just inside the class body, as shown in Listing 6-22.

Listing 6-22. *Before Filter Added in app/controllers/events_controller.rb*

```
class EventsController < ApplicationController
  before_filter :authenticate, :except => [:index, :show]

  #...
end
```

Notice how we're able to selectively apply the filter to specific actions. Here, we want every action to be protected *except* for `index` and `show`. The `:except` modifier accepts either a single value or an array. We're using an array here. If you want to protect only a few actions, you can use the `:only` modifier, which, as you would expect, behaves the opposite of `:except`.

We also want to use a filter in the `users` controller. Right now, anyone can edit a user as long as they know the user ID. This would be risky in the real world. Ideally, we want the `edit` and `update` actions to respond only to the currently logged-in user, allowing that user to edit his profile. To do this, instead of retrieving `User.find(params[:id])`, we'll retrieve the `current_user` and apply a filter to protect the `edit` and `update` actions. Listing 6-23 shows the latest version of the `users` controller, the updated code is highlighted in bold.

Listing 6-23. *Before Filter Added in app/controllers/users_controller.rb*

```
class UsersController < ApplicationController
  before_filter :authenticate, :only => [:edit, :update]

  def show
    @user = User.find(params[:id])
  end

  def new
    @user = User.new
  end

  def create
    @user = User.new(params[:user])
    if @user.save
      flash[:notice] = 'Thanks for signing up!'
      redirect_to :controller => 'events', :action => 'index'
    else
      render :action => 'new'
    end
  end

  def edit
    @user = current_user
  end

  def update
    @user = current_user
    if current_user.update_attributes(params[:user])
      flash[:notice] = 'Information updated'
      redirect_to :action => 'show', :id => current_user.id
    else
      render :action => 'edit'
    end
  end

  def login
    if request.post?
      if user = User.authenticate(params[:login], params[:password])
        session[:user_id] = user.id
        redirect_to :controller => 'events', :action => 'index'
```

```
      else
        flash[:notice] = 'Invalid login/password combination'
      end
    end
  end

  def logout
    session[:user_id] = nil
    redirect_to :action => 'login'
  end
end
```

Adding Finishing Touches

We're almost finished with our work in this chapter. Only a few tasks remain. We need to spruce up our templates a bit and make them a little cleaner. We also need to make it possible for event owners to edit and delete their events. Finally, we want to update the layout and apply some CSS styles to make things look pretty. Ready? Let's get started!

Using Action View Helpers

One of the ways we can clean up our templates is with helpers. Rails ships with a bevy of formatting helpers to assist in displaying numbers, dates, tags, and text in your templates. Here's a quick summary:

Number helpers: The `NumberHelper` module provides methods for converting numbers into formatted strings. Methods are provided for phone numbers, currency, percentage, precision, positional notation, and file size. See `http://api.rubyonrails.org/classes/ActionView/Helpers/NumberHelper.html` for more information.

Text helpers: The `TextHelper` module provides a set of methods for filtering, formatting, and transforming strings that can reduce the amount of in-line Ruby code in your views. See `http://api.rubyonrails.org/classes/ActionView/Helpers/TextHelper.html` for more information.

URL helpers: Rails provides a set of URL helpers that make constructing links that depend on the controller and action (or other parameters) ridiculously easy. For more information, see `http://api.rubyonrails.org/classes/ActionView/Helpers/UrlHelper.html` and `http://api.rubyonrails.org/classes/ActionController/Base.html`.

Let's take a closer look at two very handy URL helpers that you're likely to use often: url_for and link_to.

The url_for method returns a URL that has been rewritten according to the given options hash and the defined routes. It has the following format:

```
url_for(options={})
```

You can provide the following options:

- :anchor: Specifies the anchor name to be appended to the path. For example, url_for :controller => 'posts', :action => 'show', :id => 10, :anchor => 'comments' will produce "/posts/show/10#comments".

- :only_path: If true, returns the relative URL (omitting the protocol, hostname, and port). It's false by default.

- :trailing_slash: If true, adds a trailing slash, as in /pub/archive/2007/.

- :host: Overrides the default (current) host if provided.

- :protocol: Overrides the default (current) protocol if provided.

The URL will be generated from the remaining keys in the hash, and Routes will compose a query string for any key/value pairs not included in the route definition. For example, if you had a route defined as /events/show/:id and passed in additional parameters to url_for, such as print => true, the extra parameters would be rendered as http://example.com/events/show/1/?print=true.

The default routes setup supports a typical Rails path of controller/action/id, where action and id are optional, with action defaulting to index when not given. Here are some typical url_for statements and their corresponding URLs:

```
url_for :controller => 'posts', :action => 'recent'
  # => 'http://example.com/posts/recent'
url_for :controller => 'posts', :action => 'index'
  # => 'http://example.com/posts'
url_for :controller => 'posts', :action => 'show', :id => 10
  # => 'http://example.com/posts/show/10'
url_for :controller => 'posts', :action => 'show', :id => 10,
  :print => true, :return => false
  # => 'http://example.com/posts/show/10/?print=true&return=false'
```

When generating a new URL, missing values may be filled in from the current request's parameters. For example, url_for :action => 'some_action' will retain the current controller, as expected. This behavior extends to other parameters, including :controller, :id, and any other parameters that are placed into a route's path.

Another handy URL helper is `link_to`, which creates a hyperlink tag of the given name using a URL constructed according to the options hash given. It acts exactly like `url_for`, except that it produces an HTML hyperlink. It's possible to pass a string instead of an options hash to get a link tag that points to any URL. Additionally, if `nil` is passed as a name, the link itself will become the name. Here's the fine print:

```
link_to(name, link={}, options={})
```

This generates an HTML anchor tag using the following parameters:

- The first argument is the link's name.

- The second argument is the URL to link to, given either as a string or a hash of options used to generate the URL.

- The third argument is a hash of options for the resulting tag.

In Ruby, if the last argument to a method is a hash, the curly braces are optional. Most `link_to` helpers will therefore look like this:

```
link_to 'New', :controller => 'events', :action => 'new'
```

or, if using a named route, like this:

```
link_to 'New', new_event_url
```

If you're using all three arguments and are passing in options for HTML (like a `class` or `id` attribute), you need to disambiguate them. Consider the following example where we're using two hashes: one for the URL generation and another for the HTML options:

```
link_to 'New', {:controller => 'articles', :action => 'new'}, :class => 'large'
```

Notice that we need to use the curly braces for at least the first hash to inform Ruby that there are three arguments. Using braces on the last hash of options is still optional, and we could just have easily included them:

```
link_to 'New', {:controller => 'articles', :action => 'new'}, {:class => 'large'}
```

Escaping HTML in Templates

You should always escape any HTML before displaying it in your views to prevent malicious users from injecting arbitrary HTML into your pages (which is how cross-site scripting attacks are often carried out). The rule of thumb is that whenever you have data that is provided by the user, you can't trust it blindly. You need to escape it. This includes your model attributes, as well as parameters. Fortunately, escaping is easy to do.

While not technically a Rails helper, ERb provides a utility method to escape entities in HTML called escape_html. It's aliased to h for short, and it's easy to use. Here's an example:

```
<%=h @event.title %>
<%= link_to h(@event.title), event_url(event) %>
```

Let's update the _event.rhtml partial to make sure everything is properly escaped, as shown in Listing 6-24.

Listing 6-24. *HTML Escaping Added in app/views/events/_event.rhtml*

```
<div class="event item">
  <h3 class="title"><%= link_to h(event.title), event_url(event) %></h3>
  <ul>
    <li><%=h event.occurs_on %></li>
    <li><%=h event.location %></li>
  </ul>
  <div class="description">
    <%=h event.description %>
  </div>
</div>
```

Formatting a Description Field

While we're working with the _event partial, let's improve the display of the description field. One of the aforementioned text helpers is the simple_format helper. The simple_format helper converts text to HTML using simple formatting rules. Two or more consecutive newlines are considered as a paragraph and wrapped in <p> tags. One newline is considered as a line break and a <br /> tag is appended. We'll also use the sanitize helper to make sure there are no gremlins in the description before we format it. Listing 6-25 shows the additions.

Listing 6-25. *Formatting Helpers Added in app/views/events/_event.rhtml*

```
<div class="description">
  <%= simple_format(sanitize(event.description)) %>
</div>
```

Adding Edit Controls

We've applied our authentication filters, but we still don't have a way to prevent users from editing or deleting events that belong to other users. To do this, we'll add a method to the Event model that can tell us whether the event in question is owned by the user we pass in. When we're finished, we'll be able to ask an event whether it's owned by the current user. Open the Event model and add the owned_by? method, as highlighted in bold in Listing 6-26.

Listing 6-26. *Updated app/models/event.rb*

```ruby
class Event < ActiveRecord::Base
  belongs_to :user
  has_many :registrations
  has_many :attendees, :through => :registrations, :source => :user
  has_and_belongs_to_many :categories

  validates_presence_of :title, :location

  after_create :ensure_owner_attends
  validate     :has_not_occurred

  def is_in_the_past?
    occurs_on < Date.today
  end

  def long_title
    "#{title} - #{location} - #{occurs_on}"
  end

  def owned_by?(owner)
    return false unless owner.is_a? User
    user == owner
  end

  protected
    def ensure_owner_attends
      unless attendees.include? user
        attendees << user
      end
    end
```

```
    def has_not_occurred
      errors.add("occurs_on", "is in the past") if occurs_on && is_in_the_past?
    end
end
```

Now let's make use of this method in the _event partial by adding links to edit or delete an event *only* if it's owned by the currently logged-in user, as shown in Listing 6-27.

Listing 6-27. *Links Added in app/views/events/_event.rhtml*

```
<% if event.owned_by? current_user %>
<p>
  <%= link_to 'edit', edit_event_url(event) %> |
  <%= link_to('delete', {:action => 'destroy', :id => event},
              :method => 'delete', :confirm => 'Really?') %>
</p>
<% end %>
```

The final event partial is show in Listing 6-28.

Listing 6-28. *Complete Event Partial in app/views/events_event/rhtml*

```
<div class="event item">
  <h3 class="title"><%= link_to h(event.title), event_url(event) %></h3>

  <% if event.owned_by? current_user %>
  <p>
    <%= link_to 'edit', edit_event_url(event) %> |
    <%= link_to('delete', {:action => 'destroy', :id => event},
                :method => 'delete', :confirm => 'Really?') %>
  </p>
  <% end %>

  <ul>
    <li><%=h event.occurs_on %></li>
    <li><%=h event.location %></li>
  </ul>

  <div class="description">
    <%= simple_format(sanitize(event.description)) %>
  </div>
</div>
```

Adding Custom Helpers

Our events application is looking pretty good, but we would like to make it a bit more user-friendly. One thing we can do is add helpful cancel links beside each of the submit buttons on the forms, so that it's possible for users to back out of editing. We could do this by adding `link_to` helpers beside each button, but then we would need to do this for every form. Since we'll probably want to repeat this pattern throughout the application, this could end up being a lot of duplication. Why don't we create our own custom helper to do this for us? Listing 6-29 shows the method `submit_tag_or_cancel` added to the `application_helper`.

Listing 6-29. *The app/helpers/application_helper.rb File*

```
module ApplicationHelper
  # Creates a submit button with the given name with a cancel link
  # Accepts a hash of options in url_for format to create the cancel link
  def submit_tag_or_cancel(name, options={})
    options = 'javascript:history.go(-1);' if options.empty?
    "#{submit_tag(name)} or #{link_to 'Cancel', options, :class => 'cancel' }"
  end
end
```

Now let's use this helper on our forms. Open both the `new` and `edit` templates and update them so they look like Listings 6-30 and 6-31.

Listing 6-30. *Updated app/views/events/new.rhtml*

```
<h1>New event</h1>

<% form_tag :action => 'create' do %>
  <%= render :partial => 'form' %>
  <%= submit_tag_or_cancel "Create" %>
<% end %>
```

Listing 6-31. *Updated app/views/events/edit.rhtml*

```
<h1>Editing event</h1>

<% form_tag :action => 'update', :id => @event do %>
  <%= render :partial => 'form' %>
  <%= submit_tag_or_cancel 'Save Changes' %>
<% end %>
```

Giving It Some Style

Our events application could use a little varnish. We'll update the layout, apply a style sheet, and add a helper that will make it possible to highlight the tab the user has selected.

Updating the Layout

Let's update the main layout and add in some style hooks that we can target via CSS, as shown in Listing 6-32.

Listing 6-32. *Updated app/views/layouts/application.rhtml*

```
<!DOCTYPE html PUBLIC "-//W3C//DTD XHTML 1.0 Transitional//EN"
  "http://www.w3.org/TR/xhtml1/DTD/xhtml1-transitional.dtd">
<html>
  <head>
    <title>Events</title>
    <meta http-equiv="Content-Type" content="text/html; charset=utf-8" />
    <%= stylesheet_link_tag 'application' %>
    <%= javascript_include_tag :defaults %>
  </head>

  <body>
    <div id="application">
      <div id="header">
        <div class="container">
          <div class="statusbar">
            <div class="logo">
              <strong>Eventalicious!</strong>
            </div>
            <div class="menu">
              <% if logged_in? %>
                logged in as:
                <%= current_user.login %> (<%= link_to 'logout', logout_url %>)
              <% else -%>
                <%= link_to 'signin', login_url %>
              <% end -%>
            </div>
          </div>
          <br style="clear:both;" />
          <div class="tabs">
```

```
        <ul class="navigation">
          <li>
            <%= link_to('Events', events_url) %>
          </li>
          <% if logged_in? %>
          <li>
            <%= link_to('New Event', new_event_url)
          </li>
          <% end -%>
        </ul>
      </div>
    </div>
  </div>

  <div id="page">
    <div id="content">
      <% if flash[:notice] %>
      <div class="flash"><%= flash[:notice] %></div>
      <% end -%>

      <%= yield %>

    </div>
    <hr />
  </div>

  <div id="footer"></div>
  </div>
</body>
</html>
```

Applying a Style Sheet

We've taken the trouble to prepare a simple CSS style sheet that you can apply to make the application look pretty. Listing 6-33 shows the application.css file, which should go in the /public/stylesheets directory.

Listing 6-33. *The public/stylesheets/application.css File*

```css
/**
 * Application.css
 */

@media print { #sidebar { display: none; }
               #content { float: none; width: 90%; } }

body { background: #e1e1e1; font: normal 14px "lucida grande", arial, helvetica,
sans-serif; }

h1,h2,h3,h4,h5,h6 { font-family: helvetica, arial, sans-serif; }

h1 { font-size: 28px; margin-bottom: 15px; }
h2 { font-size: 18px; margin-bottom: 15px; }
h3 { font-size: 17px; margin-bottom: 15px; }

input  { font: normal 12px "lucida grande", verdana, sans-serif; }
textarea { font: normal 12px "bitstream vera sans mono", monaco, "courier new",
courier, monospace; }

code, pre { font: normal 80% "bitstream vera sans mono", monaco, "courier new",
courier, monospace; }

abbr { border: none; }
cite { font-style: normal; }

img { border: none; }

a { text-decoration: underline; padding: 1px; }

a:link,
a:visited { color: #03c; }

a:hover,
a:active { color: #fff; background: #000; text-decoration: none; }

a.cancel,
a.cancel:link,
a.cancel:visited { color: #c00; }
```

```css
a.delete,
a.delete:link,
a.delete:visited { color: #990000; }

hr { visibility: hidden; clear: both; }



/*====================================================
 * Definitions for layout (positioning, width, height, margin, padding)
 *
 * #application
 *    #header
 *    #page
 *       #content
 *       #sidebar
 *    #footer
 ====================================================*/

body { text-align: center; margin: 0; padding: 0; }

#header { float: left; width: 100%; }
#header .container, #footer { width: 800px; margin: auto; }
#header .statusbar { margin: auto; padding: 4px 12px; height: 16px; }
#header .statusbar .logo { float:left; }
#header .statusbar .menu { float:right; }

#page {
  width: 759px;
  margin-left: auto;
  margin-right: auto;
  margin-bottom: 5px;
  padding: 16px;
  text-align: left;
  clear: both;
}

#content { min-height: 360px; }

#footer { text-align: left; clear:both; }
```

```
/*===================================================
 * Definitions for the tabbed interface
 * Tab colors are meant to be customized to your liking
 ===============================================*/

#header .statusbar {
  color: #ddd; background: #333;
  font-size: 11px;
  border-bottom: 2px solid #272727;
}

#header { background: #141414; }

/*-------------------------------------------------
  The background color of all tabs
  ----------------------------------------------*/
#header .tabs li { background: #272727; }

/*-------------------------------------------------
  The text color of all tabs
  ----------------------------------------------*/
#header .tabs a { color: #fff; }

/*-------------------------------------------------
  The hover color of all tabs
  ----------------------------------------------*/
#header .tabs a:hover {
  background: #fff;
  color: #090;
}

/*-------------------------------------------------
  The colors of a selected tab
  ----------------------------------------------*/
#header .tabs a.selected,
#header .tabs a.selected:hover {
  background: #fff;
  color: #222;
  font-weight: bold;
}
```

```css
/*-------------------------------------------------
Tab dimensions and layout properties
-----------------------------------------------*/
#header .tabs ul {
  margin: 0 16px; padding: 0;
  list-style-type: none;
}

#header .tabs li {
  float: left;
  margin: 0; padding: 0;
  display: inline;
}

#header .tabs a {
  float: left;
  margin: 0; padding: 0.5em 1.8em;
  text-decoration: none;
}


/*=================================================
 * Main interface definitions
 * Everything other than 'layout' and 'tabs'
 ===============================================*/


/*-------------------------------------------------
Header
-----------------------------------------------*/

#header .statusbar .menu a:link,
#header .statusbar .menu a:visited { color: #ddd; text-decoration: none; }
#header .statusbar .menu a:hover,
#header .statusbar .menu a:active { color: #fff; }
#header .statusbar .menu a.selected { color: #fff; font-weight: bold; }

#header .statusbar .logo strong { color: #fff; font-size: 12px; }


/*-------------------------------------------------
Page
-----------------------------------------------*/
```

```css
#page { background: #fff;
        border-bottom: 4px solid #ccc;
        border-right:  4px solid #ccc;
        border-left:   4px solid #ccc; }


/*------------------------------------------------
 Content
 -----------------------------------------------*/


#content h1 { margin-top: 0; }

#content ul { list-style: square; padding-left: 20px; }

/* list items */
#content .item {
  margin: 0 0 0.75em 0; padding: 0.6em;
  border: 1px solid #c1c1c1; background: #f6f6f6;
}

#content .item h3 {
  margin: 0 0 0.3em 0; padding: 0.2em 0 0 0.2em;
  border-bottom: 1px dotted #bbb;
  font-size: 20px;
  background: #fff;
}

#content .item h3 a { padding: 3px; }

#content .item h3 a:link,
#content .item h3 a:visited  { color: #000; text-decoration: none; }
#content .item h3 a:hover    { background: none; text-decoration: underline; }


/*------------------------------------------------
 Footer
 -----------------------------------------------*/


#footer { color: #666; font-size: 11px; }

#footer a:link,
#footer a:visited { color: #666; }
#footer a:hover { color: #fff; background: #333; }
```

```
/**
 * Definitions for fields, buttons, and forms
 *
 * Fieldsets can be nested; those containing radio buttons
 * or checkboxes can be given a class of 'radio'
 */


form { margin: 0; padding: 0; }

form label { color: #444; font-weight: bold; margin: 0 0.8em 0.3em 0; }

form input,
form select { font-size: 14px; }

form input[type=submit] { font-size: 15px; }

form input.large {
  font-size: 18px; font-weight: bold;
  width: 80%;
  padding: 4px;
}

form input.huge {
  font-size: 22px; font-weight: bold;
  width: 90%;
  padding: 4px;
}

form textarea {
  width: 97%;
  padding: 0.3em;
  display: block;
  clear: both;
}

/**
 * Rules for ActionPack's generated selectors
 */


/*-------------------------------------------------
 Error explanations
 -----------------------------------------------*/
```

```
div.errorExplanation {
  border: 2px solid #f00;
  padding: 7px 7px 12px 7px;
  margin-bottom: 20px;
  background-color: #fff;
}

div.errorExplanation h2 {
  color: #fff !important; font-size: 12px; font-weight: bold; text-align: left;
  background: #c00;
  padding: 5px 5px 5px 15px;
  margin: -7px;
}

div.errorExplanation p {
  color: #333;
  padding: 5px;
  margin-bottom: 0;
}

div.errorExplanation ul li {
  font-size: 12px;
  list-style: square;
}

/*--------------------------------------------------
  Fields containing errors
  ------------------------------------------------*/

div.fieldWithErrors { display: inline; }

div.fieldWithErrors input,
div.fieldWithErrors select { background: #ffc; }


/*--------------------------------------------------
  Flash Messages
  ------------------------------------------------*/

div.flash {
  font-size: 12px; font-weight: bold;
  color: #390;
```

```
    background: #ffc;
    margin: 0 0 1em 0; padding: 0.3em;
    border: 1px solid #fc0;
}

div.flash h2 { margin-top: 0; }
```

Yikes! That's a lot of CSS! Don't worry, though. We've placed all the code on the book's web site (`http://beginningrails.com`), so you can download the CSS file and copy it into your project. We certainly don't expect you to copy it all by hand.

Highlighting the Selected Tab

We want to apply a CSS class to the navigation links to indicate to the user that the link is selected. To accomplish this, we'll make (you guessed it) a new helper method that wraps `link_to` and adds some functionality, as shown in Listing 6-34. Add this method to the application helper in `app/helpers/application_helper.rb`.

Listing 6-34. *Helper Addition to app/helpers/application_helper.rb*

```
def link_to_with_selected(name, url_options={}, html_options={}, &block)
  css_class = (!!block.call) ? 'selected' : nil
  link_to name, url_options, html_options.merge(:class => css_class)
end
```

This method works by applying the CSS class `selected` to the link if the given block returns `true`. We use it just as we would a regular `link_to` helper, except that we pass it a block. Inside the block, we need to do a little work to figure out whether the link should be selected. To do this, we interrogate the current environment a bit to determine whether we're showing events or adding a new event.

To see this at work, we need to update the application layout in `app/views/layouts/application.rhtml` and use `link_to_with_selected` in place of `link_to` for our tabbed navigation. The relevant code is shown in Listing 6-35.

Listing 6-35. *Updated Navigation List in app/views/layouts/application.rhtml*

```
<ul class="navigation">
  <li>
    <%=
    link_to_with_selected('Events', events_url) do
      params[:controller] == 'events' && params[:action] != 'new'
    end
    %>
```

```
  </li>
  <% if logged_in? %>
    <li>
      <%=
        link_to_with_selected('New Event', new_event_url) do
          params[:controller] == 'events' && params[:action] == 'new'
        end
      %>
    </li>
  <% end %>
</ul>
```

Now when we're in the events controller and *not* on the `new` action (`params[:action]` `!= 'new'`) or when we're *on* the `new` action (`params[:action] == 'new'`), the block yields `true`, and the correct tab is selected. Perfect!

With the CSS in place and with this helper to improve navigation, our application is really starting to look nice. If you've done everything correctly, yours should look a lot like Figure 6-5.

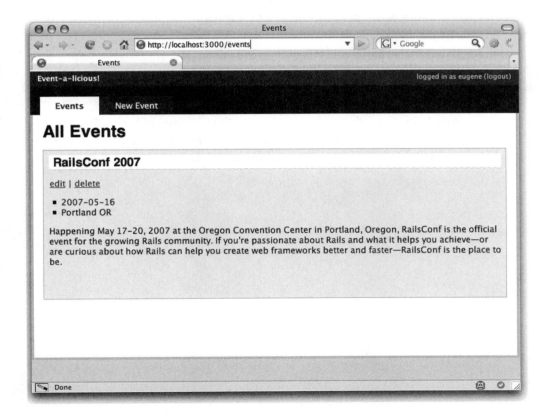

Figure 6-5. *Final layout with CSS*

Summary

This chapter covered a lot of ground. Truth be told, we probably could have made this into two or even three chapters. But as you know by now, Action Pack is a tightly integrated component of Rails, and it would have been difficult to separate the concepts while retaining continuity.

We started this chapter with a general introduction to the components that compose Action Pack, the Rails library responsible for the controller and the view. Then we launched into a controller walk-through, where we built a complete controller from scratch, eliminating our scaffolding dependency. In doing so, you learned about routes, how to generate a controller, how actions relate to views, how to create templates, and how to work with layouts. We introduced Rails' form helpers, and you learned how to easily create forms that integrate with Active Record objects. We also introduced partials, and you learned how to leverage them to keep your templates DRY and easy to maintain.

We discussed a fair number of advanced topics in this chapter as well, including sessions and state, the philosophy of the shared-nothing architecture, and how to protect actions using filters. But we didn't stop there. You also learned how to sanitize HTML to protect your application from defacement from malicious users, and how to create your own helpers to improve your interface. We even took the time to make our application look pretty, sprucing up the layout and adding some CSS.

This chapter gave you your first taste of Rails outside the model. You now have a complete understanding of how Rails divides its concerns and a first-hand look at MVC in action. We started by modeling our domain in Chapters 4 and 5, and now we've completed the first iteration of building a web application around our domain.

We've said it before, but we'll say it again: you should be proud of yourself. At this stage, you know a lot about Rails. The next chapters will build on this knowledge, starting with techniques to improve user interaction by way of a technology known as Ajax.

CHAPTER 7
■ ■ ■

Improving Interaction with Ajax

Ajax represents a fundamental shift in what the web is capable of, and is one of the defining characteristics of the Web 2.0 movement. First coined by Jesse James Garrett in his essay, *Ajax: A New Approach to Web Applications* (http://adaptivepath.com/publications/essays/archives/000385.php), Ajax stands for Asynchronous JavaScript and XML. By enabling web applications to make requests to the server behind the scenes without refreshing the browser, Ajax can dramatically improve the responsiveness and usability of the user interface. It enables live searching, in-place editing, auto-completion, drag and drop re-ordering, and a host of interface techniques that were previously only available to desktop applications. While the acronym might be new, Ajax isn't exactly new. In fact, it's been around for several years. The problem was that it was prohibitively difficult to implement successfully. Times have changed, though, and with modern web frameworks like Rails, Ajax is accessible to the masses.

In this chapter, we're going to focus on Ajax. We'll start by introducing the extensive support available for it in Rails, facilitated largely by two JavaScript libraries that come bundled with Rails: Prototype and script.aculo.us. With that out the way, we'll show you how to leverage these libraries to implement Ajax techniques in your applications. Finally, we'll look at how to use Ruby JavaScript (RJS) templates—Rails' own easy way to use JavaScript.

Ajax and Rails

Ajax is a combination of technologies centered around the XMLHttpRequest object, a JavaScript API originally developed by Microsoft, but now supported in all modern browsers. Of course, you could interface with the XMLHttpRequest API directly, but trust us, it wouldn't be fun. A far better idea is to use one of several libraries that abstract the low-level details and make cross-browser support possible.

One of Rails's main features is the promise to make Ajax easier for web developers to use. To that end, it includes a comprehensive suite of helpers that will enable you to implement event the most advanced techniques with relative ease.

Prototype and Helpers

The primary way by which Rails makes Ajax easier for developers is through the Prototype JavaScript library (http://prototypejs.org). While Prototype is a separate library, it's maintained and distributed as part of the Rails source code, and was copied to your Rails project when you ran the `rails` command. This amazingly well-thought-out library handles most of the work associated with creating the rich, highly interactive applications that characterize the Web 2.0. Even if JavaScript is not your main strength, you'll find that using Prototype makes working with it much easier.

Prototype provides several utility methods that make working with JavaScript better. Perhaps the most important of these is $(), which is more or less a shortcut for the oft-cited `document.getElementById()` function used to access an element in the web page. Truth be told, $() is far more than a simple wrapper `document.getElementById`. The real magic stems from the fact that any elements accessed using it are automatically extended by Prototype.

The biggest part of the Prototype framework is its Document Object Model (DOM) extensions. These DOM extensions allow you to write things like: $('contact'). `removeClassName('active').hide();` to get the element with the ID 'contact', remove the 'active' class name, and hide it from view. The 'contact' element wouldn't have had these methods natively. Because it was fetched using $(), Prototype automatically added them.

Table 7-1 lists some of the most commonly used Prototype utility methods. For a complete list, see http://prototypejs.org/api/utility.

Table 7-1. *Prototype Utility Functions*

Function	Description
$()	Returns the element in the document matching the given ID. For example, $('contact_form'); will return the element with ID contact_form.
$F()	Returns the value of the given form element (such as a text field or selection list) identified by the given ID. For example, $F('email_address'); will return the value of the field with ID email_address.

JavaScript Libraries

When a Rails application is created, the directory public/javascripts is created along with it. This directory is the default location for all the JavaScript files in your application. Five files are added by the rails command, as listed in Table 7-2.

Table 7-2. *JavaScript Files Automatically Created by Rails*

File	Description
prototype.js	The Prototype library.
controls.js, dragdrop.js, and effects.js	The script.aculo.us libraries. Based on Prototype, these include additional functions and visual effects.
application.js	The file to contain application-specific JavaScript code. You'll add JavaScript functions specific to your application to this file.

The files in Table 7-2 are the ones you need to import to use Ajax in your Rails applications.

Using Ajax Helpers

Now that we've explained Prototype's role in Rails, let's get cracking using it in our events application.

To start using Ajax in Rails, the first thing you need to do is import the required JavaScript files and make them available to your templates. The best place to do this is in your application's layout file. Open your layout file in app/views/layouts/application. rhtml and add the javascript_include_tag directive to the head section, as shown in Listing 7-1.

Listing 7-1. *Importing the JavaScript File in app/views/layouts/application.rhtml*

```
<html>
  <head>
    <title>Events</title>
    <meta http-equiv="Content-Type" content="text/html; charset=utf-8" />
    <%= stylesheet_link_tag 'application' %>
    <%= javascript_include_tag :defaults %>
  </head>
  ...
</html>
```

The :defaults option to javascript_include_tag instructs it to include all the JavaScript files from public/javascripts. You can also instruct it to load specific files by providing them as a comma-separated list. For example, to include only the prototype and effects libraries, you would use javascript_include_tag 'prototype', 'effects'.

To run our first examples in this chapter, we'll create a new controller called ajax_ controller, where we can experiment. In reality, you would never create a controller named like this, but for these examples, it will suit us just fine. As always, to create the controller, use the generator:

```
$ ./script/generate controller ajax
```

First, let's try out the link_to_remote helper, which will get us started in Ajax land.

Making Remote Calls with link_to_remote

The link_to_remote helper creates a link that will use Prototype to send an XmlHttpRequest from the browser to the server in the background. The server receives the request as it does any other request, executes the action, and returns the result to the browser. The only real difference between link_to_remote and link_to (which you learned about in Chapter 6) is that the request is sent in the background.

Let's start with link_to_remote in its most basic form. Create a new template in app/views/ajax/index.rhtml, and give it the code shown in Listing 7-2.

Listing 7-2. *The app/views/ajax/index.rhtml File*

```
<%= link_to_remote "Run a controller method using Ajax",
                   :update => "ajax_target",
                   :url    => { :controller => "ajax",
                                :action      => "simple_response" } %>
```

We've given link_to_remote the following information:

- The text of the hyperlink.

- The element to update with the results of the controller action. Here, we've used :update => "ajax_target" to indicate that we want to update the element with an id of "ajax_target".

- The URL to send the request to. Here we've specified a controller and action using :url => { :controller => "ajax", :action => "simple_response" }.

Make sure your local web server is running (./script/server) and point your browser to http://localhost:3000/ajax. You should see something like Figure 7-1. It looks just like a regular hyperlink, but the interesting part is yet to come.

Figure 7-1. *A simple link in your web page*

When you click the link, the browser will make a remote request, invoking the simple_response action on the ajax controller. Of course, nothing will happen yet, because that method does not exist yet.

The rendered output could be any type of output Rails is capable of rendering, as you've seen in the Chapter 6 (on Action Pack). So it could be a new template, some text, a partial, or even nothing. (It will be nothing in rare cases when your application is called but doesn't need to render any output.)

Let's add the simple_response method to the controller so we can see Ajax in action. Go ahead and add the code shown in Listing 7-3 to the ajax controller.

Listing 7-3. *Adding the simple_response Action to app/controllers/ajax_controller.rb*

```
class AjaxController < ApplicationController
  def simple_response
    render :text => "<p>Rails loves Ajax :D</p>"
  end
end
```

We also need to change the view code to include an element where the output from the controller call will be displayed. To make this happen, just add <span id="ajax_target"></span> to index.rhtml, as shown in Listing 7-4.

Listing 7-4. *Adding the Element for Displaying the Ajax Response to app/views/ajax/index.rhtml*

```
<%= link_to_remote "Run a controller method using Ajax",
                :update => "ajax_target",
                :url    => { :controller => "ajax",
                             :action     => "simple_response" } %>
<span id="ajax_target"></span>
```

Once again, run your application, point your browser to http://localhost:3000/ajax, and click the link. The result will look something like Figure 7-2. Notice how the result of the controller action is placed inside the ajax_target element.

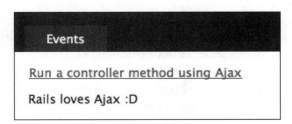

Figure 7-2. *The page after the Ajax action was called*

> **■Tip** Try to use partials in your view code to make snippets of HTML easy to reuse. If you use a few partials to render parts of a page, you can later use the same partial to update specific DOM elements, based on the user input, without having to duplicate view code. See Chapter 6 for details on using partials.

This is Ajax in its simplest form using Rails. The `link_to_remote` function has many parameters that can be used to enhance the functionality of your web page. Let's look at some common options, beginning with displaying a confirmation dialog box.

Displaying a Confirmation Dialog

By using the `:confirm` parameter of `link_to_remote`, you can have a dialog box appear when the user clicks the link. The Ajax call will happen only if the user selects the OK option in the dialog box presented, as shown in Figure 7-3.

Figure 7-3. *The confirmation box from the browser*

The following code (added in `app/views/ajax/index.rhtml`) will display the same link as the previous example, but when clicked, will display the dialog box.

```
<%= link_to_remote "Run a controller method using Ajax",
                :update  => "ajax_target",
                :confirm => "Are you sure you want to make an Ajax call?",
                :url     => { :controller => "ajax",
                              :action     => "simple_response" } %>
```

Positioning the Response

Another optional parameter of `link_to_remote` is the `position` indicator, which can have the values `:before`, `:top`, `:bottom`, or `:after`. This parameter indicates where, relative to the DOM element referenced by the `:update` parameter, the HTML response should be rendered. The following code will display the same link as the original example, but the response from the server will be displayed after the `div` referenced by the `:update` parameter.

```
<%= link_to_remote "Ajax call with position parameter",
                :update   => "ajax_target",
                :position => :after,
                :url      => { :controller => "ajax",
                               :action     => "simple_response" } %>
```

By repeatedly clicking the link, the text returned from the server will be appended just below the `ajax_target` element, as you can see in Figure 7-4.

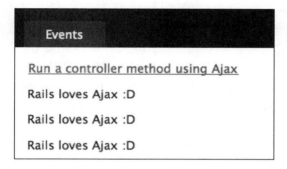

Figure 7-4. *Using the position parameter, results can be inserted after an element.*

Using Callback Methods

The `link_to_remote` function also exposes some event-based callback methods that can be used to respond to events in the life cycle of the Ajax call. These callback methods are very useful if you need to perform any action in your page together with the Ajax call, such as manipulating the HTML.

A special variable called `request` is available to callback methods. This variable holds information about the remote server call. Two of the most used `request` variables are `request.responseText` and `request.status`.

Here's a basic example of using callbacks.

```
<%= link_to_remote "Ajax call with callbacks",
                :update   => "ajax_target",
                :success  => "alert(request.responseText)",
                :failure  => "alert('Something went wrong')",
                :complete => "alert(request.status)",
                :url      => { :controller => "ajax",
                               :action     => "simple_response" } %>
```

In this example, we use the `alert` function, so that after the link is clicked, you can see the raw HTML returned by the remote call and the HTTP return code. If the request can't be fulfilled properly, the `failure` callback is triggered and the user is notified. In this example, we used three different callback methods. The user will see the response text from the server if the call is successful, or an error message if there's a failure. You will also see the status code of the request after the call is complete, regardless of its success or failure.

You can use the callback methods in the situations that best fit your application. Table 7-3 lists the callback methods that can be used in most of the Ajax helpers.

Table 7-3. *Callback Methods for Ajax Helpers*

Callback	Triggered
:loading	When the response from the remote call is loading
:loaded	After the browser is finished loading the response from the remote call
:interactive	When the user can start to interact with the results from the remote call
:success	When the remote request is completed, and the returned code is successful
:failure	When the remote request is completed, but the return code is unsuccessful
:complete	When the remote request is completed, after success or failure

Adding a Progress Indicator

All the functions we've looked at so far are very powerful, but they lack a basic usability component: user feedback. Users tend to get frustrated when an application takes a while to load and there is no indicator to tell them that something is happening. They may assume that the application isn't responding and click the reload button.

We can use the callback methods provided by the Ajax helpers in order to show a visual progress indicator. Replace the previous example we were working on with the code in Listing 7-5.

Listing 7-5. *Replacing the link_to_remote Helper in app/views/ajax/index.rhtml*

```
<%= link_to_remote "Ajax call with indicator",
                :update   => "date",
                :loading  => $('indicator').show(),
                :complete => $('indicator').hide(),
                :url      => { :controller => "ajax",
                               :action     => "current_date" } %>

<div id="date"><p>This text will be replaced.</p></div>
<%= image_tag "indicator.gif", :id => 'indicator', :style => 'display:none' %>
```

The image_tag function will generate HTML for the indicator.gif image, which you can download from the book's sample application code repository, and will change its display property to none, making it invisible to the user when the page loads. In the :loading callback, the indicator image will be displayed. Then it will be hidden after the request is completed, by the :complete callback.

Add the code shown in Listing 7-6 to the ajax controller. This is a new action called current_date, to return the server's current date and time.

Listing 7-6. *Adding the current_date Action to app/controllers/ajax_controller.rb*

```
def current_date
  render :text => "<p>#{Time.now}</p>"
end
```

Now run the example again and click the link. This time, you'll see the progress indicator before the replacement text appears, as shown in Figure 7-5.

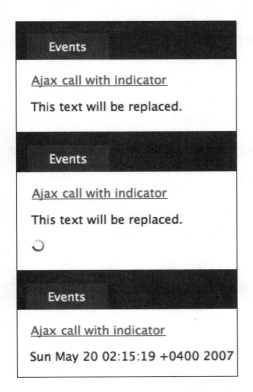

Figure 7-5. *Ajax call with a progress indicator*

■**Note** When you run this example on your local machine, the indicator image might appear and disappear really fast, so if you're not paying attention, you might miss it. When running on a remote server, the request time won't be quite so fast, and you'll appreciate the feedback the indicator provides. If you want to simulate long-running actions in development, you can use Ruby's `sleep` method, which puts a process on hold for the given number of seconds. For example, adding `sleep 2` to the `current_date` action will ensure that you get to see the progress indicator do its thing.

Posting Forms Remotely with `form_remote_tag`

You've seen the power that the `link_to_remote` helper provides, but so far you haven't seen an example that submits data entered by the user to the controller. With the `form_remote_tag` helper, you can create a regular form that sends all the parameters to the server using an `XmlHttpRequest` object; however, your controller will see the upcoming requests as regular `POST` data. On the controller side, it needs no special treatment, so you can use the `params` method, or any other methods, as you usually would.

Let's experiment by allowing users to create a new event using an Ajax call from a form. Start by creating the template for the event form in app/views/ajax/events.rhtml, as shown in Listing 7-7.

Listing 7-7. *Adding an Event Form to app/views/ajax/events.rhtml*

```
Add a new event:
<% form_remote_tag(:update   => "count",
                   :loading  => $('indicator_form').show(),
                   :complete => $('indicator_form').hide(),
                   :url      => { :controller => 'ajax',
                                  :action      => "save_event" }) do %>

  <p>Title<br/><%= text_field 'event', 'title' %></p>
  <p>Location<br/><%= text_field 'event', 'location' %></p>

  <%= submit_tag 'Save' %>
  <%= image_tag 'indicator.gif',
               :id => 'indicator_form', :style => 'display:none' %>
<% end %>

<div id="count">
  <%= render :partial => "events_count" %>
</div>
```

The code for the view contains a form with Title and Location fields, and an HTML div element that contains the number of existing events in the database. As soon as the new event is saved, the div content will be updated with the new number of items in the database.

Notice that we're putting the view code that displays the number of events in its own partial to make it easier to update that value in the browser with the same content. Let's make that partial now, adding the code shown in Listing 7-8 to app/views/ajax/ _events_count.rhtml.

Listing 7-8. *The app/views/ajax/_events_count.rhtml Partial*

```
<p>We have <%= @event_count %> great events in our application!</p>
```

Next, we need to add a couple methods to the controller to make this come together. The new code is shown in Listing 7-9.

Listing 7-9. *Adding count_events and save_event Methods to app/controllers/ ajax_controller.rb*

```ruby
class AjaxController < ApplicationController
  #...

  def events
    count_events
  end

  def save_event
    Event.create(params[:event])
    count_events
    render :partial => "events_count"
  end

  private
    def count_events
      @event_count = Event.count
    end
end
```

The first action is called to load the page the first time; it only needs to display the form and the number of events currently in the database, which we do by creating and calling a private count_events method to expose the @event_count variable to the view.

The save_event action is called when the user clicks the form's Save button. It receives all the parameters from the request, creates a new Event object, and saves it to the database. It then renders the events_count partial, which updates in the DOM object defined by the :update parameter in the form_remote_tag helper.

You can see that Rails deals with both Ajax and regular form submission in the same way, so there's nothing new to learn. This saves us a lot of time, since we can trust that the `params` method will return all the parameters without any extra effort.

Try this out now by running the application and browsing to `http://localhost:3000/ajax/events`. You'll notice that this approach makes adding new events very easy and fast.

To further enhance this example, we can clear the text box with the event title and location after the form is submitted, which will allow users to enter multiple events without having to remove their hands from the keyboard. This technique makes data entry a lot more efficient. To do this, we need to create a new JavaScript function that, in addition to hiding the progress indicator, also changes the text box value to an empty string. Enter the JavaScript code shown in Listing 7-10 into the `app/view/ajax/events.rhtml` file.

Listing 7-10. *Adding JavaScript to app/view/ajax/events.rhtml*

```
<script language="Javascript">
  function eventAdded() {
    $('indicator_form').hide();
    $('event_title').value = '';
    $('event_location').value = '';
    $('event_title').focus;
  }
</script>
```

Now we just need to change the `form_remote_tag` call to use this function in the complete callback call. Change the parameter in the `form_remote_tag` call in the `app/view/ajax/events.rhtml` file to `eventAdded()`, as shown in Listing 7-11.

Listing 7-11. *Changing the form_remote_tag Call in app/view/ajax/events.rhtml*

```
<% form_remote_tag :update   => "count",
                   :loading  => $('indicator_form').show(),
                   :complete => "eventAdded()",
                   :url      => { :controller => 'ajax',
                                  :action     => "save_event" } do %>
```

Figure 7-6 shows how this new form works.

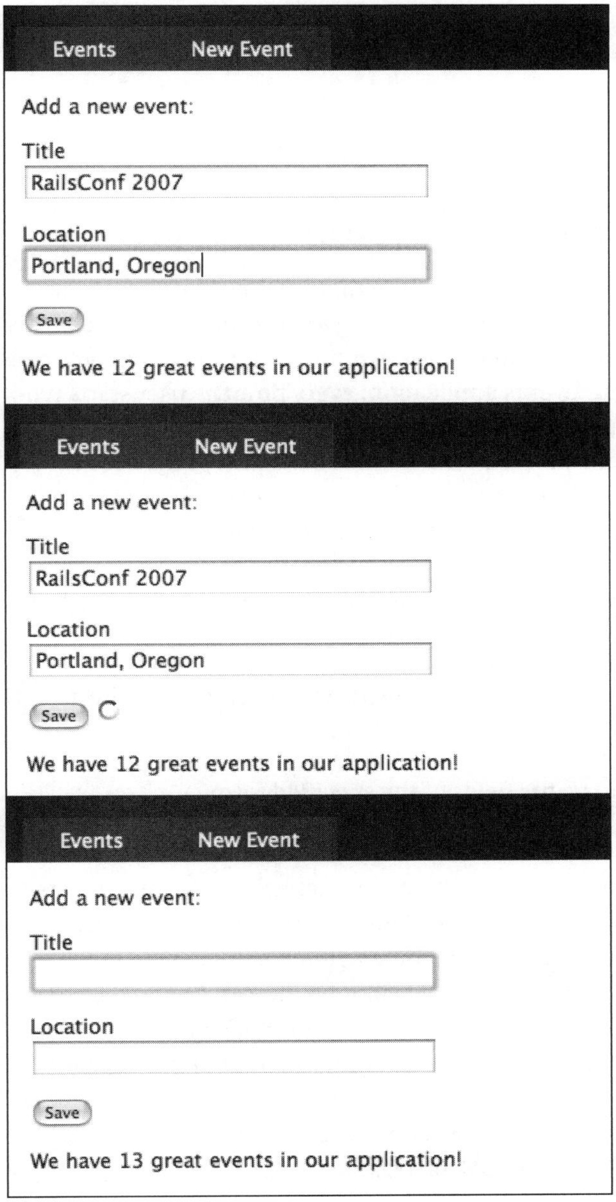

Figure 7-6. *Creating new events*

■**Tip** `link_to_remote`, `form_remote_tag`, `observe_form`, and `observe_field` all accept the same options, including the callback methods.

Polling for Changes with observe_field and observe_form

If you have ever used Gmail (`http://gmail.com`), we're sure that you love the fact that it saves a draft of the email you type as soon as you stop typing for a couple of seconds. This happens automatically in the background, without interrupting your interaction with the application. We can do the same in our events application: every time the user starts typing an event, we can save the incomplete record to a persistent storage system such as the database, cookie, or session variable. If the user's computer crashes or the browser is accidentally closed, we'll be able to retrieve the incomplete item, and bring a great smile to the user's face. We can accomplish this with the `observe_field` and `observe_form` helpers.

The `observe_field` and `observe_form` helpers work in a similar way to each other, but they act on different elements:

- The `observe_field` helper acts on a specific form field, which could be the event title or location.

- The `observe_form` helper acts on all the fields of the specified form.

The output of the `observe_field` and `observe_form` helpers is a call that instantiates a `Form.Observer` object or a `Form.Element.Observer` object, respectively. These are objects provided by Prototype that check the contents of the elements you want to observe.

To demonstrate, we'll use `observe_form` with the new event form we created in the previous section. As the user fills in the form, the page will send information to the server that will be saved to the session. This will bring the added benefit that if users accidentally navigate to a different page, the event they were entering will be kept during the session and will be shown when they return to the event form.

The code to display the form and create the `Observer` object goes in the view. Modify the existing `app/views/events/new.rhtml` file to look like Listing 7-12.

Listing 7-12. *Adding the observe_form Helper to app/views/events/new.rhtml*

```
<h1>New event</h1>

<% form_tag({:action => 'create'}, :id => "event_form") do %>
  <%= render :partial => 'form' %>
  <%= submit_tag_or_cancel "Create" %>
```

```
<% end %>

<%= observe_form "event_form",
                :frequency => 1,
                :update    => {},
                :url       => { :controller => 'events',
                                :action     => "observe_new" } %>
```

In Listing 7-12, we changed the `form_tag` call, adding the `:id` parameter so that the created form can be referenced by our soon-to-exist `Observer` object. We used the `observe_form` helper with a few options, indicating the `id` of the form on which it must act. The first option is the URL of the action to which we'll send an Ajax call. The second option is the frequency, which indicates the amount of time, in seconds, at which changes to the form will be detected. If the frequency value is 0 or less, it will indicate to the `Observer` object that we will use event-based observation, and the Ajax call will be made after the user moves the focus out of each text box.

With those small changes, as you start entering data in the new event form, you'll be able to see that Ajax requests are being made to the server. To prove this, run the application and take a look at the command prompt window where your web server is running. You should see requests like the following:

```
Processing EventsController#observe_new (for 127.0.0.1) [POST]
  Session ID: 51b4bb0ab45219045ff0630128618f7c
  Parameters: {"commit"=>"Create", "tags"=>"",
    "event"=>{"occurs_on(1i)"=>"2007",
    "occurs_on(2i)"=>"5", "title"=>"RailsConf 2008", "occurs_on(3i)"=>"20",
    "url"=>"http://railsconf.com", "description"=>"",
    "location"=>"Nobody knows"},
    "action"=>"observe_new", "categories"=>["1"], "controller"=>"events"}
```

In the controller, we need to create a method to receive the Ajax call from the `Observer` object. The method will be called `observe_new`. Inside this method, we read all the parameters from the request and save the `draft` event to the session. Add the code shown in Listing 7-13 to the `events` controller.

Listing 7-13. *Adding the observe_new Action to app/controllers/events_controller.rb*

```
def observe_new
  session[:event_draft] = current_user.events.build(params[:event])
  render :nothing => true
end
```

The observe_new method creates a new Event object with the request parameters, saves that object to the session, and finishes without rendering a response.

Note If you want to save the event in case the browser somehow crashes while the user is entering the event information, you can take the same approach, but save the draft event to a cookie. The cookies interface is the same as session.

With the event information saved in the session, we need to start using it next time the user tries to add an event. So now we need to change the new action in the events controller, to make it instantiate the @event variable from the session, if there's any data in the session. To achieve this, we only need to call session[:event_draft]. Change the new action in the events controller as shown in Listing 7-14.

Listing 7-14. *Updating the new Action in app/controllers/events_controller.rb*

```
def new
  @event = session[:event_draft] || current_user.events.build
end
```

We're almost finished. The only remaining issue is that after we create an event, we no longer want the application to remember what the draft event looked like; otherwise, the user will get the impression that the changes weren't saved. To prevent this, we just need to make sure that the Event object in the session in cleaned up after we save it to the database. All we need to do is make a small change to the create action to set the event_draft session to nil, as shown in bold in Listing 7-15.

Listing 7-15. *Updating the create Action in app/controllers/events_controller.rb*

```
def create
  @event = current_user.events.build(params[:event])
  @event.categories << Category.find(params[:categories]) ➥
    unless params[:categories].blank?
  @event.tag_with(params[:tags]) if params[:tags]

  if @event.save
    flash[:notice] = 'Event was successfully created.'
    session[:event_draft] = nil
    redirect_to :action => 'index'
  else
```

```
      render :action => 'new'
   end
end
```

To test this, run the application and start trying to create an event. Then navigate away. To your delight, you'll see that clicking the New Event link will take you back to the event form, which will still have the information you typed earlier. This is a feature your users will love to see in forms where a lot of data is entered.

Using script.aculo.us Helpers

Ajax allows for rich user interaction, moving away from the traditional hyperlinked applications of the first-generation web. Script.aculo.us (http://script.aculo.us) is a great JavaScript library, built on top of Prototype, which provides some additional functionality to make the development of Web 2.0 applications easier. For example, it supplies auto-completion and animation effects such as drag-and-drop.

As with Prototype, Rails builds on top of all that JavaScript wizardry and provides a set of helpers that make integrating script.aculo.us into your Rails applications a breeze. We'll go over some of the most useful script.aculo.us helpers in this section.

Implementing Auto-Completion

Auto-completion of text fields is a technique that helps users fill in forms quickly and more accurately, based on data that already exists for specific fields in the database. To see an example of this type of functionality, take a look at Google Suggest (http://google.com/webhp?complete=1). When you type a search term in the search text box, Google Suggest recommends search terms that possibly match the subject you're searching. In Rails, the auto_complete_for helper provides this type of functionality.

Let's enhance our events application by making it suggest possible values for the Location field, saving the user some data-input time. This will help minimize the margin for error in cases where the location is already in the database, while still allowing the user to enter the name of a new location.

To see this in action, start by adding the auto_complete_for declaration to the events controller as shown in Listing 7-16.

Listing 7-16. *Adding the auto_complete_for helper in app/controllers/events_controller.rb*

```
class EventsController < ApplicationController
  before_filter :authenticate, :except => [:index, :show]

  auto_complete_for :event, :location
  #...
end
```

This piece of code will tell the controller to return a list of the existing locations in the database.

By default, auto_complete_for limits the number of returned records to 10 and orders the query by the field being searched. As always, those are sensible defaults; however, if you need to overwrite them, just specify them in the hash passed to auto_complete_for, as follows:

```
auto_complete_for :event, :location, :limit => 25, :order => 'title DESC'
```

On the template side, we need to make an adjustment to how we're dealing with the location field. Fortunately, this is easy. Simply replace the following lines in app/views/events/_form.rhtml:

```
<p><label for="event_location">Location</label><br/>
<%= text_field 'event', 'location' %></p>
```

with the lines shown in Listing 7-17.

Listing 7-17. *Updating app/views/events/_form to Use Auto-Completion*

```
<p><label for="event_location">Location</label><br/>
<%= text_field_with_auto_complete :event, :location %></p>
```

The code is slim, and the result is quite pleasing. As you can see in Figure 7-7, as soon as you start to type the location, the auto_complete_for helper runs a database search to find existing values for the Location field that match what you're typing. If you see the location you want to enter, you can select it (with the mouse or keyboard). If you don't see the location, you can ignore the suggested values and keep typing.

New event

Title

New Event

Categories

Conferences
Parties
Concerts
Readings
Readings

Location

Po

- Portland, Oregon
- Poznan, Poland

Figure 7-7. *Auto-complete text box*

Adding an In-Place Editor

Another classic Ajax technique is the in-place editor. If you are a Flickr (http://flickr.com) user, you know that you can edit the description and title of your own photos by simply clicking the information you want to change. If you have the appropriate permissions, the text transforms into a text box that allows you to view and edit database records on a single page, making the process of editing information simpler and faster.

You can achieve the same level of functionality in Rails with a simple helper called in_place_editor. The in_place_editor helper takes a couple of parameters: the first is the name of the element that contains the data to update, and the second is a hash of options, the most important of which is the URL of the action that will receive the Ajax call.

To demonstrate, we'll make the event location editable in place by the user who owns the event. Open the event detail partial in the app/views/events/_event.rhtml and replace the following code.

```
<ul>
  <li><%=h event.occurs_on %></li>
  <li><%=h event.location %></li>
</ul>
```

with the code shown in Listing 7-18.

Listing 7-18. *Adding the in_place_editor Helper to app/views/events/_event.rhtml*

```
<ul>
  <li><%=h event.occurs_on %></li>
  <li><span id="event_location_<%= event.id %>"><%=h event.location %></span></li>
</ul>

<%= in_place_editor("event_location_#{event.id}",
    :loading_text => "Saving...",
    :cancel_text  => "Cancel",
    :save_text    => "Save",
    :url          => { :action => "update_location",
                       :id      => event }) if event.owned_by? current_user %>
```

First, we needed to wrap the location field in a <span> element and give it a specific id attribute so it can be uniquely identified. To do this, we tacked the event.id (which we know is unique) onto the end of event_location using a little ERb:

```
<span id="event_location_<%= event.id %>">
```

This will give us element id values like event_location_1 and event_location_2. We do the same thing when we tell the in_place_editor method which element we want it to work on:

```
<%= in_place_editor("event_location_#{event.id}", #...) %>
```

The in_place_editor accepts options to customize the text to show on the submit button and the cancel link. We've set these to sensible values: Cancel and Save. Finally, we've used the url option to specify the action to invoke when the Save button is clicked. Also notice how we've applied an if modifier after the call to in_place_editor that checks to make sure the event is owned by the currently logged-in user. This will effectively disable in-place editing for all but the event's owner.

When the Save button is clicked, the in_place_editor form will be serialized and the value in the text box sent to the server in a parameter called value. The controller action needs to process the value and return the updated value in the body of the response. To implement this, we need to create an update action on the controller to handle the request, which is what we'll add next.

When implementing the update action used with the in_place_editor, we need to pay attention to a specific convention: the action should be named update_*field_name*, where *field_name* is the name of the field to be updated. Since we're updating the location field, our method will be called (you guessed it) update_location. Add the update_location action to the events controller, as shown in Listing 7-19.

Listing 7-19. *Adding the update_location Action in app/controllers/events_controller.rb*

```
def update_location
  Event.update(params[:id], {:location => params[:value]})
  render :text => params[:value]
end
```

This will update the event whose id matches that of params[:id] with the changed location value before rendering the entered value using render :text—effectively, replacing the previous location with the newly entered value.

Now that we have everything set up, it's time to enjoy the fruits of our labor and see the in-place editor in action. With the application running, reload the events listing and select an event. When you click the event location, it should change to a text field that allows you to edit and save the location right there on the page, as shown in Figure 7-8.

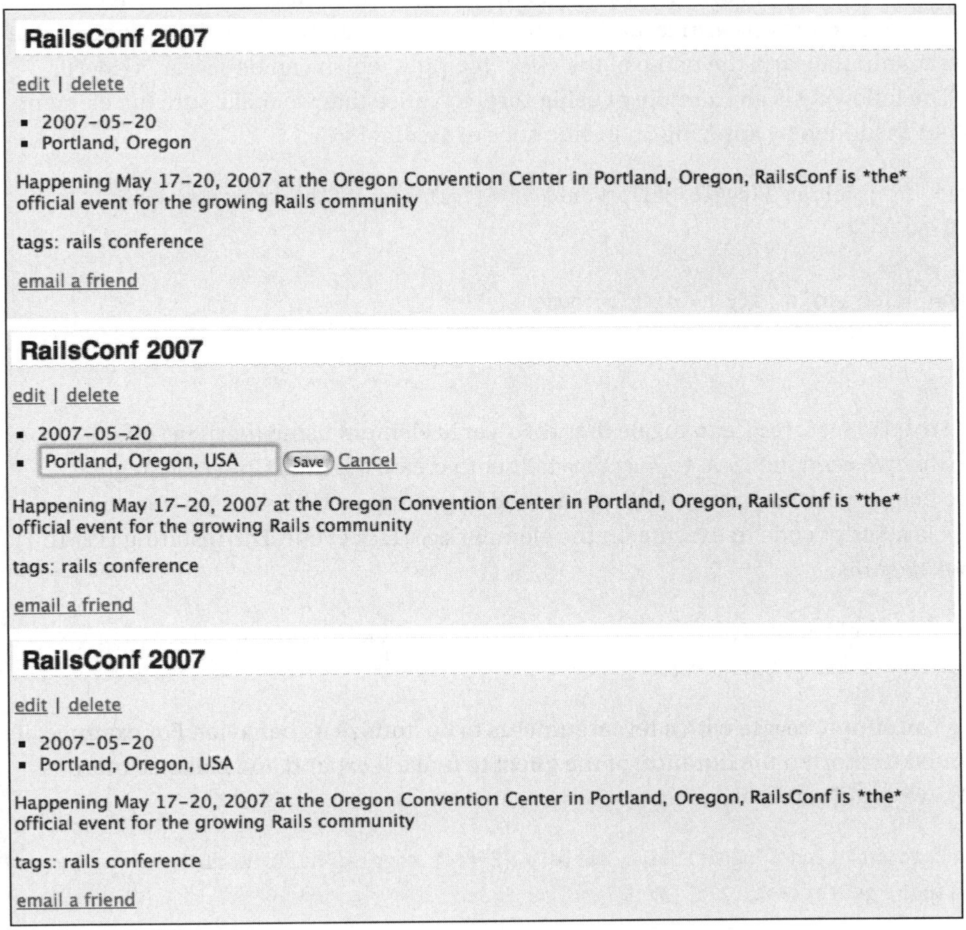

RailsConf 2007

edit | delete

- 2007-05-20
- Portland, Oregon

Happening May 17–20, 2007 at the Oregon Convention Center in Portland, Oregon, RailsConf is *the* official event for the growing Rails community

tags: rails conference

email a friend

RailsConf 2007

edit | delete

- 2007-05-20
- Portland, Oregon, USA   (Save) Cancel

Happening May 17–20, 2007 at the Oregon Convention Center in Portland, Oregon, RailsConf is *the* official event for the growing Rails community

tags: rails conference

email a friend

RailsConf 2007

edit | delete

- 2007-05-20
- Portland, Oregon, USA

Happening May 17–20, 2007 at the Oregon Convention Center in Portland, Oregon, RailsConf is *the* official event for the growing Rails community

tags: rails conference

email a friend

Figure 7-8. *In-place editor in action*

Adding Visual Effects

The script.aculo.us library also includes a rich, cross-browser animation framework that makes creating fancy effects a breeze. Like the rest of script.aculo.us, the animation framework is built on top of Prototype and includes several handy prebuilt functions. Let's take a quick look at some of the effects you can create.

Toggling Visibility

One of the rules of good interface design is to make things snappy. That is to say, the interface should be responsive and quick to load. A good way to achieve this is by loading elements (like forms or content areas) onto the page in advance, but hiding them until they're ready to be used. By doing this, you can toggle their visibility using JavaScript on the client side, which is several times faster than reloading the page from the server.

To make hiding and revealing elements easier, the script.aculo.us Effect class includes the functions show, hide, and toggle. You simply specify the id of the element you want to manipulate and the name of the effect to apply, which can be appear, slide, or blind. The following is an example of using toggle. Notice that we make sure the element starts out as hidden by applying an in-line style of display:none.

```
<%= link_to_function 'Toggle Hello World', "Effect.toggle('hello_world',
    'blind')" %>


<div id="hello_world" style="display:none">
  <p>Hello World!</p>
</div>
```

We used Effect.toggle to toggle the hello_world element using the blind effect. Notice that we used the link_to_function helper to create the link. Unlike the regular link_to helper, which accepts a URL or method to generate a URL, link_to_function accepts JavaScript code to execute on the element's onclick event. The resulting HTML will look like this:

```
<a href="#" onclick="Effect.toggle('hello_world', 'blind'); return false;">
      Toggle Hello World</a>
```

We can supply toggle with a few arguments to customize its behavior. For example, if we wanted to shorten the duration of the effect to make it expand and collapse more quickly, we could set the duration option:

```
<%= link_to_function 'Toggle Hello World', "Effect.toggle('hello_world',
    'blind', {duration: .2})" %>
```

Tip Script.aculo.us has a set of core effects that can be combined to create new visual effects, and it also has a set of combination effects that are based on the core effects. Take a look at the Combination Effects Demo page at `http://wiki.script.aculo.us/scriptaculous/show/CombinationEffectsDemo` to learn more about all the different options available.

Using the Yellow Fade Technique

In some situations, you might want to direct the user's attention to a recently updated area of your page. This is a common practice when using Ajax, since lack of a page refresh leaves little to indicate that something has happened. 37signals pioneered a technique dubbed the Yellow Fade Technique, which creates a yellow highlight that briefly identifies a change to the page before fading away after a second or two.

Script.aculo.us implements the Yellow Fade Technique using the `highlight` function. You can apply it in the same fashion as the `toggle` effect we looked at in the previous section. For example, to highlight an area of the page immediately after it loads, just add the following anywhere in your template:

```
<script type="text/javascript">
  new Effect.Highlight('some_element');
</script>
```

Rails makes it even easier to attach visual effects, however, by way of the `visual_effect` helper. This is actually a Ruby method that returns the JavaScript necessary to render the effect. Here's an example that will apply the `highlight` effect to a specific element in response to clicking a link.

```
<div id="higlightable">
  <%= link_to_function 'Click Me!',
        visual_effect(:highlight, 'higlightable', :duration => 2.0) %>
</div>
```

We could just have easily supplied the JavaScript directly, as we did with the `toggle` example, but using the `visual_effect` helper lets us stick to pure Ruby, instead of dropping down to JavaScript.

Using RJS Templates

You've seen that Rails' support for Ajax is comprehensive and fairly simple to use. However, as the complexity of web pages grows with the number of elements that need to be updated due to user interaction, the model we described becomes very complicated and starts to show signs of weakness.

To make managing complex Ajax interactions easier, a major feature was introduced (in Rails 1.1): Ruby JavaScript (RJS) templates. RJS templates allow you to express the response to user interactions in pure Ruby code, which is then transformed into JavaScript before being sent to the browser. Unlike conventional templates that are used to render the results of an action, RJS templates generate instructions on how to modify an already rendered page. This approach has the following advantages:

- You can express yourself using pure Ruby.

- You can extract Ajax responses from your ERb templates, moving them to a separate file, and making them easier to debug and maintain.

- You can call any Rails methods and assign them to JavaScript variables.

Implementing RJS in Templates

Let's go back to one of our earlier Ajax examples and implement it using RJS. When we were experimenting with the `ajax` controller, we used the `form_remote_tag` helper to create a new event using Ajax. If you'll recall, we defined callbacks to show and hide a progress indicator while the form was being submitted. Here's what it looked like:

```
Add a new event:
<% form_remote_tag(:update   => "count",
                   :loading  => $('indicator_form').show(),
                   :complete => $('indicator_form').hide(),
                   :url      => { :controller => 'ajax',
                                  :action     => "save_event" }) do %>

  <p>Title<br/><%= text_field 'event', 'title' %></p>
  <p>Location<br/><%= text_field 'event', 'location' %></p>

  <%= submit_tag 'Save' %>
  <%= image_tag 'indicator.gif',
                :id => 'indicator_form', :style => 'display:none' %>
<% end %>
```

```
<div id="count">
  <%= render :partial => "events_count" %>
</div>
```

This is all well and good, but you can see how it could get pretty unwieldy if we needed to do more than a few things on :loading and :complete. What if, in addition to showing and hiding the progress indicator, we wanted to highlight the updated count element, reset the form elements, and place the cursor in the Title field? Sure, we could probably pull it off, but it wouldn't look very pretty. RJS to the rescue.

Just like ERb templates (with the .rhtml extension), RJS templates correspond to controller actions. Our form submits to the save_event action, so we'll create a template to respond to that action, called save_event.rjs, and save it in app/views/ajax. As expected, it will be executed in response to the save_event action.

In RJS templates, you have access to a special variable named page, which represents the web page on which you'll be acting. The responsibility of the RJS file is to manipulate page elements after an Ajax request, as we did with the :update parameter. The RJS template has more flexibility, as you can access any element on the page, instead of being constrained by the element indicated by the :update parameter.

Let's get down to coding the template now. We'll start by outlining what we want the response to be, and then we'll implement the necessary RJS. After submitting the form, we want to do the following things on the rendered page:

- Update the count element.

- Highlight the count element to show that a change has taken place.

- Clear the values from the title and location form elements.

- Place the cursor inside the title element so it's ready for the next input.

- Hide the status indicator.

The RJS required to implement these actions is shown in Listing 7-20.

Listing 7-20. *The save_event RJS Template in app/views/ajax/save_event.rjs*

```
# Replace the count div
page.replace_html 'count', :partial => 'events_count'
page.visual_effect :highlight, 'count'

# Clean up the UI
page['event_title'].value = ''
page['event_location'].value = ''
page['event_title'].focus
```

```
# Hide the indicator image
page['indicator_form'].hide
```

The first line tells the RJS engine to generate JavaScript code to replace the HTML element count with the contents of event_count partial. The second line creates the code to highlight the recently changed element. Notice that we're writing all this in pure Ruby. The page variable gives us access to the rendered page, and we can call methods on it.

You can also use the page object to access elements by index. That's how we're manipulating the field values and the indicator image.

```
page[element_id] # => accesses the specified element
```

We reset the value of the event_title element using page['event_title'].value = ''. Similarly, we focus it using page['event_title'].focus. The page object also has several methods you can use to interact with your web pages, as listed in Table 7-4.

Table 7-4. *Methods Available to the Page Object in RJS Templates*

Method	Description	Example
replace	Replaces the entire element with content supplied	page.replace :content, '<div id="content">Howdy!</div>'
replace_html	Replaces the inner HTML of the given element with the content supplied	page.replace_html :content, :partial => 'content'
insert_html	Inserts HTML at the specified position relative to the given element	page.insert_html :top, 'Total', content_tag(:h3, "$150.00")
hide	Hides the given element or elements if they are visible	page.show 'savings'
show	Shows the given element or elements if they are hidden	page.show 'savings', 'account'
select	Returns an array of elements that match the given CSS selector	page.selector '#items li'
reload	Replaces the contents of the element with the output of a partial with the same name	page.reload 'content'

Our RJS template is in place, but we still need to update the call to form_remote_tag now that we've offloaded most of its work. The modified code is shown in bold in Listing 7-21.

Listing 7-21. *The Updated events Template in app/views/ajax/events.rhtml*

```
Add a new event:
<% form_remote_tag(:loading => $('indicator_form').show(),
                   :url     => { :controller => 'ajax',
                                 :action     => "save_event" }) do %>

  <p>Title<br/><%= text_field 'event', 'title' %></p>
  <p>Location<br/><%= text_field 'event', 'location' %></p>

  <%= submit_tag 'Save' %>
  <%= image_tag 'indicator.gif',
                :id => 'indicator_form', :style => 'display:none' %>
<% end %>

<div id="count">
  <%= render :partial => "events_count" %>
</div>
```

Notice that we've removed all but the `:loading` callback. This is important—if you're switching from in-line updates to RJS, remember to remove the `:update` parameter from your helper calls. If you don't, the in-line `:update` will clobber the one performed by the RJS.

Implementing RJS in the Controller

In some situations, your RJS file can be just a few lines of code, or it could even be a single call, and it might seem like overkill to create and manage a new template with such a small amount of code. In those cases, you can implement RJS responses directly from the controller action using `render :update`. If we were so inclined, we could do away with the `save_event.rjs` template and implement the entire response in the `save_event` action. Here's how it would look:

```
def save_event
  current_user.events.create(params[:event])
  count_events

  render :update do |page|
    # Replace the count div
    page.replace_html 'count', :partial => 'events_count'
    page.visual_effect :highlight, 'count'

    # Clean up the UI
```

```
      page['event_title'].value = ''
      page['event_location'].value = ''
      page['event_title'].focus

      # Hide the indicator image
      page['indicator_form'].hide
    end
end
```

Deciding whether to put RJS code in its own file or on the controller might come down to personal preference, so try both approaches and stick with the one you like best. For RJS responses that are long, we recommend that you create an RJS template, to help keep your controller clean of view code and easy to read. For RJS responses that are one or two lines long, keeping the code in the controller may save you some time when coding.

For more information about RJS templates, including usage examples, be sure to check out the Rails API documentation at http://api.rubyonrails.org/classes/ ActionView/Helpers/PrototypeHelper/JavaScriptGenerator/GeneratorMethods.html.

Summary

To be sure, Ajax is a large topic. Entire books and conferences are devoted to this subset of technology alone, so it goes without saying that we've only scratched the surface here. Still, in short order, you've learned the basics about implementing Ajax in your Rails applications, and you know where to go when you need to dig deeper.

We started by introducing the Prototype library and highlighting a few of its finer points. These include its various shortcuts for accessing elements and input fields, among other features. We also showed you how to include all the necessary JavaScript libraries, including your own application-specific JavaScript functions (application.js) using javascript_include_tag :defaults.

You learned how to make remote Ajax calls using link_to_remote, and how to post forms remotely using form_remote_tag. We also covered polling the page for changes using observe_field and observe_form.

We introduced the script.aculo.us library and showed you how it integrates with Rails to make implementing seemingly complex features, like auto-complete and in-place editing, a snap.

Finally, you learned about RJS templates and how they enable you to harness the power of Ruby to do your JavaScript bidding, be it from templates or from the controller.

At this stage, you have a solid grasp of the Action Pack side of web development with Rails. Next, we'll look at how you can conquer another common component of web application development: sending mail.

CHAPTER 8

■ ■ ■

Sending and Receiving Mail

It's a rare web application that doesn't need to send mail from time to time. For example, you may want to send messages to welcome users who sign up to your site, relay passwords, or confirm orders placed with an online store. Rails ships with a library called Action Mailer, which provides developers with an easy-to-use yet powerful tool to handle email.

In this chapter, we'll explain how Action Mailer works and how to use it in your applications. We'll start by describing how to configure it, and then we'll show you a few examples of how to send email in various formats. In addition to sending mail, Action Mailer is also capable of *receiving* mail, an advanced topic that we'll touch on briefly.

Setting Up Action Mailer

Like Active Record and Action Pack, Action Mailer is another one of the components that make up the Rails framework. It works much like the other components of Rails: mailers are implemented as models, and mailer templates are implemented as views. Because it's integrated into the framework, it's easy to set up and use, and requires very little configuration to get going.

When you send email using an email client such as Outlook or a web-based email application like Gmail or Yahoo Mail, your messages are sent via a mail server. Unlike a web server, Rails doesn't provide a built-in mail server. You'll need to tell Action Mailer where your email server is located and how to connect to it. This sounds a bit complicated, but it's really quite easy. Depending on what kind of computer you're using, you might have a mail server built in (this is true of most UNIX systems). If not, you can use the same server that you use to process your regular email. If this is the case, you can find your server information in your email client settings, as provided by your Internet service provider (ISP), or in the settings section of your web-based email application, like Gmail.

Configuring Mail Server Settings

Before you can send email from your Rails application, you need to tell Action Mailer how to communicate with your mail server. Action Mailer can be configured to send mail using either `sendmail` or an SMTP server. SMTP stands for Simple Mail Transfer Protocol and is the core Internet protocol for relaying mail messages between servers. If you're on Linux, OS X, or any other UNIX-based system, you're in luck. You can use `sendmail`, and as long as it's in the standard location (`/usr/bin/sendmail`), you don't need to configure anything. If you're on Windows, or if you want to use SMTP, you have some work to do.

Action Mailer options are set at the class level on `ActionMailer::Base`. The best place to set these options is in your `environment.rb` file, located in the `config` directory of your application. Doing your configuration in `config/environment.rb` will ensure that your settings apply for all environments. Remember, though, that settings in any of the environment-specific configuration files, (`config/environments/*.rb`) take precedence over the global `environment.rb`, so it's easy to configure Action Mailer to use different settings depending on the environment.

We're going to describe how to set up Action Mailer to use SMTP, since it will work on all systems. To do this, we set the `delivery_method` option to `:smtp` and supply the SMTP settings via the `smtp_settings` option. The `smtp_settings` method expects a hash of options, all of which are shown in Table 8-1.

Table 8-1. *Server Connection Settings*

Setting	Description
address	The address of your mail server. The default is `localhost`.
port	The port number of your mail server. The default is port 25.
domain	If your email server responds to different domain names, you might need to specify your domain name here.
authentication	If your mail server requires authentication, you need to specify the authentication type here. This can be one of `:plain`, `:login`, `:cram_md5`.
user_name	The username you'll use to authenticate when you connect to the mail server, if your server requires authentication.
password	The password you'll use to authenticate when you connect to the mail server, if your server requires authentication.

Listing 8-1 shows a typical configuration for a server that requires authentication. You can use this sample configuration as a starting point to configure your connection. You'll need to change each of the settings (authentication, username, password, and address) to connect to your own SMTP server. Again, if you're using `sendmail` as the delivery method, you don't need to set this up at all; everything should "just work" out of the box.

Listing 8-1. *Sample Action Mailer Configuration Using SMTP, in config/environment.rb*

```
ActionMailer::Base.delivery_method :smtp
ActionMailer::Base.smtp_settings = {
  :address        => 'mail.example.com',
  :authentication => :login,
  :user_name      => 'sender@example.com',
  :password       => 'secret'
}
```

Include your completed configuration code at the bottom of `config/environment.rb`, make sure you restart your server if it's running, and your application will be ready to send mail.

Configuring Application Settings

In addition to the mail server settings, Action Mailer has a set of configuration parameters that can be tweaked to make the library behave in specific ways according to the application or the environment. We're going to stick with the defaults here, so we don't need to set up any special application settings. For reference, Table 8-2 lists the most common configuration options. Just like the server settings, these can be specified in `config/environment.rb` or in the environment-specific configuration files (`config/environments/*.rb`).

Table 8-2. *Common Action Mailer Application Settings*

Option	Description
`template_root`	Indicates the base folder from which template references will be made. The default is `app/views`.
`raise_delivery_errors`	Allows you to indicate whether you want errors to be raised when an error occurs while trying to deliver email. This should be set to `true` in production (in `config/environments/production.rb`) and `false` in development (in `config/environments/development.rb`).
`perform_deliveries`	Indicates whether messages should really be delivered to the mail server.
`deliveries`	Keeps an array of all delivered email when the delivery method is set to `:test`. This is useful when you're in testing mode.
`default_charset`	Specifies the default character set to be used when sending messages. The default is `UTF-8`.
`default_content_type`	Specifies the default content type that will be used for outbound mail. The default is `text/plain`.

■**Note** When you create a new Rails application, the configuration files automatically use sensible defaults for each of the development, test, and production environments. Take a quick look in `config/ environments` to see how Action Mailer behaves in development, production, and test mode to make sure you understand your application's behavior.

Sending Email

Now that we have Action Mailer configured, it's time to see it in action. We'll explore all the possibilities in the Action Mailer world, starting with basic text-only email, and then adding extra email options such as attachments.

To demonstrate Action Mailer, we'll enhance our events application by allowing our users to send email to their friends so that they can share information about a specific event. This is a common feature in today's web applications, affectionately referred to as "send to friend."

By now, you know that Rails provides helpful generators to get started writing your own code. You've seen generators in action when we created models and controllers in previous chapters. The Mailer generator works just like the other generators.

Enter the following command to generate the `EventMailer` and a method named `email_friend`.

```
$ ./script/generate mailer EventMailer email_friend
```

```
exists   app/models/
create   app/views/event_mailer
exists   test/unit/
create   test/fixtures/event_mailer
create   app/models/event_mailer.rb
create   test/unit/event_mailer_test.rb
create   app/views/event_mailer/email_friend.rhtml
create   test/fixtures/event_mailer/email_friend
```

The generator created a mailer class named `EventMailer`, containing the `email_friend` method we specified on the command line. Notice that Action Mailer classes are created in the `app/models` directory; however, `EventMailer` is a subclass of the `ActionMailer::Base` class, making it completely different from the Active Record models located in the same folder. The generator also created a template file in the `views` directory (`app/views/ event_mailer` that corresponds to the `email_friend` method (action) we'll use to set up the mailer message.

Listing 8-2 shows the `EventMailer` class located in `app/models`. You can see that the `email_friend` method has some code that will be the starting point for most of the methods you'll be writing using Action Mailer.

Listing 8-2. *EventMailer Class, in app/models/event_mailer.rb*

```
class EventMailer < ActionMailer::Base
  def email_friend(sent_at = Time.now)
    @subject    = 'EventMailer#email_friend'
    @body       = {}
    @recipients = ''
    @from       = ''
    @sent_on    = sent_at
    @headers    = {}
  end
end
```

In the method body, you can see a set of instance variables that will be used to specify the various headers of the message. Table 8-3 lists the available instance variables you use to configure an individual message.

Table 8-3. *Mailer Instance Variables*

Variable	Description	Example
@subject	The subject of the email message to be sent.	@subject = "ActionMailer is powerful"
@body	A hash used to expose objects from the model to the email template. The @body variable will be used most of the time, enforcing the use of the MVC pattern.	@body[:time] = Time.now
@recipient	A string or array of email addresses to which the message will be sent.	@recipients = "friend@example.com"
@from	A string specifying the sender of the email message.	@from = "sender@example.com"
@sent_on	The date header. The default is the current date.	@sent_on = Time.now
@headers	A hash of specific headers to set for the message.	@headers['X-Complaints-To'] = "abuse@example.com"
@cc	A string or array of email addresses to carbon-copy with the message.	@cc = "admin@example.com"
@bcc	A string or array of email addresses to blind-carbon-copy with the message.	@bcc = ["support@example.com", "sales@example.com"]
@charset	A string that specifies the character set to use for the message. The default is UTF-8.	@charset = 'iso-8859-1'
@content_type	A string that specifies the content type for the message. The default is "text/plain", but can be set automatically in some cases (see the "Adding Multiple Parts to Messages" section later in this chapter).	@content_type = 'text/html'

The mailer generator created a template named after the action in the `EventMailer` class in the `/app/views/event_mailer` folder: `email_friend.rhtml`. This is the template that will be used to generate the body of the email sent when using the `email_friend` method. This template works similar to the templates used for regular views in Action Pack. It is an ERb file, which can contain text and markup mixed with some Ruby code. It also has the same one-to-one relationship between action and view exhibited by Action Pack—each action in your mailer class will expect one template in the `app/views` directory.

Handling Basic Email

Let's start enhancing our events application by adding "invite a friend" functionality to the event page. The first iteration will be a very basic example that sends a text email message containing a brief message and the current server date.

We want to show users a link that will toggle the display of a form where they can enter the email address of the friend to whom they want to send a message. Let's update the view now to include the new link directly after the event description. Add the code shown in Listing 8-3 to the end of the event partial in `app/views/events/_event.rhtml`.

Listing 8-3. *Invite a Friend Functionality Added to app/views/events/_event.rhtml*

```
<p>
  <%= link_to_function "invite a friend", "Element.toggle('email_friend')" %>
</p>

<div id="email_friend" style="display:none">
  <% form_tag :action => 'email_friend', :id => event do %>
    <p>Your Name:<br />
    <%= text_field_tag 'name' %></p>

    <p>Your friend's email:<br />
    <%= text_field_tag 'email' %></p>

    <p><%= submit_tag 'Send email' %></p>
  <% end %>
</div>
```

Now when you go to any events page, you'll see a link to invite a friend. Since we don't want to show the form all the time, we enclosed it in a hidden `<div>` tag. If users are interested in sending an email to a friend, they can click the link, and the form will be revealed through the help of some clever JavaScript. The end result is shown in Figure 8-1.

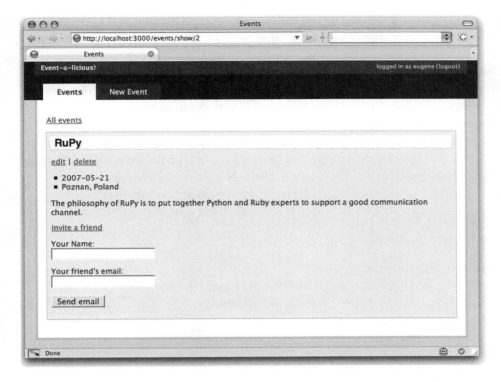

Figure 8-1. *Invite a friend form*

The interface is ready to go, but our events controller doesn't know how to handle this request yet. Our form is configured to submit to an action called email_friend, but that action doesn't exist. So, let's update the events controller and add the email_friend method shown in Listing 8-4.

Listing 8-4. *email_friend Action Added to app/controllers/events_controller.rb*

```
def email_friend
  event = Event.find(params[:id])
  EventMailer.deliver_email_friend(params[:email])
  flash[:notice] = 'Your friend has been notified about this event'
  redirect_to event_url(event)
end
```

The action we just added is short and concise, but there's something that deserves a closer look. To perform the delivery, we call a class method on the EventMailer class called deliver_email_friend; however, this method doesn't actually exist in the EventMailer class. The magic is all in the Action Mailer deliver class method. By calling `deliver_email_friend`, Action Mailer will call the `email_friend` method in the `EventMailer` class and generate an email message as per that method. After the email message is created, it is passed to the `deliver` method, which performs the actual delivery.

This is important. Every time you create a mail action, you call it directly from the mailer class (in our case, `EventMailer`), prefixed with `deliver_`. If you had a mailer class called `Notifier` and a mail action called `invitation`, you would call it using `Notifier.deliver_invitation`.

Before we try this out, our `email_friend` method still needs a bit of work. We need to augment it so that it sets a meaningful title and uses the `email` parameter we're collecting from the form and passing into the method. Listing 8-5 shows the changes.

Listing 8-5. *Subject, Recipients, and From Added to email_friend, in app/models/event_mailer.rb*

```
def email_friend(recipient)
  @subject    = '[Eventalicious] Check out this great event'
  @from       = 'Eventalicious <events@example.com>'
  @recipients = recipient
  @sent_on    = Time.now
  @body       = {}
  @headers    = {}
end
```

Notice how we've added a required argument called `recipient`, which we use to set the `@recipients` variable. We've also filled out the `@subject` and `@from` variables to make them more meaningful.

Next, we want our email message to have some sort of formatting and include the URL of our application. Let's change the template file located in `app/views/event_mailer/email_friend.rhtml` and make it look like Listing 8-6.

Listing 8-6. *event_mailer Template, in app/views/event_mailer/email_friend.rhtml*

```
One of your friends thinks you'll like the events we have listed.
Come check the event on our web site at http://eventalicio.us
Sent on: <%= Time.now %>
```

Finally, we can give this a try in a browser. Fill out the email form using your own email address, so that you can see what the email message will look like. If all goes according to plan, you should receive a message that looks something like this:

```
Date: Tue, 1 May 2007 05:22:10 +0400
From: Event Application <events@todo.com>
To: recipient@example.com
Message-Id: <44e978a7cad5e_1f5f7ba03bf@localhost.tmail>
Subject: Check out this great event
Content-Type: text/plain; charset=utf-8

One of your friends thinks you'll like the events we have listed.
Come check the event on our web site at http://eventalicio.us
Sent on: Tue May 01 05:22:10 +0400 2007
```

This is a plain text message, the default content type. In the next section, we'll show you how to send email messages that use rich, HTML formatting.

Sending HTML Email

So far, our email message is pretty plain. To make it a bit more interesting and informative, we'll add a link to the specific event being recommended and include the sender's name in the message. We'll also make it more visually appealing for users with rich email clients (like Gmail) by adding some HTML formatting. We'll start by redefining the email_friend mailer action in app/models/event_mailer.rb.

To indicate that we're sending an HTML-formatted message, we need to set the @content_type variable inside the email_friend method body. We also want to accept a few extra arguments to the method, specifically, the sender's name and the event in question. Listing 8-7 shows the required changes to email_friend.

Listing 8-7. *Sender and Event Added to email_friend, in app/models/event_mailer.rb*

```
class EventMailer < ActionMailer::Base
  def email_friend(recipient, sender_name, event)
    @subject      = '[Eventalicious] Check out this great event'
    @from         = 'Eventalicious <events@example.com>'
    @recipients   = recipient
    @content_type = 'text/html'
    @body         = { :sender_name => sender_name, :event => event }
  end
end
```

In addition to the new arguments, we've also modified the subject line, used the @content_type variable to set the content type to text/html (instead of text/plain), and added some options to the @body hash that we can use in our template.

Any key/value pairs you set in the @body hash will be available in your mailer template via instance variables named after the given keys. In our case, we'll have access to the @sender_name variable and the @event variable, initialized with the sender_name and event arguments, respectively.

Now that the mailer method can accept these additional arguments, the next thing to do is pass them in when we invoke the mailer from the controller, as shown in Listing 8-8.

Listing 8-8. *Additional Arguments Passed to the Mailer, in app/controllers/events_controller.rb*

```ruby
def invite_friend
  event = Event.find(params[:id])
  EventMailer.deliver_email_friend(params[:email], params[:name], event)
  flash[:notice] = 'Your friend has been notified about this event'
  redirect_to event_url(event)
end
```

Finally, we need to update the email template. We want to give it some HTML formatting and make sure it uses the new variables we've set up: @sender_name and @event. The modified template, located in app/views/event_mailer/email_friend.rhtml, should look like Listing 8-9.

Listing 8-9. *HTML email_friend Template, in app/views/event_mailer/email_friend.rhtml*

```html
<html>
<body>
<p>
  One of your friends, <%= @sender_name %>,
  thinks you'll like an event we have listed.
</p>

<p>
  Come check all the information about <%= @event.title %> at
  <%= url_for :only_path => false,
              :host       => "eventalicio.us",
              :controller => "events",
              :action     => "show",
              :id         => @event %>
</p>
</body>
</html>
```

Let's see the new version of our email. With your application running, go to an event details page and send yourself an invite again. The message you receive should look something like the one shown in Figure 8-2.

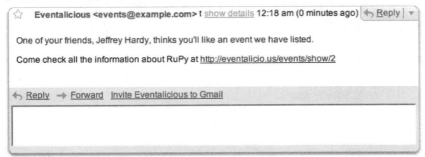

Figure 8-2. *Email received in HTML format*

That looks pretty good. But what if our users don't have a rich email client and can't read HTML mail? We can work around this by sending both HTML and plain text, which is what we'll show you how to do next.

Adding Multiple Parts to Messages

When you add different parts to an email that represent the same message, the email client will recognize that there are alternatives for the same message, and it will choose the most appropriate part based on the environment or the user preferences.

Fortunately, Action Mailer makes this ridiculously easy: simply include the name of the content type as part of the template name using the following format:

```
#{action_name}.#{content_type}.rhtml
```

So, if we create a plain-text representation of our mailer template called `email_friend.text.plain.rhtml`, and rename our existing HTML template to `email_friend.text.html.rhtml`, Action Mailer will automatically create a multiple-part message for each part. Let's go ahead and do that now.

First, rename `email_friend.rhtml` to `email_friend.text.html.rhtml`, and create a plain text representation in a file called `email_friend.text.plain.rhtml` with the code shown in Listing 8-10.

Listing 8-10. *Plain Text email_friend Template, in app/views/event_mailer/email_friend.text.plain.rhtml*

```
One of your friends, <%= @sender_name %>,
thinks you'll like an event we have listed.

Come check all the information about <%= @event.title %> at
<%= url_for :only_path  => false,
            :host       => "eventalicio.us",
            :controller => "events",
            :action     => "show",
            :id         => @event %>
```

Adding Attachments

In some cases, you might want to add attachments to an email message. Action Mailer makes this a straightforward task by providing the attachment helper. You simply tell attachment which file you want to attach to the email.

Let's walk through an example of attaching a file to an email message. Assume that we want to send a logo image of our event application every time a user sends an email about an event to a friend. Just for demonstration, we'll use the default Rails logo, which should be in the public/images directory, a vestige of the "Welcome to Rails" index.html file we deleted back in Chapter 6. To attach this image file to the email we created in the previous section, add a call to the attachment helper in the email_friend method in the EventMailer class, as shown in Listing 8-11.

Listing 8-11. *Adding an Attachment to the Mailer, in app/models/event_mailer.rb*

```
def email_friend(recipient, sender_name, event)
  @subject      = '[Eventalicious] Check out this great event'
  @from         = 'Eventalicious <events@example.com>'
  @recipients   = recipient
  @content_type = 'text/html'
  @body         = { :sender_name => sender_name, :event => event }

  attachment "image/png" do |a|
    a.body     = File.read("public/images/rails.png")
    a.filename = "event-a-licious.png"
  end
end
```

When we call the `attachment` helper, first we identify the content type of the file we want to attach, which is `"image/png"`. In the given block, we indicate the file we're attaching using the `body` property, and the filename we want the recipient to see using the `filename` property.

■Tip You can specify the body of an attachment by using the `File.read` method if the file you're sending exists on disk. Alternatively, you can generate the file on the fly if it's a dynamic file, like a personalized PDF or Word document. Just set the correct content type (such as `application/pdf`) and pass the results of your attachment generation to the `body` method.

Sending Incoming Email to a Rails Process

So far, you've seen that Action Mailer has extensive support for sending all types of mail messages. But what if your application needs to receive email? You can handle incoming email in a Rails application in a few different ways. Here, we'll explain how to use a Rails process and how to read email from your mail server. The approach you choose depends a lot on your operating system and email server.

Using a Rails Process

In an Action Mailer class, you can write a `receive` method that receives a `TMail::Mail` object as a parameter, which corresponds to an incoming email message your code can process. Inside the `receive` method, it's easy to extract details about the incoming email, such as header, subject, body text, and/or attachments.

For example, the events application could have a special email address (such as new@events.example.com) that could be monitored to create a new event whenever a new email arrives. This way, users could send an email to new@events.example.com and have a new event created without needing to open their browsers. The implementation of this feature would look something like this:

```
def receive(email)
  event = Event.new
  event.title = email.subject
  event.description = email.body
  event.save
end
```

The preceding code is pretty simple and would take care of receiving mail; however, this is just the first part of the solution. The remaining part is tricky and might demand some research and system administration skills. You'll need to tell your mail server that it should redirect messages sent to a specific address to a special process. In this case, the process is the Rails' runner script, which executes the Ruby code passed as parameter as if it were running from within your a Rails application. You can see this technique in action by saving an email message to any location on disk and invoking the receive method using the following command (POSIX only):

```
script/runner EventMailer.receive(STDIN.read) < email.txt
```

We won't go into the implementation details of configuring a script to route incoming mail to your Rails process because it's impossible to cover all setups. Visit the Rails wiki at http://wiki.rubyonrails.com/rails/pages/HowToReceiveEmailsWithActionMailer to look up information about your particular setup.

Reading Email Using POP or IMAP

If you don't have control over the email server being used and can't write a server-side script, you can still read email from your mail server as your regular email client does. To do this, you can create a separate Ruby script that fetches email, and run it as a background process that polls for new messages.

The following code connects to a mail server through POP3 and checks a specific mailbox to see if any new email has arrived. If so, the script will read that message and pass it to the EventMailer.receive method for processing. This example uses a POP3 server, but it could just as easily use an IMAP server. The only difference would be that you would use the Net::IMAP class instead of the Net::POP3 class to connect to the mail server. Both classes are part of the Ruby Standard Library.

```
Net::POP3.start("mail.example.com", nil, "username", "password") do |pop|
  if pop.mails.empty?
    logger.info "NO MAIL"
  else
    pop.mails.each do |email|
      begin
        logger.info "receiving mail..."
        EventMailer.receive(email.pop)
        email.delete
      rescue Exception => e
        logger.error "Error receiving email: #{Time.now.to_s} - #{e.message}"
      end
    end
  end
end
```

This script starts by trying to connect to the POP3 server with the credentials indicated on the first line. As soon as the connection is established, it checks to see if there are any new email messages by using the `pop.mails.empty?` method. If there are new email messages, it iterates through each of them, calling `EventMailer.receive(email.pop)`. After processing a message, it's deleted from the server to avoid reprocessing the same message the next time the script is called.

Summary

In this chapter, you learned how to send email from your web applications using Action Mailer. We started by explaining how to configure Action Mailer to talk to your mail server, and showed you the most common configuration parameters you can use to fine-tune how Action Mailer works with your application.

You learned that Action Mailer allows you to send email messages based on templates, and how to use implicit parts for text and HTML messages, as well as how to use the `attachment` helper to add attachments to your messages.

We also touched briefly on receiving mail using Action Mailer. We only scratched the surface here, this being a rather advanced technique. Still, we provided you with a good starting point should your application ever need to perform this task, and you'll know where to look when you need to find out more information.

This chapter brings us to the end of our tour of the main Rails libraries: Active Record, Action Pack, and Action Mailer. In the next chapter, we'll cover one of the most important techniques to improve the quality of your code: testing.

CHAPTER 9
■ ■ ■

Testing Your Application

Smart developers test their code. Take a minute to read that sentence again and let it sink in: smart developers test their code. The fact is, testing is one of the most important things you can do to improve the quality of your code, reduce the cost of change, and keep your software bug-free. Rails (and the Ruby community at large) takes testing seriously. Not surprisingly then, Rails goes out of its way to make testing hassle-free.

The basic idea of testing is simple: you write code that exercises your program and tests your assumptions. Instead of just opening a browser and adding a new user manually to check whether it works, you write a test that automates the process—something repeatable. With a test in place, every time you modify the code that adds a new user, you can run the test to see if your change worked, and more importantly, whether your seemingly innocuous change broke something else.

If you stop and think about it, you're already testing your software. The problem is that you're doing it manually, often in an ad hoc fashion. You might make a change to the way users log in, and then you try it in your browser. You make a change to the sign-up procedure, and then you take it for a spin. As your application grows in size, it becomes more and more difficult to manually test like this, and eventually you'll miss something important. Even if you're not testing, you can be sure that your users are. After all, they're the ones using the application in the wild, and they'll find bugs you never knew existed. The best solution is to replace this sort of visual, ad hoc inspection with automatic checking.

Testing becomes increasingly important when refactoring existing code. *Refactoring* is the process of improving the design of code without changing its behavior. The best way to refactor is with a test in place acting as a safety net. Since refactoring shouldn't result in an observable change in behavior, it shouldn't break your tests either. It's easy, therefore, to see why many programmers won't refactor without tests.

Given the importance we've placed on testing, it may seem odd that we've left it to the ninth chapter of the book. Ideally, you should be writing tests as you go, never getting too far ahead without testing what you've written. But we decided that explaining how to test would be overwhelming while you were still learning the basics of Ruby and the Rails framework. Now that you have a good deal of knowledge under your belt, it's time to tackle testing.

How Rails Handles Testing

Rails defines three different kinds of tests, each designed to test a specific piece of your application:

- *Unit* testing tests your models.

- *Functional* testing tests your controllers.

- *Integration* testing tests at a high level through multiple controllers.

Because Rails is an integrated environment, it can make assumptions about the best ways to structure and organize your tests. Rails provides the following:

- Test directories for unit, functional, and integration tests

- Fixtures for easily working with database data

- An environment explicitly created for testing

The default Rails skeleton generated by the `rails` command creates a directory just for testing. If you open it now, you'll see subdirectories for each of the aforementioned test types:

```
test
|-- unit         <-- model tests
|-- functional   <-- controller tests
|-- integration  <-- high-level testing through multiple controllers
|-- mocks        <-- stand-ins for real objects
`-- fixtures     <-- test data
```

In addition to the `unit`, `functional`, and `integration` directories, there are also a `mocks` directory and a `fixtures` directory. What are these for?

Fixtures are textual representations of table data that are loaded into the database before your tests run. You use them to populate your database with data to test against. Here's what a fixture for our `events` table might look like:

```
tiki_party:
  id: 1
  user_id: 1
  title: "Tiki Party"
  url: "http://example.com"
  description: "A wonderfully good time"
  location: "Hampton's Apartment"
  occurs_on: "2007-09-02"
```

The `mocks` directory is used to store classes that will be used in place of actual classes while your tests are running. For example, let's say you have a `CreditCard` class that processes credit card transactions. You probably don't want to actually process live transactions in your tests, so you can "mock" the `CreditCard` class and have it stand in for the actual class. For more information about mocks (and their counterparts, *stubs*), check out the following links:

- `http://en.wikipedia.org/wiki/Mock_object`

- `http://martinfowler.com/articles/mocksArentStubs.html`

You may remember that every time we generated a model or a controller while building the events application, Rails automatically generated test files for us. This is another example of its opinionated nature—Rails thinks you should test, so it goes out of its way to remind you.

You might also remember that when we originally created the databases for the events application, we created three: one for development (which is all we've been using thus far), one for production, and one for testing. Not surprisingly, Rails uses the testing database just for testing. If you didn't create the test database back in Chapter 3, you can create it now by using the following command:

```
$ mysqladmin -uroot create events_test
```

Rails will drop and re-create this test database on every run of the test suite, so make sure you don't list your development or production database in its place, or all your data will be gone.

Unit Testing Your Rails Application

So, you know that Rails generated some tests automatically. Let's open one of them now and take a look. We'll start with the `Event` test, located in `test/unit/event_test.rb`, as shown in Listing 9-1.

Listing 9-1. *Generated Event Unit Test, in test/unit/event_test.rb*

```
require File.dirname(__FILE__) + '/../test_helper'

class EventTest < Test::Unit::TestCase
  fixtures :events
```

```
  # Replace this with your real tests.
  def test_truth
    assert true
  end
end
```

While there's not much to it (all it does is test that `true` is, in fact, `true`), this test gives you a template from which to build your real tests. It has the following elements:

- The test class is a subclass of Ruby's built-in testing framework, `Test::Unit`.

- The fixtures class method makes available the given fixtures. In this case, we're loading the `events` fixture, providing access to the test data in `test/fixtures/events.yml`.

- Tests are implemented as methods prefixed with `test_`.

- Within a test case, *assertions* are used to test expectations. We'll explain how these work in the "Testing with Assertions" section coming up shortly.

If you peek inside the `test/unit` directory, you'll see a similar test case for every model we've generated so far: `Event`, `EventMailer`, `User`, and `Registration`. Each looks almost exactly the same as the `Event` test. Let's run the unit tests now and see what happens.

```
$ rake test:units
```

```
Loaded suite /usr/local/lib/ruby/gems/1.8/gems/rake-
0.7.2/lib/rake/rake_test_loader
Started
....
Finished in 0.053392 seconds.

4 tests, 4 assertions, 0 failures, 0 errors
```

Take a closer look at the output. If a test case passes, as each did this time, you'll see a `.` (dot) character. When the test case produces an error, you'll see an `E`. If any assertion fails to return `true`, you'll see an `F`. Finally, when the test suite is finished, it prints a summary.

■**Note** If you get an error like `Mysql::Error: Unknown database 'events_test'` when you run `rake test:units`, you probably didn't create your test database.

Testing the Event Model

Let's test the `Event` model. If you recall from Chapter 4, one of the first things we did with our `Event` model was basic CRUD operations. Well, testing that we can create, read, update, and delete events is a great place to start. So, let's make a quick summary of the specific things we're going to test:

- Creating a new event

- Finding an event

- Updating an event

- Destroying an event

Before we get started, we need to create a few fixtures (remember that a fixture is a textual representation of test data).

Creating Fixtures

We'll create fixtures for both users and events. Open the `test/fixtures/users.yml` file and add a couple of users to it, as shown in Listing 9-2.

Listing 9-2. *Users Fixture, test/fixtures/users.yml*

```
eugene:
  id: 1
  login: 'eugene'
  email: 'eugene@example.com'
  hashed_password: 'e5e9fa1ba31ecd1ae84f75caaa474f3a663f05f4' # => secret

lauren:
  id: 2
  login: 'lauren'
  email: 'lauren@example.com'
  hashed_password: 'e5e9fa1ba31ecd1ae84f75caaa474f3a663f05f4' # => secret
```

Next, open the `test/fixtures/events.yml` file and edit it so that it looks like Listing 9-3.

Listing 9-3. *Events Fixture, test/fixtures/events.yml*

```
tiki_party:
  id: 1
  user_id: 1
  title: "Tiki Party"
  url: "http://example.com"
  description: "A wonderfully good time"
  location: "Hampton's Apartment"
  occurs_on: <%= 1.week.from_now.to_s(:db)%>
```

That's all you need to do. The data in these fixtures will be inserted automatically into your test database before your tests run. With fixtures in place, we're ready to start creating our test cases.

■**Tip** Fixtures are parsed by ERb before they're loaded, so you can use ERb in them, just as you can in your view templates. This is useful for creating dynamic dates, as in:

`created_at: <%= 5.days.ago.to_s(:db) %>`.

We'll take each test case one at a time, beginning with create.

Adding a Create Test

Open the `test/unit/events_test.rb` file and create the first test case by deleting the `test_truth` method and replacing it with a test called `test_should_create_event`. Your file should look like Listing 9-4.

Listing 9-4. *The test/unit/events_test.rb File*

```
require File.dirname(__FILE__) + '/../test_helper'

class EventTest < Test::Unit::TestCase
  fixtures :events, :users

  def test_should_create_event
```

```
    event = Event.new

    event.title = "Test Event"
    event.url = "http://example.com"
    event.description = "Test description"
    event.location = "Test location"
    event.occurs_on = "2007-09-09"

    assert event.save
  end
end
```

The test_should_create_event case is standard event creation fare. We're creating a new event in the same way we would create one from the console. The only real difference is on the last line of the test case:

```
assert event.save
```

Before we go any further, let's take a deeper look at assertions as they pertain to Test::Unit.

Testing with Assertions

Assertions are a statement of expected outcome. As the README for Test::Unit states, assertions are like saying "I assert that x should be equal to y." If the assertion turns out to be correct, the assertion passes. If the assertion turns out to be false, the assertion fails and Test::Unit reports a failure.

Test::Unit ships with a bevy of built-in assertions, and Rails adds a bunch of its own. We'll get to the Rails-added assertions as we look at each test case, but first, here's the standard set of Test::Unit assertions for reference:

```
assert(boolean, message=nil)
assert_block(message="assert_block failed.") do ... end
assert_equal(expected, actual, message=nil)
assert_in_delta(expected_float, actual_float, delta, message="")
assert_instance_of(klass, object, message="")
assert_kind_of(klass, object, message="")
assert_match(pattern, string, message="")
assert_nil(object, message="")
assert_no_match(regexp, string, message="")
assert_not_equal(expected, actual, message="")
assert_not_nil(object, message="")
assert_not_same(expected, actual, message="")
assert_nothing_raised(*args) do ... end
```

```
assert_nothing_thrown(message="") do ... end
assert_operator(object1, operator, object2, message="")
assert_raise(expected_exception_klass, message="") do ... end
assert_respond_to(object, method, message="")
assert_same(expected, actual, message="")
assert_send(send_array, message="")
assert_throws(expected_symbol, message="") do ... end
```

The `assert` method is perhaps the most basic of the lot. It simply asserts that the return value of its first argument is true. And we know that `event.save` will return `true` if the event saves and return `false` otherwise. So, by asserting `event.save`, we successfully test that the event was saved. Pretty easy, isn't it?

■**Tip** Geoffrey Grosenbach (a.k.a. topfunky) has a useful cheat sheet that summarizes all available assertions. Download it from `http://nubyonrails.topfunky.com/articles/2006/08/24/ ruby-rails-test-rails-cheat-sheet`.

Let's run the test. First, make sure your test database is prepared and that your fixtures are loaded.

```
$ rake db:test:prepare
$ ruby test/unit/event_test.rb
```

```
Loaded suite test/unit/event_test
Started
.
Finished in 0.168879 seconds.

1 tests, 1 assertions, 0 failures, 0 errors
```

Just as the output from the test says, we ran one test (`test_should_create_event`), which included one assertion (`assert event.save`), and everything passed. Life is good!

■**Tip** You don't need to run the `db:test:prepare` task when you're running the entire test suite via Rake. When run via Rake (`rake test:units`), the test environment is prepared for you.

Adding a Find Test

Next on our list is testing that we can successfully find an event. We'll use the data in the fixture we created to help us. Add the method shown in Listing 9-5 after `test_should_create_event`.

Listing 9-5. *Test Case for Finding an Event, in test/unit/event_test.rb*

```
def test_should_find_event
  event_id = events(:tiki_party).id
  assert_nothing_raised { Event.find(event_id) }
end
```

■**Note** Fixtures can be accessed in your test cases by name. Use `fixture(:name)`, where `fixture` is the plural name of the model and `:name` is the symbolized name of the fixture you're after. This will return an Active Record object on which you can call methods. Here, we're getting at the `tiki_party` Event fixture using `events(:tiki_party)`.

Here, we're testing that we can find an event of the given id. First, we grab the `id` attribute from the fixture, and then we test that we can use `Event.find` to retrieve it. We're using the assertion `assert_nothing_raised` because we know that `find` raises an exception if the record cannot be found. If no exception is raised, we know that finding works. Again, let's run the test and see what happens.

```
$ ruby test/unit/event_test.rb
```

```
Loaded suite test/unit/event_test
Started
..
Finished in 0.133271 seconds.

2 tests, 2 assertions, 0 failures, 0 errors
```

Sure enough, finding works! So far, so good.

Adding an Update Test

Our next move is to test updating. Add the `test_should_update_event` case, as shown in Listing 9-6.

Listing 9-6. *Test Case for Updating an Event, in test/unit/event_test.rb*

```
def test_should_update_event
  event = events(:tiki_party)
  assert event.update_attributes(:title => 'New title')
end
```

First, we find the Tiki Party event from our fixture, and then we assert that changing the title via update_attributes returns true. Once again, run the test and see what happens.

```
$ ruby test/unit/event_test.rb
```

```
Loaded suite test/unit/event_test
Started
...
Finished in 0.226404 seconds.

3 tests, 3 assertions, 0 failures, 0 errors
```

Adding a Destroy Test

Only one more test to go: destroy. We'll find an event, destroy it, and assert that Active Record raises an exception when we try to find it again. Listing 9-7 shows the test.

Listing 9-7. *Test Case for Destroying an Event, in test/unit/event_test.rb*

```
def test_should_destroy_event
  event = events(:tiki_party)
  event.destroy
  assert_raise(ActiveRecord::RecordNotFound) { Event.find(event.id) }
end
```

The assert_raise assertion takes the class of the exception we expect to be raised for whatever we do inside the given block. Since we've destroyed the event, we expect Active Record to respond with a RecordNotFound exception when we try to find it by id. Run the test and see what happens.

```
$ ruby test/unit/event_test.rb
```

```
Loaded suite test/unit/event_test
Started
....
Finished in 0.215428 seconds.

4 tests, 4 assertions, 0 failures, 0 errors
```

And there you have it. We've successfully tested event CRUD.

Testing Validations

We have a few validations on our Event model, specifically for the presence of a title and location. Since we want to make sure these are working as expected, we need to test them. Add the method shown in Listing 9-8 to test that we can't create invalid events.

Listing 9-8. *Test Case for Validations, in test/unit/event_test.rb*

```
def test_should_not_create_invalid_event
  event = Event.new
  assert !event.valid?
  assert event.errors.invalid?(:title)
  assert event.errors.invalid?(:location)
  assert_equal "can't be blank", event.errors.on(:title)
  assert_equal "can't be blank", event.errors.on(:location)
  assert !event.save
end
```

This is pretty straightforward, though you might have to read it through a few times before it clicks. First, we instantiate a new Event object in the local variable event. Without having given it any attributes, we expect it to be invalid. So, we assert that it's not valid using assert !event.valid (notice the !, which negates truth). Next, we access the errors collection to explicitly check for the attributes we expect to be invalid:

```
assert event.errors.invalid?(:title)
assert event.errors.invalid?(:location)
```

We also want to check that the validation responses are what we expect. To do this, we're using the assert_equal assertion. Here's its basic syntax:

```
assert_equal(expected, actual)
```

To check the error messages, we again access the `errors` collection, but this time we ask for the specific messages associated with the given attribute.

```
assert_equal "can't be blank", event.errors.on(:title)
assert_equal "can't be blank", event.errors.on(:location)
```

Finally, we assert that `event.save` returns `false` using `!event.save`.
Run the test one more time.

```
$ ruby test/unit/event_test.rb
```

```
Loaded suite test/unit/event_test
Started
.....
Finished in 0.304773 seconds.
5 tests, 10 assertions, 0 failures, 0 errors
```

Feels good, doesn't it? Life isn't all roses, though, and requirements change. What if one day we decide to make a change to the `Event` model and remove the validation requirements for the `title` attribute? Well, if that were to happen, our test would fail. If you want to try it, open the `Event` model in `app/models/event.rb` and remove `:title` from the `validates_presence_of` declaration, and then run the tests again.

When your requirements change, you often need to update your tests. We recommend updating the tests *first*, (which should make them fail), and then updating your code (which would make them pass).

Functional Testing Your Controllers

Tests to check your controllers are called *functional* tests. When we were testing our models, we weren't testing them in the context of the web application—there were no web requests and responses, nor were there any URLs to contend with. This focused approach lets us home in on the specific functionality of the model and test it in isolation. Alas, Rails is for building web applications, and while unit testing models is important, it's equally important to test the full request/response cycle.

Testing the Events Controller

Functional tests aren't that much different from unit tests. The main difference is that Rails sets up request and response objects for you that act just like the "live" requests and responses you would get when running the application via a web server. If you open the events controller test in `test/functional/events_controller_test.rb` and examine the first few lines, as shown in Listing 9-9, you can see how this is done.

Listing 9-9. *Setup of a Functional Test, in test/functional/events_controller_test.rb*

```
require File.dirname(__FILE__) + '/../test_helper'
require 'events_controller'

# Re-raise errors caught by the controller.
class EventsController; def rescue_action(e) raise e end; end

class EventsControllerTest < Test::Unit::TestCase
  fixtures :events, :users

  def setup
    @controller = EventsController.new
    @request    = ActionController::TestRequest.new
    @response   = ActionController::TestResponse.new

    @first_id = events(:first).id
  end

  # ...
end
```

Just as in the unit test, the first thing that we do is require the `test_helper`. The `test_helper.rb` file sets up some common environment variables and generally endows `Test::Unit` with some specific methods that make testing Rails applications easier.

■**Note** You can think of the `test_helper` as being akin to the `application_helper`. Any methods you define here will be available to all your tests (since all your tests subclass `Test::Unit::TestCase`).

Next, this test requires the `events` controller itself (`require 'events_controller'`). Since controllers normally rescue errors to display a backtrace, we quickly reopen the `EventsController` class and overwrite the `rescue_action` method so as to make sure it raises any exceptions it encounters (if errors occur, we want to see them while testing). Next, we actually open a class definition for our test, `EventsControllerTest`, inside which a `setup` method is defined. It's this `setup` method that sets up the Action Controller environment, as shown in Listing 9-10.

Listing 9-10. *Initializing the Controller Environment, in*
test/functional/events_controller_test.rb

```
def setup
  @controller = EventsController.new
  @request    = ActionController::TestRequest.new
  @response   = ActionController::TestResponse.new
  @first_id   = events(:first).id
end
```

We instantiate a new `EventsController` object and store it in the instance variable
`@controller`. We also create `@request` and `@response` variables, each of which are instances
of `ActionController::TestRequest` and `ActionController::TestResponse`, respectively. As
you can no doubt tell by their names, these objects are made specifically for testing, and
they are designed to simulate the Action Controller environment as closely as possible.

Most of the time, you won't need to worry about doing this setup manually. Whenever you run the controller generator, it will automatically create a functional test file for
you and fill in all these details. Still, it's important that you know what's going on. Since
the test we're looking at was actually created by the scaffold generator, it has quite a bit
more code than you would get from the standard controller generator. There's only one
problem with this code, though: not all the test cases will pass—at least, not without
some modification. Warts and all, this gives us a rather good start and will serve well as
a template.

As you look over the `events` controller functional test file, you'll notice that each test
case tests a specific request for an action on the controller. In fact, there's a test for every
action: `index`, `list`, `show`, `new`, `create`, `edit`, `update`, and `destroy`. We'll walk through each test
case, making adjustments as we go.

We need to make a small change first, though. See the fixture that's being accessed
on the last line of the `setup` method? Well, we don't have an events fixture named `:first`,
so we'll have to fix that. Change the name of the fixture to `:tiki_party` as follows:

```
@first_id = events(:tiki_party).id
```

Creating a Test Helper

Before we get to testing our actions, a little foresight tells us that in order to create an
event, our application expects a logged-in user. So, we'll need to simulate a logged-in
user for our tests. This is a perfect job for a test helper. What we can do is create a helper
method called `login_as` that accepts the name of the user to log in as. This method can
set up the `session` object, just like our controller expects. We'll be able to use this method
for any test case that requires a login.

To begin, open up the `test_helper` file in your editor and add the `login_as` method as shown in Listing 9-11. You can find the test helper file in `test/test_helper.rb`; the method we're adding is highlighted in bold.

Listing 9-11. *The login_as Test Helper in test/test_helper.rb*

```ruby
ENV["RAILS_ENV"] = "test"
require File.expand_path(File.dirname(__FILE__) + "/../config/environment")
require 'test_help'

class Test::Unit::TestCase
  # Transactional fixtures accelerate your tests by wrapping each test method
  # in a transaction that's rolled back on completion. This ensures that the
  # test database remains unchanged so your fixtures don't have to be reloaded
  # between every test method. Fewer database queries means faster tests.
  #
  # Read Mike Clark's excellent walkthrough at
  #   http://clarkware.com/cgi/blosxom/2005/10/24#Rails10FastTesting
  #
  # Every Active Record database supports transactions except MyISAM tables
  # in MySQL. Turn off transactional fixtures in this case; however, if you
  # don't care one way or the other, switching from MyISAM to InnoDB tables
  # is recommended.
  self.use_transactional_fixtures = true

  # Instantiated fixtures are slow, but give you @david where otherwise you
  # would need people(:david). If you don't want to migrate your existing
  # test cases which use the @david style and don't mind the speed hit (each
  # instantiated fixtures translates to a database query per test method),
  # then set this back to true.
  self.use_instantiated_fixtures  = false

  # Add more helper methods to be used by all tests here...

  def login_as(user)
    @request.session[:user_id] = users(user).id
  end
end
```

The login_as method is rather simple. All it does is manually set user_id in the @request.session object (just like our login action does) to the id of the given user, as obtained from the fixture. If we give it the name of one of our users fixtures, say, :eugene, it will set session[:user_id] to users(:eugene).id.

Now that we've created a way to simulate a logged-in user, we're ready to proceed with our tests, beginning with the index action.

Testing the Index Action

The test_index case is shown in Listing 9-12. Make sure yours looks like this before you proceed.

Listing 9-12. *Test Case for the Index Action*

```
def test_index
  get :index
  assert_response :success
  assert_template 'index'
  assert_not_nil assigns(:events)
end
```

Functional tests define methods that correspond to HTTP verbs (GET, POST, PUT, and DELETE), which you use to make requests. The first line of the test_index method makes a GET request for the index action using get :index. Here's the full syntax you use for these requests:

```
http_method(action, parameters, session, flash)
```

In the case of test_index, we have no parameters to submit along with the request, so our call is quite simple. This will make a GET request to the index action in the same way as if we had done so with a browser. After the request has been made, we need to assert our expectations.

```
assert_response :success
```

The assert_response assertion is a custom assertion defined by Rails (that is, it's not part of the standard Test::Unit library), and it does exactly what its name implies: it asserts that there was a successful response to the request.

Every time you make an HTTP request, the server responds with a status code. When the response is successful, the server returns a status code of 200. When an error occurs, it returns a 500. And when the browser can't find the resource being requested, it returns a 404. In our assertion, we're actually using the shortcut :success, which is the same as 200. We could have used assert_response(200), but it's easier to remember words like *success* or *error* than HTTP status codes, which is why we avoid using the latter whenever possible. Table 9-1 lists the shortcuts available when using assert_response.

Table 9-1. *Status Code Shortcuts Known to assert_response*

Symbol	Meaning
:success	Status code was 200
:redirect	Status code was in the 300–399 range
:missing	Status code was 404
:error	Status code was in the 500–599 range

Tip You can pass an explicit status code number to assert_response, such as assert_response(501) or its symbolic equivalent assert_response(:not_implemented). See http://iana.org/assignments/http-status-codes for the full list of codes and default messages you can use.

We also want to assert that the proper template was rendered in response to the request, for which we use another of Rails' custom assertions: assert_template. Here, we expect to see the index template (from app/views/events/list.rhtml) to be rendered, so test this expectation.

```
assert_template 'index'
```

There's one more thing we need to do: assert that the correct instance variables were assigned. If you look at the events controller, you'll see that we set an instance variable called @events that contains the events collection. Rails gives us the ability to test whether this assignment was successful by way of the assigns method.

```
assert_not_nil assigns(:events)
```

This asserts that @events was, in fact, assigned (by virtue of the fact that it shouldn't be nil). We can use this technique to test for the existence of any instance variable set within our controllers. Useful, isn't it? Using assigns actually gives us access to the instance variable, so we can do with it as we please.

Testing the Show Action

Listing 9-13 shows the test_show case.

Listing 9-13. *Test Case for the Show Action*

```
def test_show
  get :show, :id => @first_id

  assert_response :success
  assert_template 'show'

  assert_not_nil assigns(:event)
  assert assigns(:event).valid?
end
```

The test_show case is almost the same as test_index, but with one notable difference: we need to identify the record we want to show. If we were requesting this in a browser, the URL would look like /events/show/1. Therefore, we need to pass in the :id parameter with a value of 1. If you look closely at the test request, you can see how this is done.

```
get :show, :id => @first_id
```

The @first_id variable is the one we set in the index method and is the id attribute of the event we grabbed from the :tiki_party fixture. We can pass arbitrary parameters in this fashion. You'll see more of this when we test the create and update actions, both of which require a set of event parameters.

One more thing to notice here: we can treat the result of assigns(:event) as we would any Event object and call methods on it.

```
assert assigns(:event).valid?
```

So, not only can we assert that there is an instance variable named @event, we can assert that it contains a valid Event object. We can safely skip the test_new case as it introduces nothing new; the test_create case, on the other hand, is full of goodies.

Testing the Create Action

Listing 9-14 shows the test_create case. Notice how we're using the login_as helper, since this action expects a logged-in user.

Listing 9-14. *Test Case for the Create Action*

```
def test_create
  login_as(:eugene)
  num_events = Event.count
```

```
  post :create, :event => { :title    => 'Test title',
                            :url       => 'http://example.com',
                            :location => 'Test location' }

  assert_response :redirect
  assert_redirected_to :action => 'list'

  assert_equal num_events + 1, Event.count
end
```

To test the create action, we actually need to submit some form parameters to create a valid event. Fortunately, this is an easy affair. All we need to do is pass a hash of parameters that contains a valid set of event attributes, just as we would using an HTML form (remember that HTML form parameters are converted into a hash object by Rails). Here's how it's done:

```
post :create, :event => { :title    => 'Test title',
                          :url       => 'http://example.com',
                          :location => 'Test location' }
```

Unlike the other test cases we've looked at so far, the test_create case uses a request method other than GET. To create a new event, we need to use the POST method. We formulate a POST request that includes a params hash with a valid event.

Next, we come across another of Rails' additions to Test::Unit, assert_redirected_to. As you can gather from its name, this lets you assert that a redirect to the expected location took place in response to the request. This match can be partial; for example, assert_redirected_to(:controller => 'events') will also match the redirection of redirect_to(:controller => 'events', :action => 'list').

```
assert_redirected_to(options, message)
```

Since we want to know whether or not a new event was created, we store the number of events in the database before we start. When we're finished, we assert that there's one more event using assert_equal.

```
assert_equal num_events + 1, Event.count
```

We're really rolling now. The test_edit case is straightforward, and test_update is almost the same as test_create, so we'll jump straight to test_destroy.

Testing the Destroy Action

Listing 9-15 shows the test_destroy case. Again, since this action expects a logged-in user, we make use of the login_as helper to log in as :eugene.

Listing 9-15. *Test Case for the Destroy Action*

```
def test_destroy
  login_as(:eugene)
  assert_nothing_raised { Event.find(@first_id) }

  post :destroy, :id => @first_id
  assert_response :redirect
  assert_redirected_to :action => 'list'

  assert_raise(ActiveRecord::RecordNotFound) { Event.find(@first_id) }
end
```

First, we test that we can find the event in question, knowing full well that find will raise an exception if the event doesn't exist. Then we formulate a POST request to the destroy action, passing in the id of the event to destroy. We assert that the response is a redirect to the list action, and finally, we ensure that the event has in fact been deleted by asserting that Active Record raises a RecordNotFound exception.

Running the Functional Test Suite

Now that our functional testing tour is complete, Listing 9-16 shows the full file.

Listing 9-16. *Complete test/functional/events_controller_test.rb File*

```
require File.dirname(__FILE__) + '/../test_helper'
require 'events_controller'

# Re-raise errors caught by the controller.
class EventsController; def rescue_action(e) raise e end; end

class EventsControllerTest < Test::Unit::TestCase
  fixtures :events, :users

  def setup
    @controller = EventsController.new
    @request    = ActionController::TestRequest.new
    @response   = ActionController::TestResponse.new

    @first_id = events(:tiki_party).id
  end

  def test_index
    get :index
```

```ruby
    assert_response :success
    assert_template 'index'

    assert_not_nil assigns(:events)
  end

  def test_show
    get :show, :id => @first_id

    assert_response :success
    assert_template 'show'

    assert_not_nil assigns(:event)
    assert assigns(:event).valid?
  end

  def test_new
    login_as :eugene

    get :new

    assert_response :success
    assert_template 'new'

    assert_not_nil assigns(:event)
  end

  def test_create
    login_as :eugene

    num_events = Event.count

    post :create, :event => { :title    => 'Test title',
                              :url      => 'http://example.com',
                              :location => 'Test location' }

    assert_response :redirect
    assert_redirected_to :action => 'index'


    assert_equal num_events + 1, Event.count
  end

  def test_edit
    login_as :eugene
```

```
    get :edit, :id => @first_id

    assert_response :success
    assert_template 'edit'

    assert_not_nil assigns(:event)
    assert assigns(:event).valid?
  end

  def test_update
    login_as :eugene

    post :update, :id => @first_id
    assert_response :redirect
    assert_redirected_to :action => 'show', :id => @first_id
  end

  def test_destroy
    login_as :eugene

    assert_nothing_raised { Event.find(@first_id) }

    post :destroy, :id => @first_id
    assert_response :redirect
    assert_redirected_to :action => 'index'

    assert_raise(ActiveRecord::RecordNotFound) { Event.find(@first_id) }
  end
end
```

Make sure your test file looks like the one in Listing 9-16 and run it using the Rake test:functionals command, which will run our entire suite of functional tests.

```
$ rake test:functionals
```

```
Loaded suite /usr/local/rake/rake_test_loader
Started
.........
Finished in 0.099709 seconds.

9 tests, 26 assertions, 0 failures, 0 errors
```

Not bad—26 assertions all in less than one second! You've got to admit, this is a lot more efficient than manually clicking through your application to test it. Moreover, since this uses the test database, you don't risk polluting your production database with bogus data while you test. Whenever you make a change to your events controller, you can run this test to see if you've broken any of your expectations.

Now that we have unit and functional tests for events in place, let's run the entire test suite, which will run both our unit and functional tests. To do this, we use the built-in Rake task, test.

```
$ rake test
```

```
Loaded suite /usr/local/rake/rake_test_loader
Started
........
Finished in 0.07121 seconds.

9 tests, 13 assertions, 0 failures, 0 errors

Loaded suite /usr/local/rake/rake_test_loader
Started
.........
Finished in 0.099508 seconds.

9 tests, 26 assertions, 0 failures, 0 errors
```

■**Note** We've omitted some of the output here to cut down on the clutter. Your actual output will look slightly different, but the summary (tests, assertions, failures, and errors) should be the same.

It may interest you to know that the default Rake task is to run all tests. That means running rake with no arguments is the same as running rake test.

Integration Testing

Rails defines one more type of test, and it's the highest level of the bunch. Integration tests go a little further than their functional equivalents. Unlike functional tests, which test a specific controller, integration tests can span multiple controllers and actions with full session support. They're the closest we can get to simulating actual interaction with a web application.

Integration Testing the Events Application

Let's get started by generating the test. Given that Rails ships with a generator for just about everything, it shouldn't surprise you that it also includes one for generating integration tests. It works just like the others you've already used.

```
$ ./script/generate integration UserStories
```

```
exists  test/integration/
create  test/integration/user_stories_test.rb
```

Open the newly generated file and take a peek, as shown in Listing 9-17.

Listing 9-17. *User Stories Test in test/integration/user_stories_test.rb*

```
require "#{File.dirname(__FILE__)}/../test_helper"

class UserStoriesTest < ActionController::IntegrationTest
  # fixtures :your, :models

  # Replace this with your real tests.
  def test_truth
    assert true
  end
end
```

At this stage, it looks a lot like the other test files you've seen so far. Notice, however, that it's a subclass of `ActionController::IntegrationTest`. That's about the only difference, but not for long.

First, we need to get our fixtures in place. We'll use both the `users` and `events` fixtures for this test, so load them immediately inside the class body.

```
fixtures :users, :events
```

Test cases are added to integration tests in exactly the same way as unit and functional test cases are added: as methods prefixed with `test_`. Integration test cases tend to look deceptively like functional tests, but they have a few subtle differences, which we'll point out as we add them.

Listing 9-18 shows a test case that goes through the process of logging in a user.

Listing 9-18. *Login Integration Test, in test/integration/user_stories_test.rb*

```ruby
def test_should_login_user_and_redirect
  get '/login'

  assert_response :success
  assert_template 'login'

  post '/login', :login => 'eugene', :password => 'secret'

  assert_response :redirect
  assert_redirected_to :controller => 'events'

  follow_redirect!

  assert_response :success
  assert_template 'index'
  assert session[:user_id]
end
```

Notice how when our response is a redirect, we're able to follow it, even when it redirects to another controller. The `follow_redirect!` method does exactly what you might think: it lets you follow a single redirect response, as long as the last response was, in fact, a redirect. If the last response wasn't a redirect, an exception will be raised.

Let's add a test case for the `logout` action as well, as shown in Listing 9-19.

Listing 9-19. *Logout Integration Test, in test/integration/user_stories_test.rb*

```ruby
def test_should_logout_user_and_redirect
  get '/logout'

  assert_response :redirect
  assert_nil session[:user]

  follow_redirect!

  assert_template 'login'
end
```

Again, we're able to follow the redirect and test that the correct template was rendered.

Let's get a little fancier by testing that we can log in, create a new event, and log out, all in a single test. We'll combine the login and logout tests we've already written and sandwich an events creation test in the middle, as shown in Listing 9-20.

Listing 9-20. *Event Creation Integration Test, in test/integration/user_stories_test.rb*

```ruby
def test_should_login_create_event_and_logout
  get '/login'

  assert_response :success
  assert_template 'login'

  post '/login', :login => 'eugene', :password => 'secret'

  assert_response :redirect
  assert_redirected_to :controller => 'events'

  follow_redirect!

  assert_response :success
  assert_template 'index'
  assert session[:user_id]

  get '/events/new'

  assert_response :success
  assert_template 'new'

  post '/events/create', :event => {:title => 'BBQ', :location => 'My back yard'}

  assert assigns(:event).valid?
  assert_response :redirect
  assert_redirected_to :action => 'list'

  follow_redirect!

  assert_response :success
  assert_template 'index'

  get '/logout'

  assert_response :redirect
```

```
  assert_redirected_to :action => 'login'
  assert_nil session[:user]

  follow_redirect!

  assert_template 'login'
end
```

Here's what we get when we run the test.

user_stories_test.rb

```
Loaded suite /usr/local/rake/rake_test_loader
Started

.

Finished in 0.248968 seconds.

1 tests, 19 assertions, 0 failures, 0 errors
```

Great—19 assertions, and we know that we've just tested the whole stack from dispatcher to database. Not too shabby, is it? If you're thinking that what we've just done looks a lot like we're telling a story (Eugene logs in, Eugene creates event, Eugene logs out), you would be right.

Story-Based Testing

Integration tests are great for creating story-based scenarios using a domain-specific language (DSL). They even go so far as to allow you to test multiple users interacting! What do we mean by story-based tests? Well, what if we could do something like this:

```
def test_creating_an_event
  eugene = registered_user
  eugene.logs_in 'eugene', 'secret'
  eugene.creates_event
  eugene.logs_out
end
```

Here, we're telling an easy-to-understand story that requires no programming knowledge to follow. Eugene logs in and proceeds to create a new event. When he is finished, he logs out. Behind the scenes, we can test every request, response, and redirect, following

Eugene's path through the entire process, just as we did in the `test_should_login_create_event_and_logout` case.

Integration tests provide a method called `open_session` that you can use to simulate a distinct user interacting with the application as if from a web browser. While this lets you simulate multiple connections with ease, we're using it to help us create an object on which to define our custom story-based methods, like `logs_in` and `creates_event`.

Let's reshape our `test_should_login_create_event_and_logout` into methods we can add straight onto a new `session` object. Listing 9-21 shows the updated `user_stories` test.

Listing 9-21. *Updated User Stories Integration Test, in test/integration/user_stories_test.rb*

```ruby
require "#{File.dirname(__FILE__)}/../test_helper"

class UserStoriesTest < ActionController::IntegrationTest
  fixtures :users, :events

  def test_creating_an_event
    eugene = registered_user
    eugene.logs_in 'eugene', 'secret'
    eugene.creates_event :title => 'BBQ', :location => 'My back yard'
    eugene.logs_out
  end

  private
    def registered_user
      open_session do |user|
        def user.logs_in(login, password)
          get '/login'

          assert_response :success
          assert_template 'login'

          post '/login', :login => login, :password => password

          assert_response :redirect
          assert_redirected_to :controller => 'events'

          follow_redirect!

          assert_response :success
          assert_template 'index'
          assert session[:user_id]
        end
```

```ruby
      def user.logs_out
        get '/logout'

        assert_response :redirect
        assert_redirected_to :action => 'login'
        assert_nil session[:user]

        follow_redirect!

        assert_template 'login'
      end

      def user.creates_event(event_hash)
        get '/events/new'

        assert_response :success
        assert_template 'new'

        post '/events/create', :event => event_hash

        assert assigns(:event).valid?
        assert_response :redirect
        assert_redirected_to :action => 'index'

        follow_redirect!

        assert_response :success
        assert_template 'index'
      end
    end
  end
end
```

See how we've created a private method called `registered_user` and created a new integration session inside it? The `open_session` method yields a `session` object onto which we attach *singleton* methods (methods that exist only on a particular instance).

```ruby
def registered_user
  open_session do |user|
    def user.logs_in(login, password)
      #...
    end
```

```
    def user.logs_out
      #...
    end

    def user.creates_event(event_hash)
      #...
    end
  end
end
```

The return value of the `registered_user`, then, is a fresh integration `session` object that responds to the methods we've created. We know what you're thinking. This means we can create as many user sessions as we want and simulate multiple connections to the application. In Listing 9-22, we've updated the `test_creating_an_event` method and renamed it to `test_multiple_users_creating_an_event`.

Listing 9-22. *Updated Event Creation Story Testing Multiple Users*

```
def test_multiple_users_creating_an_event
  eugene = registered_user
  lauren = registered_user

  eugene.logs_in 'eugene', 'secret'
  lauren.logs_in 'lauren', 'secret'

  eugene.creates_event :title => 'Punk Rock Show', :location => 'Bar'
  lauren.creates_event :title => 'BBQ', :location => 'My back yard'

  eugene.logs_out
  lauren.logs_out
end
```

This is only the tip of the iceberg. The sky is the limit on how creative you'll be able to get with this style of testing.

Running the Full Test Suite

Now that we have a respectable amount of tests for our application, let's use Rake to run the entire suite. Since the default Rake task is test, let's save ourselves five keystrokes (a space counts as a keystroke!) and run our tests with just rake.

```
$ rake
```

```
Loaded suite /usr/local/rake/rake_test_loader
Started
........
Finished in 0.116108 seconds.

8 tests, 13 assertions, 0 failures, 0 errors

Loaded suite /usr/local/rake/rake_test_loader
Started
.........
Finished in 0.129197 seconds.

9 tests, 26 assertions, 0 failures, 0 errors

Loaded suite /usr/local/rake/rake_test_loader
Started
.
Finished in 0.22396 seconds.

1 tests, 40 assertions, 0 failures, 0 errors
```

Take a moment bask in the glory of a successful test run!

Rails includes a handy task to generate a formatted display of stats about your program, including the lines of code (LOC). It's capable of showing you the ratio between your application and test code. Run it using rake stats.

```
$ rake stats
```

```
+----------------------+-------+-------+---------+---------+-----+-------+
| Name                 | Lines |  LOC  | Classes | Methods | M/C | LOC/M |
+----------------------+-------+-------+---------+---------+-----+-------+
| Controllers          |  149  |  119  |    4 |     20 |  5 |    3 |
| Helpers              |   20  |   16  |    0 |      2 |  0 |    6 |
| Models               |  106  |   80  |    5 |     11 |  2 |    5 |
| Libraries            |    0  |    0  |    0 |      0 |  0 |    0 |
| Components           |    0  |    0  |    0 |      0 |  0 |    0 |
| Integration tests    |   72  |   51  |    1 |      5 |  5 |    8 |
| Functional tests     |  132  |   90  |    6 |     15 |  2 |    4 |
| Unit tests           |  116  |   90  |    5 |     12 |  2 |    5 |
+----------------------+-------+-------+---------+---------+-----+-------+
| Total                |  595  |  446  |   21 |     65 |  3 |    4 |
+----------------------+-------+-------+---------+---------+-----+-------+
   Code LOC: 215      Test LOC: 231      Code to Test Ratio: 1:1.1
```

While the code-to-test ratio is a nice thing to know, it really doesn't tell us all that much. What really matters is how much of the code our tests is exercising. For this kind of analysis, we can use a code coverage tool, like rcov.

Measuring Test Coverage with Rcov

Rcov is a code coverage tool for Ruby written by Mauricio Fernandez (a.k.a. Eigenclass), which you can learn more about at http://eigenclass.org/hiki.rb?rcov. It's easy to install as a RubyGem.

```
$ sudo gem install rcov
```

Once you've installed the gem, running the coverage report is a simple matter of running rcov with the appropriate arguments.

```
$ rcov --rails --text-summary test/*/*_test.rb
```

```
Loaded suite /usr/local/bin/rcov
Started
.................
Finished in 0.40912 seconds.

18 tests, 78 assertions, 0 failures, 0 errors
72.7%   10 file(s)   178 Lines   143 LOC
```

Just as the text summary says, we have somewhere around 72.2% test coverage of our code base, which is quite respectable by any account. Rcov also generated an HTML report that shows us exactly which lines have been tested (and which ones haven't). Open `coverage/index.html` in your browser to see the full report, as shown in Figure 9-1.

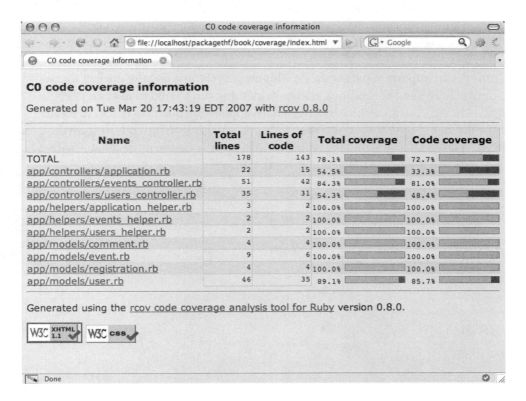

Figure 9-1. *Coverage report from rcov*

QUICK CODE COVERAGE REPORTS

Here's a task that you can add to your `lib/tasks` directory that will save you having to remember the arguments to `rcov` and make generating a coverage report a snap:

```
namespace :test do
  desc 'Measures test coverage'
  task :coverage do
    rm_f 'coverage'
    system 'rcov --rails --text-summary test/*/*_test.rb'
  end
end
```

Save this snippet in `lib/tasks/coverage.rake` and run it using `rake test:coverage`.

Summary

This chapter introduced you to the Rails philosophy behind testing and stressed its importance as part of the development cycle. You've now been on a complete tour of the baked-in facilities Rails provides for testing. You learned about testing your models with unit tests, testing your controllers with functional tests, and testing the whole Rails stack with integration tests. We even introduced some of the tools you can use to measure your test coverage.

Testing is an important part of the development cycle, and despite the fact that we've left it until near the end of this book, it's not something you should treat as an afterthought. Now that you know how to write a Rails application and how to test it, you can combine the steps: write some code, then test it. As you get into the code/test rhythm, (or better yet, test/code), you'll find that you'll be able to write better, more reliable software. And we think you'll sleep a little better at night, too.

## CHAPTER 10

Extending Rails with Plugins

Rails ships with a rich set of features and powerful functionality. It's often said that Rails is designed to solve most problems most of the time. It can't solve all problems or be all things to all people, and it doesn't try to do that. Instead, it provides a mechanism to easily extend and augment the core functionality: *plugins*. Plugins give developers the freedom to write extensions to Rails, without needing to include those additions in the Rails core code.

In this chapter, we'll show you how plugins extend the functionality of Rails and make it even more comprehensive. We'll explain how to find and install plugins, and how to use plugins to add functionality to our events application. Finally, we'll create a plugin from scratch to showcase how you can extract common functionality from an application and share it with other projects and developers.

Finding and Installing Plugins

To help you manage your plugins, Rails ships with a `plugin` command in the `script` directory. To see its usage information, run the command without arguments:

```
$ ./script/plugin
```

```
Unknown command:
Usage: plugin [OPTIONS] command
Rails plugin manager.
...
```

As indicated by the output, you need to pass a command as a parameter to the `plugin` script. Table 10-1 shows the `plugin` command options.

Table 10-1. *Plugin Command Options*

Command	Description
discover	Automatically add new plugin repositories.
list	List all available plugins from the sources.
install	Install a plugin from a known repository or a URL. Here's an example: `plugin install continuous_builder`.
update	Update installed plugins.
remove	Uninstall a plugin.
source	Install plugin from a known repository or a URL. For example: `source http://dev.rubyonrails.com/svn/rails/plugins/`.
unsource	Remove a plugin repository. For example: `unsource http://dev.rubyonrails.com/svn/rails/plugins/`.

The plugin system comes with a set of predefined Subversion repositories from which you can find and install plugins, so you don't need to learn the exact location of most of them. The list is kept internally by your Rails installation. As shown in Table 10-1, a few commands are available to help you manage this list of repositories.

Note Most developers use Subversion, a popular version control system, to manage the development of their plugins. If you don't have a Subversion client installed, you won't be able to install plugins that are distributed directly from Subversion repositories. Yet another good reason to start using Subversion (`http://subversion.tigris.org`).

Finding Plugins

If you want to find a plugin for implementing a specific feature, try a Google search. Usually, you'll get results that will lead you to the web site of an appropriate plugin with instructions on how to install it.

If you are not sure exactly what you want, but would like to explore plugins by category, such as Controllers, Models, or Testing, you can access the Rails Plugin Directory at `http://agilewebdevelopment.com/plugins`. This directory contains an extensive categorized list of plugins. Each plugin has a specific page, which includes a description, some information on how to use it, and a link to the plugin developer's page.

Another option is to go to the Plugins page in the Rails wiki: `http://wiki.`
`rubyonrails.org/rails/pages/Plugins`. This page has links to additional resources about
plugins and has a huge list of available plugins in a single page. However, the wiki plugin
list isn't structured, which sometimes makes it hard to find things. Such is the peril of the
anarchic, collaborative nature of the wiki.

After you install a plugin, you can usually find instructions on how to use it by reading the README file in the plugin root folder, located at `vendor/plugins/#{plugin_name}`.

Installing Plugins

Installing a plugin is a straightforward affair: just invoke the `plugin` script with the `install`
command and the name or URL of the plugin you want to install. Plugins are installed in
the `vendor/plugins` directory. Using the name *vendor* is common in software projects, and
generally indicates that the code contained within it is "third-party." Let's look at a couple
of installation examples.

Install a plugin using only its name. This works when the plugin's location is already
known to the plugin system via the `source` option (see Table 10-1).

```
$ ./script/plugin install simply_helpful
```

```
+ ./simply_helpful/CHANGELOG
+ ./simply_helpful/README
...
+ ./simply_helpful/test/test_helper.rb
```

Install a plugin Using a URL. This works for any plugin, and can use either the http(s)
or svn protocol.

```
$ ./script/plugin install ➡
svn://rubyforge.org/var/svn/ym4r/Plugins/GM/trunk/ym4r_gm
```

```
A    /vendor/plugins/ym4r_gm
A    /vendor/plugins/ym4r_gm/test
...
Exported revision 85.
```

To uninstall a plugin you no longer want to use, just call the `remove` command:

```
$ ./script/plugin remove simply_helpful
```

Using a Plugin in Our Application

A particular Rails plugin that is useful in many web applications is `acts_as_taggable`. This plugin implements tagging—giving users the ability to add tags to web content. *Tags* are relevant keywords that help identify a piece of content.

In this section, we'll improve our events application by adding the ability for users to organize the events by tagging them. By installing the `acts_as_taggable` plugin in our application and using it to manage tagging, we can get this feature up and running in no time.

■**Note** The `acts_as_taggable` plugin has its own page on the Rails wiki that you can reference: http://wiki.rubyonrails.com/rails/pages/ActsAsTaggablePluginHowto.

First, use the following command to install the `acts_as_taggable` plugin in our events application.

```
$ ./script/plugin install acts_as_taggable
```

```
+ ./acts_as_taggable/init.rb
+ ./acts_as_taggable/lib/README
+ ./acts_as_taggable/lib/acts_as_taggable.rb
+ ./acts_as_taggable/lib/tag.rb
+ ./acts_as_taggable/lib/tagging.rb
+ ./acts_as_taggable/test/acts_as_taggable_test.rb
```

Modifying the Database

The plugin is installed, but we still have a bit of work to do before we can begin using it. The first thing we need to do is to create the tables we'll need for tag management. Generate a new migration called AddSupportForTagging.

```
$ ./script/generate migration AddSupportForTagging
```

This command will create the `db/migrate/008_add_support_for_tagging.rb` migration. Open the file and edit it so that it looks like Listing 10-1.

Listing 10-1. *The db/migrate/008_add_support_for_tagging.rb Migration File*

```
class AddSupportForTagging < ActiveRecord::Migration
  def self.up
    create_table :tags do |t|
      t.column :name, :string
    end

    create_table :taggings do |t|
      t.column :taggable_id, :integer
      t.column :tag_id, :integer
      t.column :taggable_type, :string
    end
  end

  def self.down
    drop_table :tags
    drop_table :taggings
  end
end
```

This will create two tables that will be used to save the tags generated by our application.

Go ahead and execute the migration file by issuing the Rake command:

```
$ rake db:migrate
```

Modifying the Application to Use the Plugin

With the plugin successfully installed and the database tables created, all that's left to do is integrate it into our application. We need to allow users to add tags when they create and edit events.

The first step is to configure the Event model to accept tagging. This can be accomplished by adding the acts_as_taggable call to the Event model declaration, as shown in Listing 10-2.

Listing 10-2. *Adding acts_as_taggable, in app/models/event.rb*

```
class Event < ActiveRecord::Base
  acts_as_taggable
  #...
end
```

Just like other class-level model declarations, such as has_many and belongs_to, acts_as_taggable results in the addition of several methods to the class in which it's used. Two instance methods are supplied for adding tags to and listing the tags of a particular object: tag_with(list) and tag_list. Additionally, a class-level finder is added to enable searching of items by a list of tags: find_tagged_with.

Let's take this for a quick spin on the console so you can see how it works.

```
$ ./script/console
Loading development environment.

>> e = Event.find(:first)
=> #<Event:0x3068e04>

>> e.tag_with "interesting parties activism"
=> ["interesting", "parties", "activism"]

>> Event.find_tagged_with "activism"
=> [#<Event:0x30283cc>]

>> e.tag_list
=> "interesting parties activism"

>> e.tags
=> [#<Tag:0x3111a54, #<Tag:0x311198c>, #<Tag:0x3111964>]
```

To implement the tagging feature, we need to be able to assign tags to existing and new events. This is a simple matter of adding a tags field to our event form partial and handling the tags parameter in the controller. Modify the partial in app/views/events/ _form.rhtml to include the tags field at the very bottom of the form, as shown in Listing 10-3.

Listing 10-3. *Adding a Tags Field to the Form, in app/views/events/_form.rhtml*

```
<p><label for="event_tags">Tags <span>(space separated)</span></label><br/>
<%= text_field_tag 'tags', @event.tag_list, :size => 40 %></p>
```

We use the text_field_tag helper to create a field for tags. The second argument to text_field_tag is the field's initial value, which we set using the tag_list method, which returns a string of space-separated tags. Figure 10-1 shows the result when rendered in a browser.

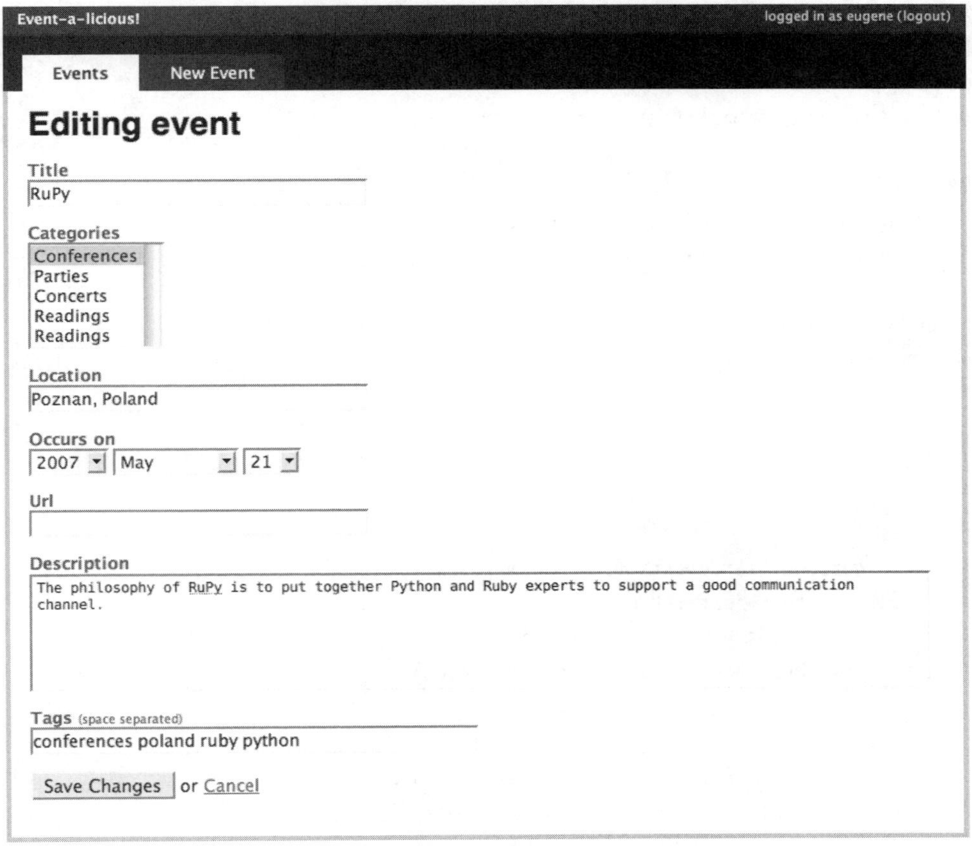

Figure 10-1. *Editing an event with tags*

All that's left to do is handle the `tags` field in the `events` controller (`app/controller/events_controller.rb`). We'll need to modify both the `create` and `update` actions to invoke the `tag_with` method, passing in `params[:tags]` (if it exists). Here's how it looks:

```
@event.tag_with(params[:tags]) if params[:tags]
```

The updated `create` and `update` actions are shown in Listing 10-4. The new code is listed in bold.

Listing 10-4. *Modified Create and Update Actions, in app/controller/events_controller.rb*

```
class EventsController < ApplicationController
  #...

  def create
```

```
    @event = current_user.events.build(params[:event])
    @event.categories << Category.find(params[:categories]) unless➥
    params[:categories].blank?
    @event.tag_with(params[:tags]) if params[:tags]

    if @event.save
      flash[:notice] = 'Event was successfully created.'
      redirect_to :action => 'index'
    else
      render :action => 'new'
    end
  end

  #...

  def update
    @event = current_user.events.find(params[:id])
    @event.attributes = params[:event]
    @event.category_ids = params[:categories]
    @event.tag_with(params[:tags]) if params[:tags]

    if @event.save
      flash[:notice] = 'Event was successfully updated.'
      redirect_to :action => 'show', :id => @event
    else
      render :action => 'edit'
    end
  end

  #...
end
```

That's all there is to it! Just a few minutes after installing the acts_as_taggable plugin, we are finished implementing tagging in our application. As you can see, plugins can definitely boost productivity.

■**Note** The acts_as_taggable plugin was originally created to demonstrate polymorphic interfaces in Active Record. We think it works great for simple cases, and it may be all you ever need. If you want something more robust, try one of the various community-supported plugins, which you can find by searching: http://agilewebdevelopment.com/plugins/search?search=acts_as_taggable.

Creating Your Own Plugin

Whenever you find yourself repeatedly writing the same code snippets in different Rails applications, you have a very strong case for extracting this functionality in your own plugin. This will help you keep the business logic for this functionality in one location, instead of in multiple applications, and make it possible to fix bugs in a single place.

To demonstrate how to create your own plugin, we'll make one to implement search functionality for a given model, so that the search code can be reused easily. We'll call this plugin `simply_searchable`.

Rails comes with a plugin generator that you can use to create the skeleton for a new plugin. You just need to tell it the name of the plugin you want to create:

```
$ ./script/generate plugin simply_searchable
```

```
create   vendor/plugins/simply_searchable/lib
create   vendor/plugins/simply_searchable/tasks
create   vendor/plugins/simply_searchable/test
create   vendor/plugins/simply_searchable/README
create   vendor/plugins/simply_searchable/MIT-LICENSE
create   vendor/plugins/simply_searchable/Rakefile
create   vendor/plugins/simply_searchable/init.rb
create   vendor/plugins/simply_searchable/install.rb
create   vendor/plugins/simply_searchable/uninstall.rb
create   vendor/plugins/simply_searchable/lib/simply_searchable.rb
create   vendor/plugins/simply_searchable/tasks/simply_searchable_tasks.rake
create   vendor/plugins/simply_searchable/test/simply_searchable_test.rb
```

The generator created quite a few files. As you can see from the generator's output, they're all in the `vendor/plugins/#{plugin_name}` directory. The structure for a plugin is quite specific and follows normal Ruby library conventions. Table 10-2 describes the function of each file and directory.

Table 10-2. *Plugin Directory Structure*

File/Directory	Description
lib	Directory where the plugin code will be located. By convention, a Ruby file named after the plugin is created here.
tasks	Directory where Rake tasks specific to this plugin can be created.
test	Directory where you can add tests for this plugin.

Continued

Table 10-2. *Continued*

File/Folder	Description
README	File that contains a description of the plugin and instructions for using it.
MIT-LICENSE	It's good practice to specify the license under which this plugin is released. Rails assumes the MIT license will be used. Feel free to use whatever license best suits your application.
install.rb	Code in this file is executed when the plugin is installed.
uninstall.rb	Similar to install.rb, this file contains code that will be executed when the plugin is uninstalled.
Rakefile	A Rake file with tasks to run the tests for this plugin and generated Ruby documentation.
init.rb	Initialization code that Rails will execute automatically to make this plugin available to your application.

As you saw when we used the acts_as_taggable plugin in the previous section, a plugin usually adds one or more methods in the class, or object, in which it is acting. We'll take a similar path—we'll add a search method, also known as an action, to the events controller, to make the search functionality external to our application.

Making the Plugin Available to Applications

First, we need to let Rails know what source files it should use. We also need to make the simply_searchable method available to any controller that wants to use it, in the same fashion that the acts_as_taggable method was made available to our Event model. We accomplish both tasks by modifying the init.rb file, as shown in Listing 10-5.

Listing 10-5. *Updates to vendor/plugins/simply_searchable/init.rb*

```
require 'simply_searchable'
ActionController::Base.send(:include, BeginningRails::SimplySearchable)
```

The require 'simply_searchable' line directs Rails to our plugin files. By calling ActionController::Base.send(:include, BeginningRails::SimplySearchable), we are including the methods in the SimplySearchable module into the ActionController::Base class, which is the class from which all our controllers inherit. Next, we'll create that module and add the plugin methods.

Creating the Plugin Module

Now it's time to dive into the plugin code. We'll create a module named `SimplySearchable` that will contain our plugin's methods. We'll build up this module in pieces, and then present the entire module in Listing 10-6 at the end of this section. We start with the following:

```
module BeginningRails
  module SimplySearchable
  end
end
```

In order to prevent namespace clashes, it's always a good idea to give your plugins a unique namespace by wrapping them in a uniquely named module. It's possible that someone else might create a plugin called `SimplySearchable` one day, which would create problems if we had them both installed at the same time. Wrapping our `SimplySearchable` module inside the `BeginningRails` module will help us avoid this (admittedly unlikely) situation.

The first piece of code we need to add inside the `SimplySearchable` module is the `included` hook. Just like Active Record's callbacks, which allow you to hook into specific events in the object life cycle (create, destroy, and so on), Ruby modules have hooks that allow you to respond to events that occur in your modules and classes. The `included` hook is triggered whenever your module is included (or *mixed in*) to a class.

You can't create class methods through inclusion, because `self` inside a module is the module itself, not the class in which it might be eventually included. This is easier to illustrate with code, so here's an example:

```
module Greetable
  # An instance method
  def say_hello
    puts "hello"
  end

  # A class method
  def self.say_cheers
    puts "cheers"
  end
end

# A class that mixes-in Greetable
class Bar
  include Greetable
end
```

```
# The instance method, say_hello, will be available to the Bar class
b = Bar.new
b.say_hello # => hello

# The class method, say_cheers, doesn't exist on Bar
Bar.say_cheers # => NoMethodError: undefined method `say_cheers' for #<Bar:0x346bb0>

# Since self is the Greetable module, say_cheers exists on it
Greetable.say_cheers # => cheers
```

When you need a mixed-in module to define class methods, you use the extend hook. Here's how we would rewrite the Greetable module to correctly create the say_cheers class method on classes that include it.

```
module Greetable
  # The included hook is triggered whenever this module
  # is included in another class
  def self.included(base)
    # base is the receiving class (the class in which
    # this module is included). The extend method works
    # like include: it accepts a module and extends the
    # receiving class with the methods defined in it
    base.extend ClassMethods
  end

  # An instance method
  def say_hello
    puts "hello"
  end

  # A module to contain class methods that will extend
  # the receiving class
  module ClassMethods
    # A class method
    def say_cheers
      puts "cheers"
    end
  end
end

# A class that mixes in Greetable
class Bar
  include Greetable
end
```

```
# The instance method, say_hello, will be available to the Bar class
b = Bar.new
b.say_hello # => hello

# The say_cheers class method now exists on Bar
Bar.say_cheers # => cheers
```

For our plugin, we want simply_searchable to be available as a class method inside
our controllers, so we use the technique demonstrated in the preceding example. We create a module called ClassMethods and use extend in the included hook to make its methods
available as class methods on the receiving class. Here's how it looks:

```
module BeginningRails
  module SimplySearchable
    def self.included(base)
      base.extend ClassMethods
    end

    module ClassMethods
      def simply_searchable(options = {})
        class_inheritable_accessor :fields, :template

        raise "Please specify the fields to search on" unless options[:fields]

        self.fields = options[:fields]
        self.template = options[:template] || 'index'

        include SearchMethods
      end
    end
  end
end
```

The ClassMethods module has a single method called simply_searchable, which
is the class method we'll use in our controllers to declare them as searchable. The
simply_searchable method accepts a hash of options that will allow us to provide some
configuration parameters to customize the search.

The first value accepted by the options hash is called fields, and will include a list of
database fields on which to search. This is a required parameter, so we raise an exception
if it's empty. The second value specified by the options hash is called template. We'll use
this option to specify which template to render in response to the search, defaulting to
index if it's not set.

Now that we've got the setup covered, it's time to write the code that performs the actual search—what the user will reach when calling /events/search after we add the plugin to the EventsController.

We required the plugin user to specify the fields for the search. Since the search parameters that come in via the params hash might include fields not specified, we need to do a little filtering. If we didn't do this, our query might include fields we don't want to expose publicly, which would be a security concern. With the parameters we want, we create conditions and values arrays, to which we add the criteria for our search.

```
module SearchMethods
  def search
    # Initialize the conditions and values arrays
    conditions = []
    values = []

    # Filter out all params that don't match the specified fields
    searchable_fields = params.reject {|k,v| !self.fields.include?(k) }

    # Build the conditions and values arrays from the parameters
    searchable_fields.each_pair do |field, value|
      conditions << "#{field} LIKE ?"
      values << "%#{value}%"
    end
  end
end
```

At this point, we know the fields and values on which we'll perform the search. However, because this code has no idea what it needs to search for, the approach we will take is to run a search in the model that corresponds to a controller. This means that for the EventsController, we'll be performing searches in the Event model. By following this convention, we'll be able to reuse the plugin in other controllers without requiring changes to the plugin, The new parts are in bold.

```
module SearchMethods
  def search
    # Initialize the conditions and values arrays
    conditions = []
    values = []

    # Filter out all params that don't match the specified fields
    searchable_fields = params.reject {|k,v| !self.fields.include?(k) }
```

```
    # Build the conditions and values arrays from the parameters
    searchable_fields.each_pair do |field, value|
      conditions << "#{field} LIKE ?"
      values << "%#{value}%"
    end

    # Get the model class name from the controller class name
    model_name = self.class.name.chomp('Controller').singularize

    # Create a variable named after the controller
    variable_name = "@#{self.controller_name.pluralize}"
  end
end
```

Note While we're inferring the model name from the controller name here, you might consider making the options hash accept a :model parameter to specify the model explicitly in the event that the model you want to search on can't be inferred.

We needed to do some work to figure out the name of the model on which we want to search, and created an instance variable to hold the resultset. With that out of the way, we have everything we need to perform the search. Let's do that now. Again, the new parts are in bold.

```
module SearchMethods
  def search
    # Initialize the conditions and values arrays
    conditions = []
    values = []

    # Filter the params to have only the specified fields
    searchable_fields = params.reject {|k,v| !self.fields.include?(k) }

    # Add each field to the conditions array
    searchable_fields.each_pair do |field, value|
      conditions << "#{field} LIKE ?"
      values << "%#{value}%"
    end
```

```
    # Get the model class name from the controller class name
    model_name = self.class.name.chomp('Controller').singularize

    # Create a variable named after the controller
    variable_name = "@#{self.controller_name.pluralize}"

    if searchable_fields.any?
      # If there are conditions we add :conditions => conditions.join(' AND ')
      instance_eval <<-EOS
        @#{model_name.downcase}_pages, #{variable_name} = paginate(
          :#{model_name.pluralize.downcase},
          :conditions => [conditions.join(' AND '), *values],
          :per_page => 10
        )
      EOS
    else
      # If there are no conditions, just do a find(:all)
      instance_eval <<-EOS
        @#{model_name.downcase}_pages, #{variable_name} = paginate(
          :#{model_name.pluralize.downcase},
          :per_page => 10
        )
      EOS
    end
  end
end
```

Assuming all goes well, we'll have some results to display. This is a simple matter of rendering the template specified with the :template option. If no template is specified, we'll fall back on the index action. If the index action doesn't exist, an exception will be raised. The render code is listed in bold.

```
module SearchMethods
  def search
    # Initialize the conditions and values arrays
    conditions = []
    values = []

    # Filter the params to have only the specified fields
    searchable_fields = params.reject {|k,v| !self.fields.include?(k) }
```

```
  # Add each field to the conditions array
  searchable_fields.each_pair do |field, value|
    conditions << "#{field} LIKE ?"
    values << "%#{value}%"
  end

  # Get the model class name from the controller class name
  model_name = self.class.name.chomp('Controller').singularize

  # Create a variable named after the controller
  variable_name = "@#{self.controller_name.pluralize}"

  if searchable_fields.any?
    # If there are conditions we add :conditions => conditions.join(' AND ')
    instance_eval <<-EOS
      @#{model_name.downcase}_pages, #{variable_name} = paginate(
        :#{model_name.pluralize.downcase},
        :conditions => [conditions.join(' AND '), *values],
        :per_page => 10
      )
    EOS
  else
    # If there are no conditions, just do a find(:all)
    instance_eval <<-EOS
      @#{model_name.downcase}_pages, #{variable_name} = paginate(
        :#{model_name.pluralize.downcase},
        :per_page => 10
      )
    EOS
  end

  if self.template
    render :template => self.template
  else
    render :action => 'index'
  end
  end
end
```

Listing 10-6 shows the complete plugin code.

Listing 10-6. *Complete SimplySearchable Module, in*
vendor/plugins/simply_searchable/lib/simply_searchable.rb

```ruby
module BeginningRails
  module SimplySearchable

    def self.included(base)
      base.extend ClassMethods
    end

    module ClassMethods
      def simply_searchable(options = {})
        class_inheritable_accessor :fields, :template

        raise "Please specify the fields to search on" unless options[:fields]

        self.fields   = options[:fields]
        self.template = options[:template]

        include SearchMethods
      end

    module SearchMethods
      def search
        # Initialize the conditions and values arrays
        conditions = []
        values = []

        # Filter the params to have only the specified fields
        searchable_fields = params.reject {|k,v| !self.fields.include?(k) }

        # Add each field to the conditions array
        searchable_fields.each_pair do |field, value|
          conditions << "#{field} LIKE ?"
          values << "%#{value}%"
        end

        # Get the model class name from the controller class name
        model_name = self.class.name.chomp('Controller').singularize

        # Create a variable named after the controller
        variable_name = "@#{self.controller_name.pluralize}"
```

```
      if searchable_fields.any?
        # If there are conditions we add :conditions => conditions.join(' AND ')
        instance_eval <<-EOS
          @#{model_name.downcase}_pages, #{variable_name} = paginate(
            :#{model_name.pluralize.downcase},
            :conditions => [conditions.join(' AND '), *values],
            :per_page => 10
          )
        EOS
      else
        # If there are no conditions, just do a find(:all)
        instance_eval <<-EOS
          @#{model_name.downcase}_pages, #{variable_name} = paginate(
            :#{model_name.pluralize.downcase},
            :per_page => 10
          )
        EOS
      end

      if self.template
        render :template => self.template
      else
        render :action => 'index'
      end
    end
  end
 end
 end
end
```

■**Note** Unlike most of the components of Rails (models, controllers, and so on), plugins don't automatically reload when they've been changed. Whenever you modify a plugin, you'll need to restart the web server before you'll see the changes take effect.

Updating the Controller and Views

Now that we have written the simply_searchable plugin, we need to make some changes to the controller and views to use it. In the EventsController class, add the line shown in Listing 10-7 to the class body.

Listing 10-7. *Addition to app/controllers/events_controller.rb*

```
simply_searchable :fields => %w(title location), :template => 'events/index'
```

Now let's move to the view. We'll add to a new partial called search to contain the fields available for searching. This is fairly straightforward—we create a form that submits to the search action on the events controller and include a couple of text fields for title and location. Listing 10-8 shows the search form.

Listing 10-8. *The app/views/events/_search.rhtml File*

```
<h2><%= link_to_function "Find an event", "Element.toggle('search')" %></h2>

<div id="search" <%= 'style="display: none"' unless request.post? %>>
  <% form_tag :action => 'search' do -%>
    <p>Title:<br />
    <%= text_field_tag 'title', params[:title], :size => 30 %></p>

    <p>Location:<br />
    <%= text_field_tag 'location', params[:location], :size => 30 %></p>

    <p><%= submit_tag 'Search!' %></p>
  <% end -%>
</div>
```

Now let's modify the index template in app/views/events/index.rhtml template so that it loads the search partial we just created. The updated index template is shown in Listing 10-9.

Listing 10-9. *Updates to app/views/events/index.rhtml*

```
<h1><%= link_to "All Events", events_url %></h1>

<%= render :partial => 'search' %>
<%= render :partial => 'event', :collection => @events %>

<%= link_to 'Previous page', { :page => @event_pages.current.previous }
    if @event_pages.current.previous %>
<%= link_to 'Next page',     { :page => @event_pages.current.next }
    if @event_pages.current.next %>
```

That's all there is to it. Restart your web server and try performing a search. You should see something like the results in Figure 10-2.

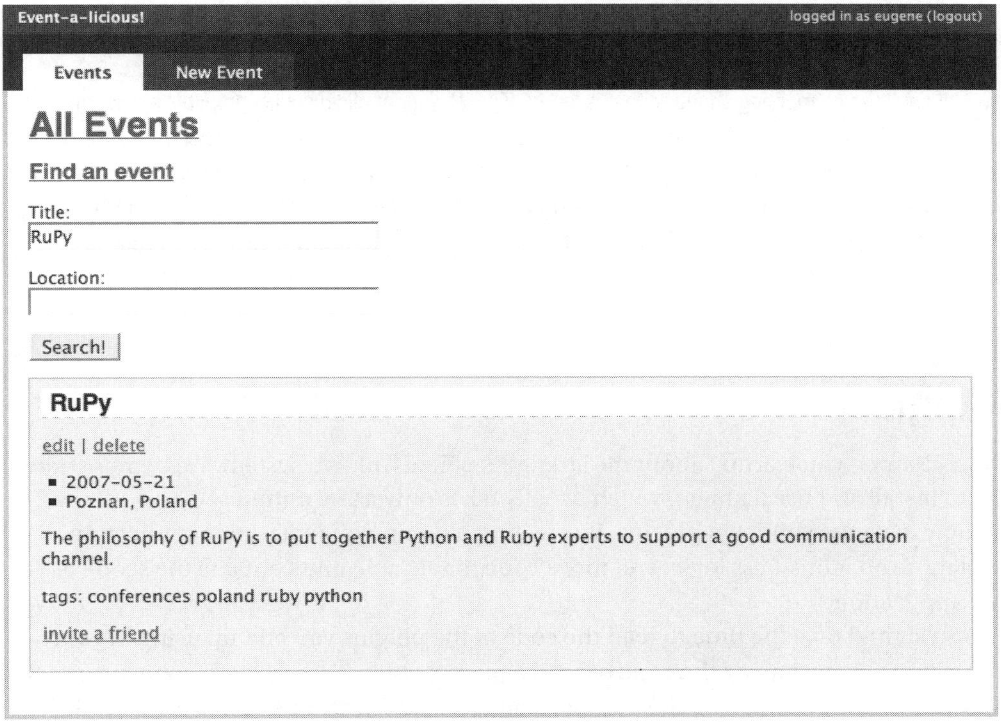

Figure 10-2. *Search functionality added to our events application*

You'll now be able to use the `simply_searchable` plugin in other applications whenever you need simple search functionality. And you'll be able to come back to it for reference when you're building more plugins in the future.

WHEN SHOULD YOU USE A PLUGIN?

You will find that there are hundreds of plugins available for Rails developers, and you might want to try a few in your applications. However, in some cases, plugins might not work to your advantage, and might even slow you down. There's no magic formula for knowing when to use a plugin or when to write your own code, but we'll try to give you a few tips to help you decide whether or not you should go for a plugin.

If the functionality you need to create is very common and your implementation has nothing very specific, you can assume that using a plugin will be safe and will save you some time. Examples of this type of common functionality are tagging, allowing users to post comments, using external applications like Google Maps, or using a specific API.

If you are implementing a common feature that has a very specific design in your application, you might still save some time by using a plugin if you feel comfortable adapting the plugin code to your own needs. This depends not only on your situation, but also on how the plugin has been written. Usually, it's not too complicated to adapt a plugin to suit your needs.

If you're implementing a feature that is very unique to your application, it's probably a wise move to code the feature directly into the code base of your application. This applies especially if the implementation depends on other parts of your code, such as an authorization and authentication system. If this specific feature is to be shared with other applications under your control, then you might want to extract the functionality into its own plugin to make the code easy to share among applications.

Summary

In this chapter, you learned about the strengths of Rails' plugin system. We demonstrated how to install and use a plugin, which usually takes only a few minutes. We also showed you how to create your own plugins. By creating plugins, you make your application focus more on it business logic, and move code to reusable units outside the scope of your application.

You should take the time to read the code of the plugins you end up using in your applications. By reviewing the code behind a plugin, you will likely learn some new tricks, and you will understand how the new methods your code inherited have been implemented. You might even be able to help the development of a plugin by spotting a bug or a better/faster implementation for a specific feature or method.

CHAPTER 11

■ ■ ■

Deploying Your Rails Applications

If you're ready to turn the world on its head by unleashing your million-dollar web application to the public, then let this chapter be your starting point.

The various web application development platforms in use today have very different deployment methods. If you're using PHP, deployment is usually as simple as dropping the right files into a directory on the remote server (usually via FTP), and then visiting them with your web browser. For PHP applications, there are thousands of hosts, and deployment is simple enough for your parents to accomplish. However, as we all know, with simplicity comes lack of options. And, as anyone who has developed in a language like PHP knows, simplicity can lead to some pretty complicated situations with your development. Luckily, Rails deployment is nothing like PHP deployment.

In the opposite camp, Java/Struts people have some deployment schemes that would make a PhD candidate panic and run away in a cloud of network diagrams. Java deployments can be terribly complex, with a lot of little details to worry about and huge amounts of memory required. Fortunately, Rails is much simpler than that.

With Rails, the porridge is just right. Rails takes some setup to get the system purring, but thanks to an ingenious deployment tool known as Capistrano, you can ensure that your ongoing use and maintenance of the server are easier than with something like PHP or Java.

Deploying with Capistrano

How does Capistrano make Rails deployment easier? The secret is that Capistrano knows a lot about what a typical Rails deployment looks like, so you don't need to tell it a lot. It makes many assumptions about your application and your deployment setup, but also provides you with a myriad of ways to override and customize those defaults.

Would you like to see how complicated it is to deploy a new release to the server? Here's an example:

```
$ cap deploy
```

```
  * executing task deploy
  * executing task update
 ** transaction: start
  * executing task update_code
  * querying latest revision...
...
  * executing task restart_mongrel_cluster
  * executing "sudo  mongrel_rails cluster::restart -C /var/www/apps/example/
    current/config/mongrel_cluster.yml" servers: ["one.example.com"]
    [one.example.com] executing command
 ** [out :: one.example.com] Stopping 3 Mongrel servers...
 ** [out :: one.example.com] Starting 3 Mongrel servers...
    command finished
```

Basically, you tell Capistrano (cap) to deploy, and it remotely grabs a new version of your application from your version control repository (usually Subversion), swaps the old code with the new, and then restarts the servers. (In this example, we're using Mongrel servers, which we'll talk about in the next section.)

It's that easy to deploy to production. The best part about this is that it's repeatable. Every time that you make a change to an application and want to deploy the changes, you simply issue the cap deploy command.

The only difficult part is the server setup. There are nearly an infinite number of ways to configure your Rails stack, and most of the configuration requires a good grasp of *nix (UNIX, Linux, OS X, and so on) system administration. For instance, Capistrano requires that you have Secure Shell (SSH) configured on your deployment box, with associated users and permissions set up for application deployment. Most novice Rails programmers aren't experts in such things, so we're going to punt here and avoid getting into server specifics. Instead, we'll show you the basics of getting started with Capistrano from the client side.

Capistrano Installation

Before you start using Capistrano, you need to install it. Fortunately, Capistrano is incredibly easy to install using the RubyGems package manager.

```
$ gem install capistrano --include-dependencies
```

```
Bulk updating Gem source index for: http://gems.rubyforge.org
Successfully installed capistrano-1.4.1
```

That's all it takes to install a full working version of Capistrano on your client computer (your development box, most likely). Part of the installation is the addition of a
new command-line utility called cap. You can read the help information for most
command-line utilities by passing in the --help directive. Let's do that now.

```
$ cap --help
```

```
Usage: /usr/local/bin/cap [options] [args]

Recipe Options ----------------------

-a, --action ACTION          An action to execute. Multiple actions may
                             be specified, and are loaded in the given order.

-f, --file FILE              A recipe file to load. Multiple recipes may
                             be specified, and are loaded in the given order.

-p, --password [PASSWORD]    The password to use when connecting. If the switch
                             is given without a password, the password will be
                             prompted for immediately. (Default: prompt for
                             password the first time it is needed.)

-r, --recipe RECIPE          A recipe file to load. Multiple recipes may
                             be specified, and are loaded in the given order.
                             (This option is deprecated--please use -f instead)

-s, --set NAME=VALUE         Specify a variable and its value to set. This
                             will be set after loading all recipe files.

-S, --set-before NAME=VALUE  Specify a variable and its value to set. This
                             will be set BEFORE loading all recipe files.

-x, --skip-config           Disables the loading of the default personal config
                             file. Specifying -C after this option will reenable
                             it. (Default: config file is loaded)
```

```
Framework Integration Options --------

-A, --apply-to DIRECTORY        Create a minimal set of scripts and recipes to use
                                capistrano with the application at the given
                                directory. (Currently only works with Rails apps.)


Miscellaneous Options ----------------

-h, --help                      Display this help message

-P, --[no-]pretend              Run the task(s), but don't actually connect to or
                                execute anything on the servers. (For various
                                reasons this will not necessarily be an accurate
                                depiction of the work that will actually be
                                performed. Default: don't pretend.)
-q, --quiet                     Make the output as quiet as possible (the default)

-v, --verbose                   Specify the verbosity of the output.
                                May be given multiple times. (Default: silent)
-V, --version                   Display the version info for this utility
```

You can use the --apply-to switch to generate a minimal set of capistrano scripts and recipes for an application. Just specify the path to the application as the argument to --apply-to, like this:

```
  cap --apply-to ~/projects/myapp
```

You'll wind up with a sample deployment recipe in config/deploy.rb and some new rake tasks in lib/tasks.

(Currently, --apply-to only works with Rails applications.)

As you can see, the cap command has a lot of options that you can pass it. Some of these will be useful to you in the future, and it's important to feel comfortable to ask for --help when working on the command line.

For now, the Capistrano option of interest is the --apply-to directive. You can use this directive to start enabling your Rails applications to have their deployment managed by Capistrano. Let's do that now. Execute the following command from your application's root directory.

```
$ cap --apply-to .
```

```
exists   config
create   config/deploy.rb
exists   lib/tasks
create   lib/tasks/capistrano.rake
```

Capistrano created two files: `deploy.rb` and `capistrano.rake`. The `deploy.rb` file is commonly referred to as the *deployment recipe*. It contains all of the basic configuration information for Capistrano. We'll look at that file in the next section. The `capistrano.rake` file is a collection of basic Rake tasks that allow you to deploy using the `rake` command instead of `cap`, if you prefer.

Note The Capistrano Rake tasks (capistrano.rake) are deprecated in favor of using `cap` directly and will be removed from future versions of Capistrano.

Capistrano Recipes

As we mentioned above, the `config/deploy.rb` file contains the "recipe" that tells Capistrano how you want your application to be deployed. It answers many simple questions, such as these:

- Where do you want to deploy?

- How should you log in to the remote system?

- Where do you want to put the application?

- Where is your source control repository?

Along with this information, the recipe provides many other details vital to any deployment procedure.

The default recipe is too long to print in these pages, but let's look at the important parts towards the top of the file.

```
# REQUIRED VARIABLES

set :application, "eventalicious"
set :repository, "http://svn.example.com/#{application}/trunk"
```

```
role :web, "www01.example.com", "www02.example.com"
role :app, "app01.example.com", "app02.example.com", "app03.example.com"
role :db,  "db01.example.com",  :primary => true
role :db,  "db02.example.com",  "db03.example.com"

# OPTIONAL VARIABLES

# set :deploy_to, "/path/to/app" # defaults to "/u/apps/#{application}"
# set :user, "eugene"            # defaults to the currently logged in user
```

The first two variables listed here are central to every recipe. The `application` variable gives a name to the application. It helps Capistrano know what name to give directories on the server, the name of the repository, and so on. The `repository` variable is where you give a URL pointing to your version control repository. Capistrano requires you to be using some type of version control system, and defaults to Subversion since it's arguably the most popular version control system used by Rails developers. Your repository must be available *from* the deployment server. If its on your local file system (and your local system is not accessible remotely), the deployment server will have no way to access the code.

Note If you are not familiar with Subversion, you can refer to many great tutorials on the web for information about how to get started with this version control system. Version control is essential for developers, no matter what language or framework they're working with. For more information about Subversion, visit `http://subversion.tigris.org`, read the online manual at `http://svnbook.red-bean.com`, or check out *Practical Subversion* by Garrett Rooney (Apress, 2006).

The large set of options in the middle of the recipe defines your deployment servers. Most likely, you'll use one computer as your web server, application server, and database server. You'll typically assign a single server to the `:web`, `:app`, and `:db` roles, like this:

```
role :app, "myserver.com"
role :web, "myserver.com"
role :db,  "myserver.com"
```

However, if your application is a huge success and generates a ton of traffic, you'll probably need to define many servers with different roles. Capistrano is built to be able to handle very complex deployments as it does as single-server architectures. It makes no difference to Capistrano if it's deploying to 15 servers or 1; it simply repeats the same actions on each server in sequence. Anyone who has ever attempted to synchronize deployment of an application to 15 servers manually has our respect, because it's a Sisyphean task of epic proportions. But with Capistrano, it's easy to control that complexity and ease most of the pain.

Let's look into exactly what Capistrano *does* on each application server when you deploy an application.

Capistrano on the Deployment Server

Whenever you set up a Capistrano deployment on the actual remote deployment server, Capistrano creates a specific folder structure, which looks like this:

```
my_app/
|-- current          # A link to the current release
|-- releases
|   |-- 200701011200 # An older release of the application
|   `-- 200701031140 # The current (most recent) release
`-- shared
    |-- config       # Symlinked to current/config
    |-- logs         # Symlinked to current/logs
    `-- tmp          # Symlinked to current/tmp
```

The releases folder contains every version of the application that you have ever deployed since your last "cleanup." Any time you do a new deployment, Capistrano puts a new version of the application in this folder, named by the timestamp of when it was deployed.

The current folder uses UNIX's built-in symlink (think *alias*) feature to create a shortcut that always points to the currently deployed release. Keeping older revisions of the application ready to go means that if something goes wrong during a deployment, you can easily roll back to an earlier version of the application with the cap rollback command. All that Capistrano needs to do in that instance is point current towards an older release.

Since you probably will frequently swap out your current release, it's important to keep some things common between each release, such as the logs, temporary files, and production configuration. The shared folder is used to house all of this information. You must manually tell Capistrano which shared files you want relinked on each deployment. However, this usually comes preconfigured with most Capistrano-based hosts.

Custom Capistrano Tasks

You can teach Capistrano to perform many other tasks. Suppose you would like to clear out a temporary folder every time you deployed? With Capistrano, defining custom tasks like this is easy.

As an example, here's a simple custom deployment task that allows us to quickly restart our particular web server on every `:web` server that we have:

```
task :restart_web, :roles => [:web] do
  sudo "/etc/init.d/lighttpd restart"
end
```

This custom task can be run from the command line on the client by simply issuing `cap restart_web`.

■**Tip** To learn more about customizing and working with Capistrano, see the manual at `http://manuals.rubyonrails.com/read/book/17`. It's a great resource that can answer many of the more advanced questions you might have when you start deploying your applications with Capistrano.

Setting Up Your Server Architecture

First things first. You're probably not a system administrator. If you want to learn how to be one, we suggest grabbing a book on the subject and spending your time getting well versed in the details of administration. Instead of focusing on the details of server administration, we're going to cover some of the high-level ideas that dominate the server architectures in the Rails world. You'll find these concepts helpful when you're discussing your options with different Rails hosting providers or server administration professionals, so that you will understand most of the terminology being used.

There are two schools of thought regarding how to set up your web server architecture. The traditional way is what we refer to as *monolithic*. The other way is called *proxy-cluster server* configuration.

Monolithic Architecture

In a monolithic architecture, a web server like Apache is used as both the web-facing end of the server and the Rails stack, as illustrated in Figure 11-1. If a remote computer requests an image, Apache handles it directly. If a remote computer requests a dynamic page, Apache handles the request using its own captive Rails running inside the server. This means that Apache handles the request end to end, as the web server and the Rails server. In this setup, the glue that goes between Apache and the actual Rails code itself is FastCGI (FCGI), which is a protocol for interfacing any interactive programs with a web server. FCGI is a vast improvement over traditional CGI bindings.

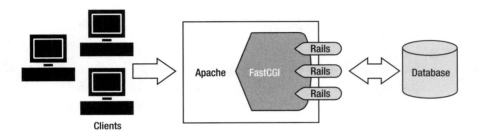

Figure 11-1. *Monolithic setup*

The problem with this setup is that occasionally your Rails applications might crash. Now, don't get into a panic. This is fairly rare. But what if someone sends you a packet of information that confuses your Rails application and it fails? In a monolithic setup, if this happens, it very well may take Apache down with it.

Another disadvantage is that if you need to upgrade the Rails code, you have to restart the whole stack *at the same time*. This results in downtime. Any request coming into the server while you are restarting fails. Even worse, if your code update contained a bug, you'd be stuck with a server that is dead in the water.

Monolithic web application architectures are extremely well tested and well worn. They are what drive most of the applications on the web today. The reason for this popularity is its maturity and the fact that you only need to understand how to run one type of system: Apache (or your web server of choice).

Proxy-Cluster Server: The New Kid on the Block

A proxy-cluster server is a new and very powerful way to deploy your Rails application stack. This type of architecture has come to dominate the Rails deployment world in recent months due to its stability, flexibility, and ease of use.

In this configuration, the web server and the Rails server are two separate entities, as shown in Figure 11-2. The web server handles the incoming requests on the standard HTTP port (80), and then redirects those requests to separate Rails server instances that are running either on the same machine or separate machines.

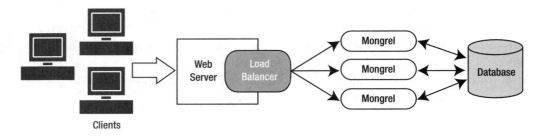

Figure 11-2. *Proxy-cluster server configuration*

As you can see from Figure 11-2, all requests to the application initially go to the web server. Then the web server acts as a proxy handler and passes the request on to a specialized Rails server. By far, the most popular of these servers at the moment is Mongrel (created by Zed Shaw).

Using Mongrel Clusters

Mongrel (`http://mongrel.rubyforge.org`) has some interesting features. First, it's single-threaded; that is, a single running Mongrel process can respond to only a single request at a time. This is why we need a cluster of several Mongrel processes. Mongrel gets a request, sends back the response, and is ready for another request. By running two or more processes, we are allowing the operating system to handle the resource sharing.

Mongrel doesn't need to use a protocol like FCGI to interface with a Rails application, because it works natively in Ruby. That's right—Mongrel is written in Ruby. Small parts of the application are compiled from C on the native system, so you end up getting a very fast wrapper around Rails.

Making this even more interesting is that a Mongrel process acts as a web server itself, but a very specialized one. On a system, you might launch five Mongrel processes and have them take up ports 8000, 8001, 8002, 8003, and 8004. A request to `http://mywebserver.com:8000` will positively respond by displaying the application. You've skipped the proxy and gone straight to one instance. A request to `http://mywebserver.com` (on the default port 80) will end up being proxied to any of the available Mongrel processes. This might mean it gets passed on to port 8002, or it might go to port 8003. The proxy balancer makes the decision.

The web server (it could be Apache, Lighttpd, Pound, or several others) isn't doing anything dangerous and definitely doesn't need to be restarted when new code is deployed. So the end result is that your front-end server is always up. Web servers are built to be as stable and fast as possible. This is even more true when they are doing the simple task of proxying. So you always know you have a friend on the front lines. Even if all of the Mongrel instances choke and die, your web server is still there to react. You can set your web server to have a "Temporary Problem" page that's displayed if the pack of Mongrels is dead.

Let's talk about when you're upgrading the code base. You upgrade the code, then tell each of the Mongrel instances to restart, in sequence only. This means that port 8000 goes down and then comes back up, while the other four are waiting their turn. Because each Mongrel restarts in sequence, you can ensure that any requests during the upgrade are serviced. The proxy server notices the few seconds that each Mongrel is down and just moves on to the next one.

Picking a Proxy Server

Three popular servers can act as your front-end web server that handles the proxy to the Mongrel instances:

LightTPD (`http://lighttpd.net`)**:** LightTPD, or "Lighty," was designed to be a simple front-end server without all of the features of Apache or IIS. It handles file serving and proxying. It also provides extensive support for virtual hosts.

Apache (`http://apache.org`)**:** The granddaddy of all open source web servers, Apache can do everything. If you want to run Subversion, virtual hosts, a chat server, and a proxy, Apache can do all that and more.

Pound (`http://apsis.ch/pound`)**:** Pound is only a proxy server. It won't send out any of the static file requests. It sends every request to Mongrel. While this makes file serving a bit slower, it means that Pound lets your Mongrel cluster run at very fast rates, because it simply gets out of the way of dynamic content.

Nginx (`http://nginx.net/`)**:** Nginx is a super fast, high-performance HTTP server that makes a great front-end for Mongrel. It boasts a small resource footprint, stands up under heavy load, and is easy to configure.

■**Tip** The absolute best and most up-to-date source for Apache/Mongrel configuration is Charles Brian Quinn's article "Apache Best Practice Deployment" (`http://mongrel.rubyforge.org/docs/apache.html`). You'll find this an extremely helpful resource if you want to use a proven, workhorse server.

Becoming an Instant Deployment Expert

As you saw earlier in this chapter, deploying with Capistrano is a piece of cake. However, how you configure your server directly impacts the way your Capistrano scripts are written. If you want to learn about that, you can find literally thousands of sources and books available on the subject. But there's another way: outsource!

It makes sense to find people who you can trust to take care of the things that aren't within your area of expertise. For instance, you don't memorize tax codes or build CPUs for your computers. Instead, you hire an accountant and pay Intel for those chips. Knowing how to deploy is very useful. But when you're launching an important product into production mode, you should go with the best.

You can find several relatively cheap Rails hosts out there. If you're going toward production with an important project, do *not* use them. The reason they are cheap is because they are cheap. You will be disappointed. Trust us—we learned the hard way.

If you're going to spend hundreds of hours of your life building something that you hope will make you some money, you'll want to host it properly. No matter how genius the application is, if people can't access it due to downtime, that application won't be getting rave reviews.

We recommend two services:

Slingshot Hosting (`http://slingshothosting.com`): Slingshot is run by a group of very intelligent Rails developers, including Charles Brian Quinn (CBQ), one of the world's foremost experts on Rails deployment. Slingshot has prewritten and preconfigured scripts that you can use to deploy your application with Capistrano. Slingshot provides dedicated, preconfigured boxes and fantastic support. You simply drop their Capsitrano recipe into your application, fire off a few commands from the terminal, and your application is ready for the wild.

Engine Yard (`http://engineyard.com`): Like Slingshot, Engine Yard also provides you with a simple set of Capistrano scripts that make deployment a breeze. Ezra Zygmuntowicz is Engine Yard's primary developer and is a legend in the Rails deployment community. Instead of focusing on dedicated boxes, Engine Yard has a scalable deployment system made up of "slices." Basically, this means that you can quickly scale your application with very little effort. The service takes care of the details of building a cluster of slices. Engine Yard is more expensive than Slingshot, but its scalability factor may be worth the difference if you plan on becoming the next Digg.

Summary

In this chapter, we showed you only some of the myriad of deployment choices. Rails deployment is as new and wild as Rails and is more of an art than a science these days. But with the help of great tools like Capistrano and the new architectures being explored, deployment gets easier with every passing month.

In this chapter, you got an idea of the power that a tool like Capistrano can give you when you're wrestling with something as complicated as application deployment and maintenance. You learned some of the basic concepts and ideas related to building deployments for Rails applications. We also gave you an easy out from dealing with this complexity—sometimes calling in the experts is the best course of action.

The only thing left for you to do is launch your application and sell it for millions of dollars. That's nearly guaranteed with a good deployment strategy![1]

---

1. No warranty of truthiness. Some limitations apply. See store for details.

■ ■ ■

Ruby, a Programmer's Best Friend

Rails is a great framework for the development of web-based applications. One of its greatest advantages over other web frameworks is that it's written in Ruby, a very consistent and elegant object-oriented programming language. In order to increase your productivity as a Rails developer, it's important that you master Ruby. If you're new to programming, don't worry. We'll explain the concepts in a way that you'll understand.

In this appendix, we'll give you an overview of the features of the Ruby language. We'll explain how the language is organized and its fundamentals. After reading this appendix, you should better understand how the Ruby language that Rails is built on works, and be able to create classes and methods, and use control flow statements in your code.

Ruby has far more features than we are able to mention in this short introduction. We encourage you to investigate more of the complex features of Ruby as you continue using Rails.

Instant Interaction

A lot of languages require that you write some code, compile, and then run the program to see the results. However, Ruby is *dynamic*, which means that you can work with the language live.

Ruby comes with a great little tool: an interactive interpreter. It's called irb (for Interactive Ruby). You can start up an irb session whenever you want by typing irb at the command prompt. Using irb, you can play around with code and make sure it works as you expect before you write it into your programs.

You can execute any arbitrary Ruby code in irb and do anything you might otherwise do inside your Ruby programs: set variables, evaluate conditions, and inspect objects. The only essential difference between an interactive session and a regular old Ruby program is that irb will echo the return value of everything it executes. This saves you from having to explicitly print the results of an evaluation. Just run the code, and irb will print the result.

You'll be able to tell whenever you're inside an `irb` session by looking for the double greater-than signs (`>>`), which indicate the `irb` prompt, and the arrow symbol (`=>`), which indicates the response.

To start an `irb` session, just go to the command prompt and type `irb`. You should see the `irb` prompt waiting for your input.

```
$ irb
irb(main):001:0>
```

Look at that. You're inside Ruby! If you press Enter, you'll see that it will just ignore the line and give you another prompt. It can only get more exciting from here.

When learning a new programming language, traditionally, the first thing you ever do is make the language print the string "Hello, World!" In Ruby, you can print something out on the screen by using the `puts` command.

```
>> puts "Hello, World!"
Hello, World!
=> nil

>> "Hello, World!"
=> "Hello, World!"
```

The first example used the `puts` command to print "Hello, World!" to the console and returned `nil`, Ruby's way of expressing *nothing*. This is because the return value of the `puts` command is `nil`.

In the second example, we just typed "Hello, World!" in quotes, without the `puts`. This creates a literal Ruby `String` object. True to form, `irb` prints the return value, which in this case is the string itself, "Hello, World!".

Ruby Types

A data type is a constraint placed upon the interpretation of data. Numbers and strings are just two of the data types that the Ruby interpreter distinguishes between, and the way Ruby adds numbers is different from the way in which it adds strings. For example, 2 + 3 evaluates to 5, but, "2" + "3" evaluates to "23". The second example might seem surprising at first, but it's really quite simple: numbers surrounded by quotes are interpreted as strings. Read on to find out more.

Strings

A *string* is a sequence of characters that usually represents a word or some other form of text. In Ruby, you can create `String` objects by putting together the characters inside single or double quotation marks.

```
>> "Ruby is a great language"
=> "Ruby is a great language"

>> 'Rails is a great framework'
=> "Rails is a great framework"
```

The main difference between strings delimited by single and double quotes is that the latter is subject to substitutions. Those substitutions are identified by Ruby code inside the #{} construct, which will be evaluated and replaced by its result in the final String object.

```
>> "Now is #{Time.now}"
=> "Now is Sun Dec 10 22:12:55 GST 2006"

>> 'Now is #{Time.now}'
=> "Now is \#{Time.now}"
```

When you use that hash symbol (#) with the curly braces, Ruby notices and tries to evaluate whatever is in between the braces. *Evaluate* means to process it like any other line of code. So, inside the braces, we say Time.now, which happens to return the current time. However, when you use single quotes, Ruby doesn't check the string for substitutions before sending it through. Remember that just typing out a string doesn't mean that the user will see it appear. You are just creating the string. If you want the user to see it (outside of irb), you need to add a puts to the front, as you saw in the previous section.

The String class has a large number of methods you will probably need when doing string manipulation, like concatenation and case-changing operations. In the following examples, a few of those methods are listed.

```
>> "Toronto - Canada".downcase
=> "toronto - canada"

>> "Dubai UAE".upcase
=> "DUBAI UAE"

>> "a " + "few " + "strings " + "together"
=> "a few strings together"

>> "HELLO".capitalize
=> "Hello"
```

■**Tip** To get a list of methods available for any object, just call the methods method using an instance of the object you want to inspect. Type "a string".methods in irb to see all the methods you can call on the String object.

Numbers

Ruby has a few classes to represent numbers: `Fixnum`, `Bignum`, and `Float`. As the names of the classes suggest, `Fixnum` and `Bignum` represent whole numbers, and are both subclasses of `Integer`. `Float` objects represent real numbers, meaning a number with a fractional part. As in most programming languages, you can perform basic arithmetic operations in Ruby, as you would using a calculator.

```
>> 1 + 2
=> 3

>> 2323 + 34545
=> 36868

>> 9093 - 23236
=> -14143

>> 343 / 4564
=> 0

>> 3434 / 53
=> 64

>> 99 * 345
=> 34155

>> 34545.6 / 3434.1
=> 10.059578928977
```

Symbols

Symbols are not a common feature in most languages. However, as you'll learn while reading this book, symbols are extremely useful. A `Symbol` is a data type that starts with a colon, like `:controller`. You can think of symbols as little named pointers (if you're a C programmer). They are used to point at some data that isn't a traditional `String` object, in a human-readable format. In fact, they are almost like strings, except you can't modify them.

```
>> :my_symbol
=> :my_symbol

>> :my_symbol + :second
```

```
NoMethodError: undefined method `+' for :my_symbol:Symbol
     from (irb):1

>> "my_string" + "second"
=> "my_stringsecond"
```

In computer science, we refer to this as being *immutable*, which is a fancy way of saying that you can't modify it. So, use symbols where you want to name something nicely, and you don't want it changed at all, for example by having something appended to the end of it.

You can even use symbols in method calls, something that Rails does quite frequently. Because Ruby allows you to omit the braces when passing hashes as method arguments (so long as the hash is either the only argument or the last argument), this has the effect of creating what look like named arguments.

```
has_many :users, :class_name => "Person"
```

We are using the :users and :class_name symbols to point at some data. Specifically, we are using them to tell ActiveRecord::Base.has_many what type of relationship it should have with the Person class.

Arrays and Hashes

Sometimes you have a lot of data that you need to keep track of—maybe a list of students, users, or anything that you might keep in a collection. Ruby has two different types of *container* objects for storing collections. First is the array, which is in almost every modern language. Arrays keep information in order. You can ask for the first item or the last item, or to put items in a certain order. You can think of an Array object as a long series of boxes in which you can put things. You define arrays by using the [ ] notation. One thing to note is that in Ruby, we always refer to the first element in an array as 0. Read carefully what we are doing here.

```
>> array = ['Toronto', 'Dubai', 'Paris']
=> ["Toronto", "Dubai", "Paris"]

>> array[0]
=> "Toronto"

>> array[2]='New York'
=> "New York"

>> array << 'Jacksonville'
=> ["Toronto", "Dubai", "New York", "Jacksonville"]
```

The `Hash` object offers another way to keep a collection. Hashes are different from arrays, because they don't care in which order the items are placed. They store items by a key. A good metaphor for a hash is a coat check. You give your coat to the coat-check attendant and tell him your name. He tags the coat with your name. When you come back, it doesn't matter in what order coats were dropped off. The attendant will find your coat by looking for the tag with your name on it. In Ruby, we often use symbols for hash keys, but in reality, *any* object can function as a key.

You define hashes with the curly braces, {}. You can create a `Hash` object by defining it with `{ :key => "value", :other_key => "other value" }`. Then you can pull out data by using square brackets on the end of the list. For instance, you would retrieve a value by saying `@my_hash[:key]` from the `@my_hash` variable. Here are some examples:

```
>> hash = { :canada => 'Toronto', :france => 'Paris', :uae => 'Dubai' }
=> {:france=>"Paris", :uae=>"Dubai", :canada=>"Toronto"}

>> hash[:uae]
=> "Dubai"

>> hash[:canada] = 'Calgary'
=> "Calgary"

>> hash
=> {:france=>"Paris", :uae=>"Dubai", :canada=>"Calgary"}
```

Also notice that on the third line, we are redefining what goes into the `:canada` key. By passing in `"Calgary"`, we are overriding the value of `"Toronto"` from the preceding command.

Language Basics

Like other programming languages, Ruby includes variables, operators, control flow statements, and methods. Here, we'll show you how to use them.

Variables

Variables are used to hold values you want to keep for later processing. When you perform a calculation, you'll probably want to use the result of that calculation somewhere else in your application code, and that's when you need a variable. In Ruby, variables are easily created. You just need to give a variable a name and assign a value to it; there's no need to specify a data type for the variable or define it in your code before you use it.

Let's create a few variables to hold some values we might need later. Notice that we can reuse a variable name by reassigning a value.

```
>> test_variable = 'This is a string'
=> "This is a string"

>> test_variable = 2007
=> 2007

>> test_variable = 232.3
=> 232.3
```

We have just created a variable named `test_variable` and assigned a few different values to it. Because everything in Ruby is an object, the `test_variable` variable holds a reference to the object we assigned.

Variable names can be any sequence of numbers and letters, as long as they start with a letter or an underscore; however, the first character of a variable indicates the type of the variable. Variables also have a *scope*, which is the context within which the variable is defined. Some variables are used in a small snippet of code and need to exist for only a short period of time; those are called *local variables*. Table A-1 lists the different types of variables supported by Ruby and shows how to recognize them when you're coding. Go ahead and type some variable names in `irb`, and you'll get results similar to the ones we're showing here.

Table A-1. *Ruby Variables*

Example	Description
@@count	Class variables are created by starting a variable name with @@. Class variables are variables that exist in the scope of a class, so all instances of a specific class will have a single value for the class variable.
@name	Instance variables are created by prefixing the variable name with @. Instance variables are unique to a given instance of a class.
SERVER_IP	You can create a constant in Ruby by naming your variable in all uppercase characters. Constants are variables that don't change throughout the execution of a program. In Ruby, constants can be reassigned; however, you'll get a warning from the interpreter if you do so.
var	Local variables start with a lowercase letter, and they live for only a short period of time. They usually exist only inside the method or block of code where they were first assigned.

In Ruby, it is considered best practice to use long and descriptive variable names. For example, in Java, we might have a variable named `phi`, but in Ruby, we would write out `place_holder_variable` for clarity. The basic idea is that your code will be much more readable if the person looking at the code (probably you) does not have to guess what `phi` stands for.

Operators

Ruby code can be combined by the use of operators. A lot of classes already implement operators as methods. Table A-2 lists the most common operators and their functions.

Table A-2. *Ruby Operators*

Operator	Description
[] []=	Assignment
* / % + **	Arithmetic
<= >= < >	Comparison
.. ...	Range
& ^ |	AND, exclusive OR, regular OR (bitwise)
|| && not or and	Logical operators

Ruby contains a ternary operator that can be used as a short notation for if-else-end. The ternary operator uses the form expression ? value_if_true : value_if_false.

```
a = 10
b = 20
a > b ? a : b
# => 20
```

Blocks and Iterators

Any method in Ruby can accept a code block. Whether the method in question calls the given block is up to it. Code blocks are fragments of code between curly braces or do..end constructs. The block always appears immediately after the method call, with the start of the block coming on the same line as the method invocation.

Here's an example using the times method. times executes the given code block once for each iteration. In this case, "Hello" will be printed 5 times.

```
5.times { puts "Hello" }
```

```
Hello
Hello
Hello
Hello
Hello
```

If a method yields arguments to a block, the methods are named between two pipe characters (|) on the same line as the method call. Observe:

```
[1,2,3,4,5].each {|item| puts item }
```

```
1
2
3
4
5
```

Here, each number is yielded to the block in succession. We store the number in the block variable, item, and use puts to print it on its own line.

The convention is to use braces for single-line blocks and do..end for multiline blocks. Here's a similar example to the one given above, except that we're using each_with_index, which yields the item and its index in the array.

```
["a", "b", "c"].each_with_index do |item, index|
  puts "Item:  #{item}"
  puts "Index: #{index}"
  puts "---"
end
```

```
Item:  a
Index: 0
---
Item:  b
Index: 1
---
Item:  c
Index: 2
---
```

Control Structures

In all the previous examples, the Ruby interpreter has executed our code from top to bottom. However, in the majority of cases, you'll want to control which methods are to be executed and when they should be executed. The statements you want to be executed might depend on many variables, like the state of some computation or the user input. For that purpose, programming languages have control flow statements, which allow you to execute code based on conditions. Here are a few examples on how to use if, else, elsif, unless, while, and end. Notice that control structures in Ruby are terminated using the end keyword.

```
now = Time.now
# => Tue Dec 05 23:25:56 GST 2006

if now == Time.now
  puts "now is in the past"
elsif now > Time.now
  puts "nonsense"
else
  puts "time has passed"
end
# => time has passed
```

A trick that makes simple conditionals easy to read is to place if and unless conditional statements at the end of a code line so they act as *modifiers*. Here's how it looks:

```
a = 5
b = 10

puts "b is greater than a" if a < b
```

```
b is greater than a
```

```
puts "a is greater than b" unless a < b
```

```
nil
```

You can also use while statements, as in all major programming languages.

```
a = 5
b = 10
```

```
while a < b
  puts "a is #{a}"
  a += 1
end
```

```
a is 5
a is 6
a is 7
a is 8
a is 9
```

Methods

Methods are the little programmable actions that you can define to help your development. Let's leave irb for the moment and just talk about pure Ruby code. However, all of this should work if you type it into irb.

Suppose that, several times in the application we're writing, we need to be able to get the current time as a string. To save ourselves from having to retype Time.now.to_s over and over, we can just build a method. Every method starts with def.

```
def time_as_string
  Time.now.to_s
end
```

Anywhere in the application that we want to get the time, we just say time_as_string.

```
puts time_as_string
```

```
"Wed Jan 31 11:24:19 EST 2007"
```

See how easy that was? Methods can also take in variables.

```
def say_hello_to(name)
  "Hello, #{name}!"
end
```

```
puts say_hello to "Hampton"
```

```
"Hello, Hampton!"
```

Next we will look at how you can put methods together into groups to make them really powerful.

Note You already know that local variables must start with a lowercase letter, and can't contain any characters other than letters, numbers, or underscores. Method names are restricted to the same rules. This means they can often look just like variables, and keywords (like if, or, when, and, and others) share the same set of properties. So, how does the Ruby interpreter know the difference?

When Ruby encounters a word, it sees it as either a local variable name, a method invocation, or a keyword. If it's a keyword, then Ruby knows it and responds accordingly. If there's an equals sign (=) to the right of the word, Ruby assumes it's a local variable being assigned. If it's neither a keyword nor an assignment, Ruby assumes it's a method being invoked and sends the method to the implied receiver, self.

Classes and Objects

We've reviewed all of the basic types of items in a Ruby application, so let's start using them for useful things.

Objects

Ruby is what we refer to as an object-oriented (OO) programming language. If you've never worked in an OO language before, the metaphors used can be quiet confusing the first time you hear them. Basically, *objects* are simple ways to separate your code and the data it contains.

Let's say that we are writing a program to help track the athletic program at a school. We have a list of all of the students who are currently participating on a team, along with their student IDs. For this example, we're going to look at the rowing team. We could just keep an array of arrays representing the students on the team.

```
rowing_team = [[1982, "Hampton", "Catlin"], [1954, "Ryan", "McMinn"], ...]
```

So, we're just keeping an array of [id, first_name, last_name]. We would probably need to add a comment to explain this. And then if we wanted to keep multiple teams, we could wrap this all in a hash.

```
teams = { :rowing => [[1982, "Hampton", "Catlin"], [1954, "Ryan", "McMinn"], ...],
          :track  => [[1982, "Hampton", "Catlin"], [1900, "Mark", "Twain"], ...]
        }
```

That works for now. But this is kind of ugly and we could very easily get confused, especially if we keep adding teams. This style of coding is referred to as *procedural*, and it's not object-oriented. We're just keeping track of huge data collections that are made up of simple types. Wouldn't it be nice to keep all of this data more organized?

Classes

A *class* is like the blueprint for creating an object. We've been using classes all over the place—Array, String, User, and so on. They are the plans for how to build an object. Let's construct a Student class and a Team class.

Here is the basic blueprint for a Student class:

```
class Student
  def first_name=(value)
    @first_name = value
  end

  def first_name
    @first_name
  end

  def last_name=(value)
    @last_name = value
  end

  def last_name
    @last_name
  end

  def full_name
    @last_name + ", " + @first_name
  end
end
```

Right now, we're just keeping track of the student's first_name and last_name strings. As you can see, we defined a method named first_name=(value), and we take value and put it into an instance variable named @first_name. Let's try using this class we just made.

```
# Take the Class, and turn it into a real Object instance
@student = Student.new
@student.first_name = "Lucas"
@student.last_name = "Porter"
puts @student.full_name
```

```
"Porter, Lucas"
```

So, instead of building a stupid array, we have built a smart class. We create an instance of the class called an object, by calling new on the class. It builds a version of itself called an *object*, which is then stored in the @student variable. In the next two lines, we use those = methods that we built to store the student's first and last name. Then we're able to use the method full_name to give a nicely formatted response.

It turns out that creating reader and writer methods like we've just done is a pretty common practice in object-oriented programming. Fortunately, Ruby saves us the effort of creating them by providing a shortcut: attr_accessor.

```
class Student
  attr_accessor :first_name, :last_name, :id_number

  def full_name
    @last_name + ", " + @first_name
  end
end
```

This behaves in exactly the same way as the first version. The attr_accessor bit just helps us by automatically building the methods that we need, such as first_name=. Also, this time we added an @id_number.

Let's build a Team class now.

```
class Team
  attr_accessor :name, :students

  def initialize(name)
    @name = name
    @students = []
  end

  def add_student(id_number, first_name, last_name)
    student = Student.new
    student.id_number  = id_number
```

```ruby
      student.first_name = first_name
      student.last_name  = last_name
      @students << student
    end

    def print_students
      @students.each do
        puts @student.full_name
      end
    end
end
```

We have added something new to this class. We are using the `initialize` method. So, now when we call `new`, we can pass in the name. For example, we could say `Team.new('baseball')`, and the `initialize` method is then called. Not only is `initialize` setting up the name, it's also setting up an instance variable named `@students` and turning it into an empty array. The method `add_students` uses that array to fill it up with new `Student` objects.

Let's see how we might use this class.

```ruby
team = Team.new("Rowing")
team.add_student(1982, "Hampton", "Catlin")
team.add_student(1984, "Lucas", "Porter")
team.print_students
```

```
Catlin, Hampton
Lucas, Porter
```

Containing things in objects really cleans up our code. If we were going to build a `School` class, it wouldn't be very complex. By using classes, we make sure that each object needs to worry about only its own concerns. If we were writing this application without objects, everyone's business would be shared. The variables would all exist around each other, and there would basically be one *huge* object. Objects let us break things up into small working parts.

By now, you should have a general idea of what is going on with some of the Ruby code that you have seen floating around Rails. There is a *lot* more to Ruby that we haven't even touched on here. Ruby has some really amazing metaprogramming features that you can read about in a book more specifically about Ruby, such as *Beginning Ruby: From Novice to Professional* by Peter Cooper (Apress, 2007).

RUBY STYLE

Style is important when programming. Ruby programmers tend to be picky about style, and generally adhere to a few specific guidelines, summarized below.

- Indentation size is two spaces

- Spaces are preferred to tabs

- Variables should be lowercase and underscored: `some_variable`, not `someVariable` or `somevariable`

- Method definitions should include parentheses and no unnecessary spaces: `MyClass.my_method(my_arg)`, not `my_method( my_arg )` or `my_method my_arg`

Whatever your personal style, the most important thing is that you remain consistent. There's nothing worse than looking at code that switches between tabs and spaces, or mixed and lowercase variables.

Ruby Documentation

You can refer to the following documentation for more information about Ruby:

Core library: The Ruby distribution comes with a code set of classes, known as the Ruby Core library, which includes base classes such as `Object`, `String`, `Array`, and others. In the Ruby Core application programming interface (API) documentation, you'll be able to find all the classes and methods included in the Core library. In this short appendix, you've already seen a few classes in action. One of the secrets to effectively using Ruby is knowing which classes and methods are available to you. We recommend that you go to the Ruby Core API documentation page at `http://www.ruby-doc.org/core/` and start to learn more about Ruby classes and methods.

Standard library: In addition to the Core library, the Ruby distribution comes bundled with the Ruby Standard library, which includes a set of classes that extends the functionality of the Ruby language by adding classes to help developers perform common programming tasks, such as network programming and threading. Make sure you spend some time reading through the Standard library documentation at `http://www.ruby-doc.org/stdlib/`.

Online resources: The Ruby documentation project home page is located at `http://www.ruby-doc.org`. There, you can find additional reading resources to help you learn Ruby, such as articles and tutorials, as well as the Core and Standard Ruby API documentation.

Databases 101

Let's begin with a simple definition. *A database is a piece of software that governs the storage, retrieval, deletion, and integrity of data.*

Databases are organized into tables. Tables have *columns* (or if you prefer, *fields*), and data is stored in *rows*. If you're familiar with spreadsheets, then the idea is fairly similar. Of course, databases blow spreadsheets out of the water in terms of power and performance.

Structured Query Language (SQL) is the standard way of communicating with databases. Using SQL, you can view column information, fetch a particular row or a set a rows, and search for rows containing certain criteria. You also use SQL to create, drop, and modify tables, as well as insert, update, and destroy the information stored in those tables. SQL is a fairly large topic, so a complete treatment is beyond the scope of this book. That said, you need to know the basics, so consider this a crash course.

Examining a Database Table

Here's an example definition for a table called `articles`. Note that we're using MySQL for our examples, as we do throughout this book (see Chapter 2). If you're following along using a different piece of database software, the response you see may be slightly different.

```
SHOW COLUMNS FROM articles;
```

```
+------------+--------------+------+-----+---------+----------------+
| Field      | Type         | Null | Key | Default | Extra          |
+------------+--------------+------+-----+---------+----------------+
| id         | int(11)      | NO   | PRI | NULL    | auto_increment |
| title      | varchar(255) | YES  |     | NULL    |                |
| author     | varchar(255) | YES  |     | NULL    |                |
+------------+--------------+------+-----+---------+----------------+
```

We're using the SQL SHOW command to peek at the table's columns.

As you can see, it has three columns: id, title, and author. Each field has a *type*, which defines the kind of data it can store. The id fieldhas a type of *integer*; title and author are both *varchar* fields. While it may sound strange, a type of varchar simply means that the field has a variable length of characters up to a defined maximum. In this case, the maximum is 255 characters, which is the typical limit for varchar fields. (If you needed to store more than 255 characters, you would use the *text* field type.)

The id column is the one to pay attention to here. It's the *primary key*—a unique identifier for a particular row. Since this key absolutely needs to be unique, we let the database manage its value for us by automatically incrementing its number each time a new row is created. Notice how this is specified in the articles table column description: the Key is set to PRI (primary) and the Extra attribute is set to auto_increment. These are special commands that tell MySQL how to handle this particular field.

Now let's take a look at some data from this table.

```
SELECT * FROM articles;
```

```
+----+-----------------+--------------+
| id | title           | author       |
+----+-----------------+--------------+
|  1 | Beginning Rails | Packagethief |
+----+-----------------+--------------+
1 row in set (0.00 sec)
```

Here, we're using the SQL SELECT command to view this table's data. As you can see, we have one record in the table.

Working with Tables

The most common use of databases (especially within the context of Rails) is to implement something we call *CRUD* functionality: create, read, update, and delete. Corresponding to the CRUD components are the most commonly used SQL commands INSERT, SELECT, UPDATE, and DELETE, as shown in Table D-1.

Table D-1. *Common SQL Commands*

Operation	SQL Command
Create	`INSERT`
Read	`SELECT`
Update	`UPDATE`
Delete	`DELETE`

We'll use the `articles` table presented in the previous section to show you some examples of how these commands work. Remember that it's not necessary for you to have a complete understanding of SQL to work with Rails. After all, the whole point of Active Record is to alleviate the tedium of needing to construct complex SQL statements to view and otherwise manipulate your data.

Selecting Data

The `SELECT` statement is a powerful and useful SQL command. Using `SELECT`, you can query (or request information from) the database and mine it for information. You can also give `SELECT` any number conditions, a limit to the number of rows it returns, and instructions on how to order its results.

Earlier, we used the `SELECT` statement to see the data in the `articles` table:

```
SELECT * FROM articles;
```

The asterisk (*) character is a wildcard that means *every column*. This statement is like saying, "Show me the values in every column for every row." This is the easiest way to look at the contents of a table. But it's not too often that you need to see every single row, and for tables with a lot of data, you could end up with a really large list. So, sometimes it's not very efficient to select everything. Fortunately, you can also select specific columns by name. For example, to select only the `title` column, we would do this:

```
SELECT title FROM articles;
```

```
+-----------------+
| title           |
+-----------------+
| Beginning Rails |
+-----------------+
1 row in set (0.00 sec)
```

Instead of returning all fields, it returns only the one requested: title.

To return both the title and the author fields, just add author to the list of columns to select.

```
SELECT title, author FROM articles;
```

```
+-----------------+--------------+
| title           | author       |
+-----------------+--------------+
| Beginning Rails | Packagethief |
+-----------------+--------------+
1 row in set (0.00 sec)
```

In both cases, the command returns all rows. If there were 100 rows in the table, they would all be returned.

But what about when you need to find a particular row? This is where *conditions* come in to play. To supply conditions to a SELECT statement, you use the WHERE clause.

```
SELECT fields FROM table WHERE some_field = some_value;
```

Let's apply this to the articles table by finding a row by its primary key.

```
SELECT * FROM articles WHERE id = 1;
```

```
+----+-----------------+--------------+
| id | title           | author       |
+----+-----------------+--------------+
|  1 | Beginning Rails | Packagethief |
+----+-----------------+--------------+
```

This query returns only the row whose primary key, id, matches the condition. You can use this technique on any field—id, title, or author—or all of these combined. Conditions can be chained together using AND and further modified using OR. For example, the following query returns only records whose titles and authors match the specified criteria.

```
SELECT * FROM articles WHERE title = 'Beginning Rails' AND author = 'Packagethief';
```

Inserting Data

To insert a row into a table, you use the INSERT command. INSERT requires a table name, a list of fields, and a list of values to insert into those fields. Here's a basic INSERT statement for the articles table:

```
INSERT INTO articles (title, author) VALUES ('Intro to SQL', 'ccjr');
```

```
Query OK, 1 row affected (0.01 sec)
```

The response tells us that our command was successful and that it affected one row. To see what was inserted, we again use the SELECT command.

```
SELECT * FROM articles;
```

```
+----+-----------------+--------------+
| id | title           | author       |
+----+-----------------+--------------+
|  1 | Beginning Rails | Packagethief |
|  2 | Intro to SQL    | ccjr         |
+----+-----------------+--------------+
```

Great! We now have two rows in our table. Notice that in our INSERT statement, we didn't specify the id field. That's because, as you'll recall, it's handled automatically by the database. If we were to insert a value ourselves, we wouldn't have a reliable way to guarantee its uniqueness and could cause an error if we attempted to insert a duplicate value. MySQL has automatically inserted an id of 2 into the field.

Updating Data

If you want to change the values in a row, you use the UPDATE statement. UPDATE is similar to INSERT, except that like SELECT, it can be modified (or constrained) by *conditions*. If we want to change the author for the "Intro to SQL" article, we can do so like this:

```
UPDATE articles SET author = 'Eugene' WHERE id = 1;
```

```
Query OK, 1 row affected (0.07 sec)
Rows matched: 1  Changed: 1  Warnings: 0
```

MySQL tells us that one row was matched by the query and that the row was success-fully changed. The fact that we used the primary key to find and update the row is significant. While we could have matched any value in any column, the only surefire way to ensure we're updating the row we want is to use the primary key. We can confirm that the value was updated with another query.

```
SELECT author FROM articles WHERE id = 1;
```

```
+--------+
| author |
+--------+
| Eugene |
+--------+
```

Sure enough, the author field has been updated.

Deleting Data

Of course, not all information in a database is going to stay there forever. Sometimes you need to delete records, such as when a product goes out of stock or a user cancels her account. That's the purpose of the DELETE statement. It works a lot like the UPDATE statement in that it accepts conditions, and deletes the rows for any records that match the conditions. If we wanted to delete the article with the id of 1, our DELETE statement would be as follows:

```
DELETE FROM articles WHERE id = 1;
```

```
Query OK, 1 row affected (0.08 sec)
```

MySQL tells us that one row was affected. And, of course, if we subsequently search for the record, we'll find that it no longer exists.

```
SELECT * FROM articles WHERE id = 1;
```

Empty set (0.01 sec)

Understanding Relationships

It's good practice to avoid duplication in your database by creating distinct tables to store certain kinds of information. You relate two tables to one another using an *association*. This will make more sense when you see it in action, so let's take a look at the `articles` table again. This time, the table has more data in it.

```
SELECT * FROM articles;
```

```
+----+----------------------+--------------------+
| id | title                | author             |
+----+----------------------+--------------------+
|  1 | ActiveRecord Basics  | Jeffrey Hardy      |
|  2 | Advanced ActiveRecord| Cloves Carneiro Jr.|
|  3 | Setting up Subversion| Cloves Carneiro Jr.|
|  4 | Databases 101        | Jeffrey Hardy      |
+----+----------------------+--------------------+
```

There's quite a bit of duplication in the `author` field. This can potentially create a few problems. While we could search for all articles by a particular author using a standard `SELECT` query, what would happen if someone's name were misspelled? Any articles by the misspelled author wouldn't show up in our query. And if there were such a typo, we would need to update a lot of records in order to fix it. Moreover, searching on a text field like `author` is both unreliable and rather slow when compared to searching using an integer type.

We could improve this design significantly by putting authors in their own table and referencing each author's unique `id` (primary key) in the `articles` table instead of the name. Let's do that now. We'll create a new table called `authors` and change the `author` field in the `articles` table so it can store an integer instead of text. The new `authors` table looks like this:

```
SHOW COLUMNS FROM authors;
```

```
+-------------+--------------+------+-----+---------+----------------+
| Field       | Type         | Null | Key | Default | Extra          |
+-------------+--------------+------+-----+---------+----------------+
| id          | int(11)      | NO   | PRI | NULL    | auto_increment |
| name        | varchar(255) | YES  |     | NULL    |                |
+-------------+--------------+------+-----+---------+----------------+
```

The modified `articles` table looks like this:

```
SHOW COLUMNS FROM articles;
```

```
+-------------+--------------+------+-----+---------+----------------+
| Field       | Type         | Null | Key | Default | Extra          |
+-------------+--------------+------+-----+---------+----------------+
| id          | int(11)      | NO   | PRI | NULL    | auto_increment |
| author_id   | int(11)      | YES  |     | NULL    |                |
| title       | varchar(255) | YES  |     | NULL    |                |
+-------------+--------------+------+-----+---------+----------------+
```

Note how instead of a text field called `author`, we now have a numeric field that *references* the author's primary key from the `authors` table called `author_id`. This field holds what is called a *foreign key*, which is a reference to the primary key of the table it relates to; in this case, the author who wrote the article. If we now look at the data from both tables, we'll see that we've eliminated the duplication.

```
SELECT * FROM articles;
```

```
+----+-----------+----------------------+
| id | author_id | title                |
+----+-----------+----------------------+
|  1 |         1 | ActiveRecord Basics  |
|  2 |         2 | Advanced ActiveRecord |
|  3 |         2 | Setting up Subversion |
|  4 |         1 | Databases 101        |
+----+-----------+----------------------+
```

```
SELECT * FROM authors;
```

```
+----+--------------------+
| id | name               |
+----+--------------------+
|  1 | Jeffrey Hardy      |
|  2 | Cloves Carneiro Jr. |
+----+--------------------+
```

We can now use this relationship in our SELECT queries by joining the two tables together using their association. In this association, the author_id in the articles table is equal to the id column in the authors table. This requires only a slight change to our SQL to add the JOIN directive.

```
SELECT id, title, name FROM articles JOIN authors ON articles.author_id =
authors.id;
```

```
+----+----------------------+--------------------+
| id | title                | name               |
+----+----------------------+--------------------+
|  1 | ActiveRecord Basics  | Jeffrey Hardy      |
|  2 | Advanced ActiveRecord | Cloves Carneiro Jr. |
|  3 | Setting up Subversion | Cloves Carneiro Jr. |
|  4 | Databases 101        | Jeffrey Hardy      |
+----+----------------------+--------------------+
```

Now we get the author names returned with our query, which effectively spans two tables. This is the crux of relational databases. Updating an author's name is now easy because there is only one instance of a given author. Updating that author will affect all of his associated articles.

```
UPDATE authors SET name = 'Packagethief' WHERE id = 1;
```

That will change the name of the author with the id of 1 to Packagethief. When we run the JOIN query again, we'll see that all instances of the author's name have been updated.

```
SELECT id, title, name FROM articles JOIN authors ON articles.author_id =
authors.id;
```

```
+----+----------------------+--------------------+
| id | title                | name               |
+----+----------------------+--------------------+
|  1 | ActiveRecord Basics  | Packagethief       |
|  2 | Advanced ActiveRecord | Cloves Carneiro Jr. |
|  3 | Setting up Subversion | Cloves Carneiro Jr. |
|  4 | Databases 101        | Packagethief       |
+----+----------------------+--------------------+
```

We get the same result, but with the first author name updated.

SQL and Active Record

This brings our database crash course to a close. This was by no means a complete reference, nor was it intended to be. Its purpose is merely to illustrate the basics about how databases work and to introduce you to their native language: SQL. Now that you have a taste, you can safely enter the world of Active Record, where most of this tedious work is handled for you.

Why did we bother showing you this if Active Record takes care of most of it for you? Because it's important to know what Active Record is doing behind the scenes. While you'll effectively be able to use Active Record like a black box, you will eventually need to debug your programs and figure out why something isn't working the way you expect. Having a basic understanding of SQL will help. Moreover, every bit of SQL that Active Record generates is logged by Rails. You can find the logs in the log/ directory of your application. Now when you see these SQL commands in the logs, you'll have a good idea about what they mean.

■ ■ ■

The Rails Community

Rails development is driven by a vibrant and passionate community of open source developers. The Rails community encourages its members to participate actively in Rails development. You can start by asking questions and discussing new features.

As your knowledge increases, you can help others by writing about your own experiences in a personal blog, answering questions on the mailing list, contributing to the wiki, and fixing bugs and writing patches to make Rails even better. Whatever your intention, be assured that participating in the community will help you get the most out of Rails.

Rails Mailing Lists

You can subscribe to several Rails-related mailing lists:

- **Talk mailing list:** A high-volume list where users can seek help, announce open source or commercial Rails projects, and discuss any miscellaneous matters about the Rails framework. You can subscribe to this list at `http://groups.google.com/group/rubyonrails-talk`.

- **Core mailing list:** A low-volume list for those interested in Rails development. You can discuss changes in the Rails framework or, if you have found a bug in the framework, you can discuss proposed soultions. You can subscribe to this list at `http://groups.google.com/group/rubyonrails-core`.

- **Security mailing list:** This list is for those who want to keep abreast of any Rails security concerns. You can subscribe to this read-only mailing list at `http://groups.google.com/group/rubyonrails-security`.

Rails IRC Channel

If you want to interact with other Rails developers live, you can try the Rails IRC channel. Open your favorite IRC client and connect to the Freenode IRC network at irc.freenode.net. Enter the #rubyonrails channel, and you'll find hundreds of Rails developers at any time of the day (or night) willing to help you and chat about their favorite web framework.

■**Note**   Internet Relay Chat (IRC) is a type of real-time Internet chat, where users talk about their interests in topic-specific areas called *channels*. All you need to connect to IRC is IRC client software. The most commonly used IRC clients are the shareware mIRC (http://mirc.com) for Windows and the open source Colloquy (http://colloquy.info) for the Mac.

Rails Blogs and Podcast

The number of blogs dedicated to Rails information is growing very fast, and most of the new Rails features are covered here even before they are released to the public. You can subscribe to the blogs of your choice to keep up with news in the Rails world.

The following are some of the more rewarding Rails-related blogs you can visit, including the official Rails podcast.

- http://weblog.rubyonrails.org: The official Rails blog. You'll find information about upcoming releases, new functionality in Rails, and news considered impor-tant (such as documentation updates and Rails adoption worldwide).

- http://weblog.jamisbuck.org: A blog by Jamis Buck. From his unique perspective as a Rails core team member and employee of 37signals, Jamis writes often about Rails internals, best practices, and useful tricks. See also The Rails Way (http://therailsway.com), a blog he co-writes with core member Michael Koziarski, wherein the pair review Rails projects and offer valuable suggestions.

- http://ryandaigle.com: A blog by Ryan Daigle called Rya's Scraps. Ryan posts regu-larly about cutting-edge developments in the Rails source code. This is a great blog to subscribe to if you're interested in all the new features that will be coming down the pipe in the next version of Rails.

- http://blog.hasmanythrough.com: A blog by Josh Susser. Josh writes frequently about advanced Rails topics, and also writes for the official Rails blog.

- http://rubyinside.com: A Ruby blog by Peter Cooper, author of *Beginning Ruby* (Apress, 2007). It contains a lot of Ruby information that will likely be very helpful in your Rails adventures.

- `http://planetrubyonrails.com`: A feed aggregator that aims to make the best of Ruby/Rails-related blogs accessible from a single site.

- `http://beginningrails.com`: A blog we've created to discuss all matters related to this book, including updates, errata, and so on. Feel free to check it out periodically.

- `http://podcast.rubyonrails.org`: The Rails podcast. You can listen to Rails news and interviews with Ruby and Rails developers. The Rails podcast is a great way to hear from industry experts and learn about how other developers have been using Rails.

Rails Wiki

The Rails wiki (`http://wiki.rubyonrails.org`) is a collaborative effort to enhance the amount of documentation about Rails. You will find information about everything related to Rails in the wiki, so feel free to visit it when you have some spare time and make sure you explore as much as you can. Along with a lot of source code, it also contains information about open source and commercial products, job posts, Rails training, tools, screencasts, tutorials, and much more. You can also easily contribute to the wiki.

■**Note** Like most wikis, it's a frequent target of spam, rendering some pages difficult to read. All changes are versioned, so when you see a page that's been defaced, it's easy to roll it back to a good version.

Rails APIs

It's close to impossible to remember the name, methods, and possible parameters of all the functions and classes in Ruby and Rails. To help you with your coding tasks, we recommend that you keep the Ruby and Rails Application Programming Interface (API) documentation open, or at least that you put it in your favorites. The API documentation will have all the information about a specific function you are trying to use, and you'll even find the function source code.

The Rails API documentation can be found at `http://api.rubyonrails.org`, and the Ruby API can be found at `http://www.ruby-doc.org/core`. For more user-friendly and searchable API documentation, head over to `http://gotapi.com` and select the Ruby/Rails option.

Rails Trac

The Rails development server can be found at `http://dev.rubyonrails.org`. It's powered by the powerful Trac application, an enhanced wiki and issue tracking system specifically for software projects.

You can participate in the development of Rails by submitting bug reports and patches to the Trac (don't forget to read the submission guidelines). You can also check the Rails source code using a web interface, and even subscribe to the Subversion change log using RSS, which will allow you to be notified when changes happen to the Rails source code.

Working with Rails Directory

Now that you are a Rails developer, you can add your name to the Working with Rails directory at `http://www.workingwithrails.com`. In this directory, you can find Rails developers by country, company, and even popularity, as measured by their recommendation and ranking system.

Index

Windows XP, installation on, 28–32
    installing MySQL, 29–30
    installing Rails, 31–32
    installing Ruby, 30–31
    overview, 28
:within option, using with
        validates_length_of, 124
Working with Rails directory, 344
writer method, 71, 73
:wrong_length option, using with
        validates_length_of, 124

X

Xcode (Apple Developer Tools), installing,
    20
Xcode Tools, 20
XmlHttpRequest object, 201, 210

Y

YAGNI (you ain't gonna need it)
        philosophy, 7
YAML, 48
Yahoo Mail, 229
yield keyword, 150
you ain't gonna need it (YAGNI)
        philosophy, 7

Z

Zygmuntowicz, Ezra, 312

FIND IT FAST

with the Apress *SuperIndex*™

Quickly Find Out What the Experts Know

L eading by innovation, Apress now offers you its *SuperIndex*™, a turbocharged companion to the fine index in this book. The Apress *SuperIndex*™ is a keyword and phrase-enabled search tool that lets you search through the entire Apress library. Powered by dtSearch™, it delivers results instantly.

Instead of paging through a book or a PDF, you can electronically access the topic of your choice from a vast array of Apress titles. The Apress *SuperIndex*™ is the perfect tool to find critical snippets of code or an obscure reference. The Apress *SuperIndex*™ enables all users to harness essential information and data from the best minds in technology.

No registration is required, and the Apress *SuperIndex*™ is free to use.

❶ Thorough and comprehensive searches of over 300 titles

❷ No registration required

❸ Instantaneous results

❹ A single destination to find what you need

❺ Engineered for speed and accuracy

❻ Will spare your time, application, and anxiety level

Search now: *http://superindex.apress.com*

You Need the Companion eBook

Your purchase of this book entitles you to buy the companion PDF-version eBook for only $10. Take the weightless companion with you anywhere.

We believe this Apress title will prove so indispensable that you'll want to carry it with you everywhere, which is why we are offering the companion eBook (in PDF format) for $10 to customers who purchase this book now. Convenient and fully searchable, the PDF version of any content-rich, page-heavy Apress book makes a valuable addition to your programming library. You can easily find and copy code—or perform examples by quickly toggling between instructions and the application. Even simultaneously tackling a donut, diet soda, and complex code becomes simplified with hands-free eBooks!

Once you purchase your book, getting the $10 companion eBook is simple:

❶ Visit **www.apress.com/promo/tendollars/**.

❷ Complete a basic registration form to receive a randomly generated question about this title.

❸ Answer the question correctly in 60 seconds, and you will receive a promotional code to redeem for the $10.00 eBook.

2855 TELEGRAPH AVENUE | SUITE 600 | BERKELEY, CA 94705

Offer valid through 1/08.